Rock & Pop
The Complete Story

This is a **FLAME TREE** book
First published in 2006

Publisher and Creative Director: Nick Wells
Project Editor: Sara Robson
Picture Research: Melinda Révèsz
Designer: Mike Spender

Special thanks to: Chris Herbert, Julia Rolf, Rosanna Singler, Elena Verrecchia, Claire Walker and Polly Willis

06 08 10 09 07

1 3 5 7 9 10 8 6 4 2

Created and produced by
FLAME TREE PUBLISHING
Crabtree Hall, Crabtree Lane
Fulham, London SW6 6TY
United Kingdom

www.flametreepublishing.com

Flame Tree Publishing is part of the Foundry Creative Media Co. Ltd.

ISBN 1–84451–395–5

Rock & Pop
The Complete Story

**Bob Allen, Lloyd Bradley, Richard Brophy, Richard Buskin, Leila Cobo, Cliff Douse, Colin Irwin,
Dave Ling, Carl Loben, Bill Milkowski, Garry Mulholland, Douglas J Noble, Ed Potton**

General Editor: Michael Heatley

Foreword by Sir George Martin

Consulting Editors
Ian Anderson, Paul Du Noyer, Geoff Brown, Richard Buskin, Paul Kingsbury,
Chrissie Murray, Michael Paoletta, Philip Van Vleck

**FLAME TREE
PUBLISHING**

Contents

Contents

Rock

How to use this *Book*

The reader is encouraged to use this book in a variety of ways, each of which caters for a range of interests, knowledge and uses.

- The book is divided into the two main **categories** – rock and pop.
- Each **category** is divided into the main **styles** of music to enable the reader to quickly locate specific areas of interest. For rock this list includes styles such as Blues Rock, British Blues and Country Rock.
- Each **style** has a leading page that introduces the reader to the section. The remaining pages in each style discuss the context within which it was created, the key artists and the development of the style.
- Within each style, there are normally three **entries** (including the leading page). Each **entry** is introduced at the head of the page to enable ease of reference to specific areas of interest.
- Quotes from artists, producers and commentators are used throughout to enable the reader to get to grips with the feel and passion of the music.
- Lists of key artists and key tracks or albums relating to each style of music are used throughout to give a flavour of the artists and records that defined the music.
- Album covers are often shown where they characterize the style of music.
- Detailed picture captions give further information on the artists included.

Entry title

Introduction to the entry

Style of music

East Meets *West*

Naturally, New York was not going to be left out of the picture for too long. By the early 1990s, the Big Apple had its own thriving gangsta rap scene, but didn't achieve much wider acclaim until Notorious BIG released his *Ready To Die* album in 1994 which proved him to be one of the best gangsta rappers.

In his slipstream were the Junior MAFIA posse, MOP, Capone-N-Noriega, Mobb Deep and Jay-Z, all of whom were a match for most of what came out of LA, shifting the power base eastwards. Too often, though, the rivalry between the two coasts, which occasionally escalated from merely a war of words, became the industry's and the media's focus and the quality of some of the music got overshadowed.

Key artists, tracks or albums that define the style

Key Albums:
All Eyez On Me Tupac Shakur
Doggy Dogg Style Snoop Dogg
OG Ice-T
Ready To Die Notorious BIG
Straight Outta Compton NWA

But whereas gangsta rap may originally have been an expression of black rage or frustration, it was quickly co-opted as a kind of ghetto-style entertainment for thrill-seeking, socially rebelling whites. The audience changed and the artists began to play up to what was required of them. By the end of the 1990s, two of gangsta's biggest stars – Notorious BIG and Tupac – had been shot dead and the form had become a caricature of itself.

Information about the music

Ironically, the narrative power and vocabulary of the medium was taken up in spectacular fashion by Eminem to create a situation where the world's greatest rapper is white. But then the world's greatest golfer is black, so anything's possible.

The biggest waves in the new rap millennium were made by Eminem protégés 50 Cent and the Game. Both members of the group G Unit made top-selling solo records, while "50" managed to branch out into movies with his 2005 autobiographical feature *Get Rich Or Die Tryin'*. Fellow rappers Jay-Z and P Diddy also harboured wider ambitions, launching clothing lines. Meanwhile in 2005, producer turned artist Kanye West came up with his classic second album *Late Registration*, having put his neck on the line with political statements in the press knocking George Bush's administration and slating hip-hop's homophobia.

Detroit rapper Eminem has raised the credibility of white rap through his phenomenal worldwide success. His song 'Lose Yourself', from the semi-autobiographical film 8 Mile, *won the singer an Academy Award.*

Picture captions

Foreword

I seem to have spent my entire life enjoying music: making it, writing it, orchestrating it, working with countless great musicians in performances of it and, of course, listening to it. Oh my word, have I *listened* to it! If you turned me upside down I am sure notes would tumble out of my ears! Music has always been my friend and comfort in good times and bad, for it has a magic that will always give us what our heart desires. There is such an infinite variety of different forms of music that has evolved over the course of time, be it Bach or Mahler or Bacharach or McCartney, that there is something for everyone. Music, of all the arts, touches the human soul like nothing else: it is the most sublime, the most primeval, the very core of our beings. I believe our ancestors were able to make music before they could speak.

Music evolved and mutated fairly slowly over the years, but it was changed forever with the invention of the commercial recorder around a hundred years ago. This device immediately brought unknown types of music within reach of everyone in the Western world, and many new stars were born. Jazz thrived, once brilliant improvisations could be captured on disc, and along with radio, recorded music became a necessary part of our lives. Not only were we charmed and entertained, but we were able to learn from it, and I remember listening time and again to great jazz piano solos and copying them in my own way. Without the record, many of our greatest talents would still be doing their day jobs!

I had the good fortune to enter the music business at a crucial time. I began as a specialist in Baroque music in the 1950s, and part of my job was to advise the conductor where he should make a break in the score, so as to split the music into the different sections demanded of the shellac 78 rpm system, which only allowed four and a quarter minutes a side. My joy knew no bounds when the vinyl 33 1/3 rpm disc gave us up to half an hour a side, and later the introduction of the CD and digital recording which broke down all barriers on the road to perfection. Becoming head of a small record label, I found myself working alongside many fine artistes in all kinds of music, from folk and jazz to classical and pop, and I learned so much from them as my career advanced. It was an extraordinary plunge into the mainstream of good music, and I knew I was privileged indeed. You could say I was spoiled.

Nowadays, however, it is the consumer who is spoiled for choice. Music proliferates in every part of our lives, sometimes intrusively, and that may not be the best thing, either for us or for music. It is such a precious asset that is so easy to squander, most of us hearing a great deal by *listening* to little. Oscar Wilde spoke disparagingly of someone "who knew the cost of everything and the value of nothing." Well, have no fear: this book will give its readers the true value of music, exploring the incredible variety of evolving styles and explaining the importance of each genre. It will broaden their knowledge and point the way to a far deeper understanding and enjoyment of music. In an age where the visual image tends to dominate our minds, I hope this book will make us realise how very vital and precious is our sense of sound.

We all need to look less and listen more, which will make us all the more discerning. And we will find that the world *can* be a better place.

Sir George Martin

Pop *Introduction*

Across the centuries and around the globe, many different forms of music have enjoyed mass appeal for a limited period of time. None, however, have been able to match the widespread influence of the popular music that erupted in America during the mid-1950s and, by the second half of the decade, was exerting its grip over much of the world.

Attaching doo-wop songs and soulful ballads to the main catalyst of rock'n'roll, this new youth-oriented pop, with its sometimes earthy lyrics and often grating beat, was the first to meld sexual energy with long-repressed feelings of teen angst and rebelliousness.

"Pop music is the mass medium for conditioning the way people think."
Graham Nash

No longer prepared to do their parents' bidding by dressing and behaving like young adults, the postwar generation of kids demanded to be recognized on their own terms, and pop music was the vehicle that enabled them to achieve this. Forget those slick crooners, strict-tempo dances and sterile hits such as 'How Much Is That Doggie In The Window?'. The new music was all about unleashing inhibitions and having unrestrained fun, not hanging out on street corners to kill time – and it was also about emphasizing the gulf between Mum, Dad and their over-sexed, under-compliant offspring.

Suddenly, teen emotions were being expressed in the words as well as in the rhythms, while the music was all the more accessible for the fact that vocal and instrumental virtuosity were not prerequisites for performing it yourself. Commencing in the mid-1950s, pop was, for the first time, truly music for the teen masses, to be enjoyed and even performed by teens. In the wake of Elvis Presley and Buddy Holly, guitar sales went through the roof, and it was not long before tens of thousands of juvenile bands began springing up on both sides of the Atlantic. Indeed, in cash-strapped Britain, which was still suffering from the ravages of the Second World War, R&B-based skiffle music served as a practical solution for kids who often did not have the funds to purchase decent instruments, while also providing them with a grounding in the basic skills that some would employ to great advantage just a few years later.

Perhaps the ultimate pop icon, Elvis Presley. Presley brought attitude and sexuality into the mainstream at a time when it was far from acceptable.

13

In the meantime, before pop's second big explosion could take place, its first phase had to run its course. As the 1950s segued into the 1960s, white adults were still running the show, and a combination of social pressure and self-destructive circumstances helped to spell the end for the black-derived rock'n'roll that some whites referred to as "jungle music". Chuck Berry was jailed for statutory rape, Jerry Lee Lewis was ostracized for marrying his 13-year-old cousin, Little Richard joined the Church, Buddy Holly and Eddie Cochran were killed in tragic accidents, and after Elvis emerged without sideburns from a two-year stint in the US Army, he threw himself head-first into a revamped scene that saw the old heavy brigade replaced by clean-cut, parent-approved smoothies: Fabian, Frankie Avalon, Connie Francis, Pat Boone, Bobby Vinton, Ricky Nelson. For now, the older generation had won the battle, even though the long term would see them forced to concede the war.

Still, the era that coincided with Cold War crises and President Kennedy's tenure in the White House was not just about soapy ballads and itsy bitsy teeny weeny yellow polka dot bikinis. It was also about the classic, three-minute pop songs that were being turned out by the brilliant young composing/ production teams housed inside New York City's Brill Building, as recorded by artists ranging from the Drifters to the Shirelles; about a uniquely solo dance craze known as The Twist; about the innovative "Wall of Sound" hits produced by wunderkind Phil Spector; about the nonstop flow of pulsating dance material being written, produced and recorded inside Motown's Hitsville facility in Detroit; and about the surf-and-hot-rod sounds emanating from Californian outfits such as the Beach Boys.

In ironic contrast with the global tensions taking place during the nuclear age, pop music was espousing youthful optimism – serving as a welcome diversion from a troubled world, it was, for now, less a means of expression than a form of escapism. Nevertheless, although America had led the way with regard to popular music for much of the twentieth century, the status quo was about to change. Some British kids, whose lives had been irrevocably changed by rock'n'roll as well as by R&B, were stamping their own distinctive style and personality on the music. When they transported it back across the Atlantic, the shock waves reverberated throughout the industry, sweeping away virtually all before them.

5 Top UK Artists (Since Charts Began):	*5 Top US Artists (Since Charts Began):*
1 Cliff Richard	1 Michael Jackson
2 Elvis Presley	2 Elvis Presley
3 Elton John	3 Madonna
4 Diana Ross	4 Mariah Carey
5 David Bowie	5 Whitney Houston

New York's Brill Building on Broadway was the hub of American pop music for many years.

In the vanguard of the mid-1960s "British Invasion" were the seemingly happy-go-lucky Beatles, whose guitar-and-drums-based sound infused the entire pop scene. Meanwhile, R&B-influenced rockers such as the Animals and the Rolling Stones, as well as mod outfits such as the Who, also provided contrast by way of their devil-may-care attitudes and slightly less clean-cut image. For a short time, many American artists found themselves in the unprecedented position of having to imitate their Brit counterparts in order to make the charts, although in the second half of the decade West Coast acts such as the Turtles and the Mamas & the Papas helped to redress the balance.

By then, pop's fun and carefree attributes were charting a parallel but distinct course from the outspoken, introspective and experimental traits associated with the newly defined genre of rock music, as they were from the characteristics of numerous other musical categories that started to emerge. Largely appealing to pre-teens, early teens and middle-agers, pop would increasingly be associated with infectious commercialism at its best and crass exploitation at its worst.

While the emergence of reggae, rap and dance would see beat and rhythm jumping to the musical forefront during the ensuing decades, melody has continued to be at the centre of mainstream pop material. This has ranged from the teeny-bop product of the Osmonds and Bay City Rollers in the 1970s, Wham! and New Kids On The Block in the 1980s and Hanson and the Spice Girls in the 1990s, to the catchy Europop sounds of ABBA, the homogenous, production-line-type output of British songwriting/production team Stock, Aitken & Waterman, the slick recordings of new romantics such as Duran Duran, and the even smoother product of boy bands such as Take That and the Backstreet Boys. Indeed, by tapping into other veins of music and infusing them with melody, sub-genres have fallen into the pop category – such as new wave (an offshoot of punk) and 2-Tone (a by-product of ska). Having split off from rock while incorporating anything from funk to Latin, pop music keeps evolving. Even so, its most consistent feature is its propensity for instant gratification. "If you can really get it together in three minutes," Blondie's lead singer Debbie Harry once observed, "that's what pop songs are all about."

5 Top UK Tracks (Since Charts Began):	5 Top US Tracks (Since Charts Began):
1 'Candle In The Wind' Elton John	1 'Candle In The Wind' Elton John
2 'Do They Know It's Christmas' Band Aid	2 'We Are The World' USA For Africa
3 'Bohemian Rhapsody' Queen	3 'I Will Always Love You' Whitney Houston
4 'Mull Of Kintyre' Wings	4 'Macarena' Los Del Rio
5 'Rivers Of Babylon' Boney M	5 'Whoomp! (There It Is)' Tag Team

As Wham!, George Michael and Andrew Ridgeley went from having minor hits with cynical songs like 'Wham! Rap' to phenomenal commercial success with pop anthems such as 'Wake Me Up Before You Go Go'.

Fifties *Pop*

During the mid-1950s, the American and British pop scenes experienced a complete shake-up of the old order. Up until the decade's halfway point, the airwaves, record stores and jukeboxes were filled with sentimental ballads, novelty songs and instrumentals that largely reflected the tastes of white adults.

American artists such as Frankie Laine, Frank Sinatra, Dean Martin, Perry Como, Guy Mitchell, the McGuire Sisters, Eddie Fisher, Al Martino, Doris Day, Rosemary Clooney, Tony Bennett and Tennessee Ernie Ford dominated the charts on both sides of the Atlantic, while the British also enjoyed an array of homegrown acts, including pianist Winifred Atwell as well as singers such as Dickie Valentine, Ruby Murray, Alma Cogan, Anne Shelton, Jimmy Young and Vera Lynn. The one genuine teen heart-throb during this era was Johnnie Ray, a latter-day bobbysox idol whose early hits, 'Cry' and 'The Little White Cloud That Cried', coupled with a bawling style of singing that had his female fans in floods of tears,

"Rock'n'roll... smells phoney and false. It is sung, played and written for the most part by cretinous goons."
Frank Sinatra

led to him being dubbed the "Prince of Wails" and, somewhat awkwardly, the "Nabob of Sob". Still, neither Ray nor any of his white contemporaries performed material that spoke to youthful vitality or rebellion. With his 1955 covers of Otis Williams & The Charms' 'Two Hearts' and Fats Domino's 'Ain't That A Shame', Pat Boone commenced his highly profitable enterprise of taking R&B songs originated by black artists, cleaning up their earthier lyrics, and crooning them in a style that, in line with his wholesome smile and white buck shoes, was deemed more acceptable to "moral" white audiences. Boone's sanitized covers of material by Domino, Little Richard, Ivory Joe Hunter, The Flamingos and The El Dorados would help him sell more records during the 1950s than any artist except Elvis Presley, yet it is debatable whether he helped push open the door for these innovative black artists or simply ensured that they continued to be marginalized.

Johnnie Ray was one of the first white pop performers to really play the audience, taking the microphone from the stand, moving around the stage and emphasizing his songs with screams and real tears.

Shake, Rattle and *Rock'n'Roll*

In 1954, Bill Haley did much the same when he covered Big Joe Turner's 'Shake, Rattle And Roll' and substituted many of composer Charles E. Calhoun's racier lyrics – "Get outta that bed, wash your face and hands" was transformed into "Get out from that kitchen and rattle those pots and pans", although the less explicit but actually more risqué "I'm like a one-eyed cat peepin' in a seafood store" remained, despite Haley assuring a reporter that "We stay clear of anything suggestive."

The previous year, blending country and western with R&B, Haley had introduced rock'n'roll to the charts by way of 'Crazy Man Crazy'. But it was his energetic recording of a song originally conceived as a "novelty foxtrot" by its veteran Tin Pan Alley composers that marked the first significant shift of power in the pop charts. 'Rock Around The Clock', tracked by Bill Haley & his Comets in 1954 and subsequently played over the title credits to juvenile delinquency film *The Blackboard Jungle*, displaced Pérez Prado's massively successful instrumental 'Cherry Pink And Apple Blossom White' atop the *Billboard* charts on 9 July 1955. After sharing pole position with Frank Sinatra's 'Learnin' The Blues' for a couple of weeks, it then occupied the summit all by itself. The old guard was giving way to a new era.

5 Top 1950s UK Artists:	*5 Top 1950s US Artists:*
1 Elvis Presley	1 Elvis Presley
2 Frank Sinatra	2 Frank Sinatra
3 Frankie Vaughan	3 Johnny Mathis
4 Nat "King" Cole	4 Isley Brothers
5 Pat Boone	5 Patsy Cline

Blind in his left eye since childhood, Bill Haley was self-conscious about his appearance. To draw attention away from his eye Haley wore his hair in a kiss curl, which became his trademark and sparked a craze.

The Soundtrack of *Youth*

Those restless teens who had idolized Marlon Brando in *The Wild One* (a biker movie that was banned in Britain) and James Dean in *Rebel Without A Cause* were now lining up at the box office to see *The Blackboard Jungle* because of its theme song.

Suddenly, youth had a soundtrack, and it was not long before numerous other artists began to jump on the bandwagon. In America, where *Billboard* magazine published three separate charts between 1955 and 1958 – "Bestsellers In Stores", "Most Played By Jockeys" and "Most Played In Jukeboxes"– before merging them into the "Hot 100", there was an almost immediate change in the record-buying demographic.

In addition to a string of definitive rock'n'roll hits by Elvis Presley, who represented the complete teen-friendly, parent-threatening package, the upper regions of the charts were soon dominated by an assortment of rockers and pop-flavoured doo-woppers, ranging from Buddy Holly, Jerry Lee Lewis, Paul Anka and the Everly Brothers to the Platters and Frankie Lymon & the Teenagers. Indeed, if 1956 was a year of transition, 1957 was the year when the balance changed once and for all. This was also true for Britain, where the aforementioned American artists shared their success with a number of homegrown innovators and imitators. These included skiffle king Lonnie Donegan, Cliff Richard and Larry Parnes's stable of imaginatively named teen idols, such as Tommy Steele, Billy Fury, Georgie Fame and Joe Brown.

Both musically and culturally, young was in and old was square. Yet as the 1950s wound down, hardcore rock'n'roll was virtually dead, and a telling sign as to the short-term future arrived in the form of 'Venus', a sentimental, chart-topping ballad by clean-cut smoothie Frankie Avalon. For the time being, pop music was becoming acceptable once again.

5 Top 1950s UK Tracks:

1. 'Rock Around The Clock' Bill Haley and his Comets
2. 'I Believe' Frank Sinatra
3. 'Mary's Boy Child' Harry Belafonte
4. 'Hound Dog' Elvis Presley
5. 'Heartbreak Hotel' Elvis Presley

5 Top 1950s US Tracks:

1. 'Hound Dog' Elvis Presley
2. 'Cherry Pink And Apple Blossom White' Perez "Prez" Prado
3. 'Sincerely' The McGuire Sisters
4. 'Singing The Blues' Guy Mitchell
5. 'Mack the Knife' Bobby Darin

Blackboard Jungle was a controversial film and was banned in some areas amidst fears that it would incite violence. However, the teenagers flocked to see it, above all for the theme song 'Rock Around The Clock'.

Fifties Pop *Singer/Songwriters*

Until the advent of rock'n'roll, pop singers and songwriters were, for the most part, divided into two separate camps. The singers were typically faced with the daunting task of unearthing new hit material, unless, like Frank Sinatra, they were so esteemed that they had the best songwriters in the business lining up to write for them.

All of this began to change in the mid-1950s, however, as pop music commenced its evolution into a do-it-yourself art form in which, as with country and western and the blues, the performance of a song was often less about perfection than about feel.

"A lot of songs I sang to crowds first to watch their reaction, that's how I knew they'd hit."
Little Richard

Rockabilly singer/songwriter Carl Perkins secured his own place in pop history by way of his one major chart hit, 'Blue Suede Shoes', which became a rock'n'roll anthem when it was covered by Elvis Presley in 1956. At around the same time, the R&B field delivered the likes of Little Richard (real name Richard Penniman), an electrifying, gospel-rooted singer/pianist who co-wrote many of his biggest hits, including 'Tutti Frutti', 'Lucille', 'Long Tall Sally', 'She's Got It', 'Keep A Knockin'', 'Slippin' And Slidin'' and 'Jenny, Jenny'; and singer/guitarist Bo Diddley (born Otha Ellas Bates), innovator of the pounding, Latin-tinged rhythm and beat that infused not only self-referential compositions such as 'Bo Diddley' and 'Diddley Daddy', but also numerous classic songs by other artists down the years, such as The Strangeloves' 'I Want Candy', Buddy Holly's 'Not Fade Away', Johnny Otis's 'Willie And The Hand Jive', Shirley And Company's 'Shame, Shame, Shame', George Michael's 'Faith' and U2's 'Desire'.

The Iowa plane crash in 1959 in which Buddy Holly died also killed fellow singers J. P. Richardson (aka The Big Bopper) and Ritchie Valens. The tragic event was commemorated in Don McLean's 1972 single 'American Pie'.

Pure Poetry for a New *Generation*

Nevertheless, perhaps the single most influential singer/songwriter of the era was Chuck Berry, whose driving guitar licks and topical, witty and ingeniously quick-fire, poetic lyrics pretty much defined rock'n'roll.

A native of St. Louis, Missouri, Charles Edward Anderson Berry threw country, R&B and boogie-woogie into the mix when concocting major chart hits such as 'Maybellene', 'Roll Over Beethoven', 'Rock And Roll Music', 'Sweet Little Sixteen', 'Carol' and 'Johnny B. Goode'. The results were pure poetry for a new generation of car-cruising, guitar-strumming, record-playing, dancing and dating teens. As John Lennon once said, "If you tried to give rock'n'roll another name, you might call it Chuck Berry."

As attested to by his chart success and influence over 1960s superstars ranging from the Beach Boys and the Beatles to Bob Dylan and the Rolling Stones, Berry had little trouble appealing to white audiences. Meanwhile, another singer/songwriter who made a more concerted effort in that regard was Sam Cooke, who crossed over from his gospel origins as the lead singer with the Soul Stirrers to lend his sublime voice to self-penned mainstream white pop, flavoured with an assortment of soul, R&B and, on occasion, unadulterated kitsch. In 1957, Cooke enjoyed his first solo American number 1 with 'You Send Me', a romantic ballad complemented by white backing vocalists, and moved even further away from his roots with overtly commercial follow-ups such as 'Everybody Likes To Cha Cha Cha' and 'Only Sixteen' before really hitting his stride during the early part of the ensuing decade.

Key Artists:

Paul Anka
Chuck Berry
Sam Cooke
Bobby Darin
Buddy Holly

The ingenious songs of Chuck Berry combined clever and witty lyrics with fast-moving tunes and intricate guitar playing. Onstage, Chuck was known for the famous "duck walk".

Inspiring the Composers of *Tomorrow*

While Sam Cooke stood as a symbol of African-American achievement and prosperity, writing most of his hit material in addition to running his own management and publishing companies alongside an independent record label, several of his white contemporaries were also inspiring the composers of tomorrow by honing their skills as singer/songwriters.

Bobby Darin (born Walden Robert Cassotto) enjoyed his first chart success in 1958 with the co-written novelty number 'Splish Splash', and he built on that the following year by penning the smash hit 'Dream Lover'. At the same time, while 'Words Of Love' was a Buddy Holly solo composition that would later be covered by the Beatles, Holly co-wrote several of his most memorable songs with members of his backing band The Crickets, as well as with producer Norman Petty; among them were 'That'll Be The Day', 'Peggy Sue', 'It's So Easy', 'Well ... All Right', 'Think It Over' and 'True Love Ways'.

Shortly after his death in a plane crash in February 1959, Holly topped the UK charts with the posthumous (and ironically titled) single 'It Doesn't Matter Anymore'. This had been penned by Paul Anka, yet another multi-talented youngster who had enjoyed international success by recording his own material. A native of Ontario, Canada, Anka was only 16 when 'Diana', his 1957 paean to a girl four years his senior, made him an international star, and during the next couple of years he capitalized on this with a string of highly dramatic ballads focusing on teen romance (or the lack thereof), including 'You Are My Destiny', 'Lonely Boy' and 'Put Your Head On My Shoulder'. He also wrote the lyrics to the big Sinatra hit, 'My Way'.

Key Tracks:
'Diana' Paul Anka
'Dream Lover' Bobby Darin
'Peggy Sue' Buddy Holly
'Roll Over Beethoven' Chuck Berry
'You Send Me' Sam Cooke

Unlike the veteran Tin Pan Alley composers, Anka was able to connect with teenagers and convey their emotions because he was one himself. This trend would pick up pace during the decades to follow.

Sam Cooke's magnificent voice made an easy transition from gospel music to mainstream pop.

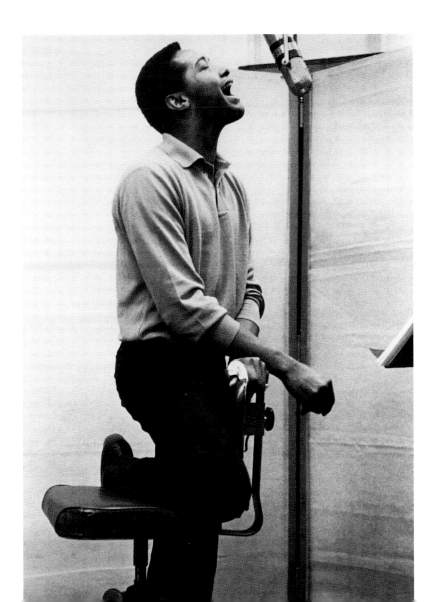

Rhythm & *Blues*

Rhythm & blues (R&B) music evolved out of jump blues rhythms during the late-1940s, but it also had riffs and lyrics that were beginning to point more towards the emergence of rock'n'roll. Using sparser instrumentation than jump blues, R&B was based upon traditional blues chord changes played over a steady backbeat.

R&B placed more emphasis on the singer and the song than on the band's instrumentalists. Although it branched out into rock'n'roll during the 1950s, and soul during the 1960s, it always retained its own following, and R&B artists continue to draw large audiences all over the world.

R&B's First Lady

As rock'n'roll continued to emerge, R&B developed into further distinct styles, including doo wop, electric blues and New Orleans. Each of these exerted its influence on other R&B forms, as well as popular music in general. During the late 1940s and early 1950s, a number of great singers began to emerge from the R&B scene. Ruth Brown was perhaps the first of these. Initially inspired by jazz singers such as Sarah Vaughan, Billie Holiday and Dinah Washington, Ruth developed her own expressive tone and was recommended to the bosses of a fledgling Atlantic Records in 1948. After she was promptly signed up, they produced a string of R&B classics, including 'So Long' (1949), 'Teardrops From My Eyes' (1950), 'I'll Wait For You' (1951), '(Mama) He Treats Your Daughter Mean' (1953) and 'Mambo Baby' (1954). She became well known as "Miss Rhythm", appeared on the TV program *Showtime At The Apollo* with Miles Davis and Thelonious Monk, and proved to be a big influence on subsequent female R&B singers.

"I was born with music inside me. That's the only explanation I know of." Ray Charles

---

Owing to the seemingly endless string of hits enjoyed by Ruth Brown on Atlantic Records, the then fledgling label came to be known as "The House That Ruth Built".

Legendary R&B *Singers*

Ray Charles was another hugely influential figure in the 1950s R&B movement, and one of the forefathers of soul music. Born Ray Charles Robinson in Albany, Georgia, on 23 September 1930, and blind since the age of seven, he studied composition and learned to play a number of musical instruments at the St. Augustine School for the Deaf and the Blind in Florida.

Charles drew from gospel and Southern blues music to develop a unique singing and songwriting style, which encouraged Atlantic Records to sign him up in 1953. He and Atlantic hit the jackpot: 'I Got A Woman' was a number two R&B hit in 1955, and Charles followed it with a string of other chart-toppers, combining his unmistakably soulful vocal delivery with R&B rhythms. Ray influenced countless R&B singers and became one of the first soul superstars in the 1960s. He later worked with many popular artists, including Aretha Franklin and Michael Jackson.

Key Artists:

Ray Charles
Ruth Brown
Clyde McPhatter
Johnny "Guitar" Watson
Bo Diddley

Another important name in early R&B music is Clyde McPhatter. Originally a gospel singer with the Mount Lebanon Singers in New York, Clyde switched over to R&B when he joined the Dominoes in 1950. They signed to Syd Nathan's King label and recorded 'Sixty Minute Man' (1951), the biggest R&B hit of the year and, according to some, the earliest identifiable example of a rock'n'roll song. He quit the Dominoes in early 1953 and formed his own band, the Drifters, the same year. They recorded 'Money Honey' (1954) and several other big R&B hits for Atlantic Records during the mid-1950s and McPhatter's extremely versatile tenor voice proved capable of handling both sensitive ballads and raucous rock'n'roll. He left the band for a solo career and released several other hits during the late-1950s, but he had less success in the following decade and, undeservedly, faded into obscurity. Other notable R&B singers from the 1950s included Jackie Wilson and James Brown, who both became soul superstars during the 1960s.

Clyde McPhatter's compelling vocals combined blues and gospel influences, and his stunning, emotionally charged tenor voice served as a forerunner to the 1960s and 1970s soul sounds.

R&B Guitar *Icons*

Other R&B artists, such as Bo Diddley and Johnny "Guitar" Watson, were associated with their instruments as much as their singing. Diddley developed an unorthodox, "hambone" rhythm guitar style, which he played on a trademark rectangular guitar. Perhaps his most famous hit was the two-sided 'Bo Diddley'/'I'm A Man' (1955), which he recorded for Chess records.

Watson grew up listening to bluesmen T-Bone Walker and Clarence "Gatemouth" Brown and developed a biting, high-treble guitar tone, which he used to strong effect on albums such as *Gangster Of Love* (1958) and *Johnny Guitar Watson* (1963). An eccentric performer, he was reputed to have played the guitar standing upside-down, using a 46m (150 ft) cord so he could get on top of the auditorium with his instrument. "Those things Jimi Hendrix was doing; I started that shit!" he said to a music journalist.

Key Tracks:

'Bo Diddley' Bo Diddley
'I Got A Woman' Ray Charles
'Money Honey' Clyde McPhatter
'Sixty Minute Man' Clyde McPhatter
'Teardrops From My Eyes' Ruth Brown

Although R&B branched off into a number of different music styles between the 1950s and 1970s, countless blues and soul stars have released R&B hits over the past 40 years. Recent R&B revival artists, such as Big Boy Bloater & his Southside Stompers, continue to ensure that the genre is very much alive.

(Right) Johnny "Guitar" Watson, whose stinging guitar style complemented his decorative vocals. (Above) Bo Diddley, whose insistent, driving rhythms and hard-edged guitar sound made him a key figure in the transition of blues into rock'n'roll.

Rock'n'Roll

Although he did not coin the term "rock'n'roll" – an African-American slang term for sex – New York disk jockey Alan Freed did popularize it when he attached it to a teen-oriented form of music that evolved from a fusion of rockabilly, R&B and, to a lesser extent, gospel and boogie-woogie.

In its early forms, rock'n'roll was often so similar to R&B (known as "race music" until *Billboard* journalist Jerry Wexler provided it with a more appropriate name) in terms of structure and feel that it is not easy to discern which of the categories certain records fell into or even to ascertain what was, in fact, the first true rock'n'roll record.

"Let's face it – rock'n'roll is bigger than all of us."
Alan Freed

Jackie Brenston's 1951 classic, 'Rocket 88', which he cut as a member of Ike Turner and the Kings of Rhythm, is one of the most popular choices in this regard, but there are many, many other contenders, ranging from 1948 recordings such as Wynonie Harris's 'Good Rockin' Tonight' and Wild Bill Moore's 'We're Gonna Rock, We're Gonna Roll' to Jimmy Preston's 'Rock The Joint' in 1949 and Muddy Waters' 'Rollin' And Tumblin' ' in 1950. Waters' assertion that "the blues had a baby and they called it rock'n'roll" was only part of the story; other musical genres also played a major role in the evolutionary process.

(Right) Little Richard's breathlessly delivered lyrics marked a decidedly new style of music. Many credit him as the architect of rock'n'roll.

(Above) His Fabulous Little Richard album presents the usually frenetic star in a slightly more mellow mood.

A Hybrid *Sound*

'Rocket 88' was produced by the legendary Sam Phillips a year before he formed Sun Records, the small independent label which, along with his tiny Memphis Recording Service studio, soon became synonymous with the birth of rock'n'roll.

Phillips worked with local country acts while searching for a white artist who could bring black music to the masses by conveying the true feel and passion of the blues. As it turned out, that artist was Elvis Presley, who, through a process of trial and error, under guidance from Phillips, utilized his innate talent, steeped in country, gospel and the blues, to contrive a hybrid sound that would shake the world. In 13 months at Sun, from July 1954 to August 1955, Presley released five singles, each of which featured an R&B standard on one side and a souped-up country track on the other. While the latter category helped to define rockabilly, the former held the key to rock'n'roll. When white Southerners heard the first of these R&B cuts, Elvis's feverish, yearning cover of Arthur "Big Boy" Crudup's 'That's All Right (Mama)', many of them assumed they were listening to a black singer; by the time of the second, a heavily suggestive version of 'Good Rockin' Tonight', they knew not only that he was white, but that it was time to lock up their daughters.

After Elvis's contract was sold to the huge RCA corporation in late 1955, he recorded the seminal 'Heartbreak Hotel', a sombre, haunting single that not only sustained its predecessors' blues feel and levels of sexual insinuation, but also gained him worldwide recognition. With its blues-laced piano, strident guitar solos and depressive, self-pitying lyrics, 'Heartbreak Hotel' served as a call to arms for disgruntled teenagers; from then on, Presley, whose youthful good looks and Brando-like sexuality stood in sharp and favourable contrast to the pudgy, kiss-curled visage of Bill Haley, pressed home his advantage with a series of blistering rock'n'roll recordings. 'Blue Suede Shoes', 'Hound Dog' and 'Jailhouse Rock' were just a few of the many classic tracks he laid down during a four-year period, yet while they epitomized the genre, some also smacked of manufactured pop rather than heartfelt R&B.

Key Artists:

Jerry Lee Lewis
Little Richard
Elvis Presley

Being considered threatening and corruptive by the authorities only further ensured Elvis Presley's iconic status. In fact, despite his risqué onstage moves, Presley was really a sweet, home-loving boy.

Energy and *Attitude*

Meanwhile, another Sam Phillips discovery was Jerry Lee Lewis, "The Killer" from Ferriday, Louisiana, whose arrogant, aggressive performances quickly established him as one of rock'n'roll's most inspirational figures during its halcyon period.

Melding country and R&B with frenetic, boogie-style piano, Lewis turned out songs that would get the whole joint jumping: 'Whole Lotta Shakin' ', 'Great Balls Of Fire', 'Breathless' and 'High School Confidential'. If Elvis Presley was rock'n'roll's greatest sex symbol, Jerry Lee Lewis was certainly its wildest white performer.

Nevertheless, whereas Lewis belted out his songs' lyrics with manic intensity, and Presley traversed the musical boundaries to sound alternately raucous, gospel-tinged, crooner-like, countrified and bluesy, neither man could match Little Richard, another classic voice of rock'n'roll, for raw, throat-grating, lightning-quick delivery.

Key Tracks:

'Good Golly Miss Molly' Little Richard
'Great Balls Of Fire' Jerry Lee Lewis
'Heartbreak Hotel' Elvis Presley
'Hound Dog' Elvis Presley
'Rocket 88' Jackie Brenston

Richard's exhaustingly energetic singing, punctuated with falsetto shrieks and breathless asides, perfectly matched his flamboyant appearance and short-changed no one, least of all the kids for whom "awop-bop-a-loo-bop-a-lop-bam-boom" had complete meaning. Gibberish or not, it was a language they could instantly identify with, for it somehow encapsulated the energy and attitude prevalent in numbers such as 'Tutti Frutti', 'Long Tall Sally', 'Rip It Up', 'She's Got It', 'Lucille' and 'Good Golly Miss Molly'. What's more, it was a language that most parents could in no way understand, and that had to make it all the more pertinent.

"The Killer" performs a storming rendition of the title track in the opening scenes of High School Confidential, *a film that involved a tongue-in-cheek exposé of drug abuse in American schools.*

Rockabilly

A slapped upright bass, twanging lead guitar and acoustic rhythm guitar; a blues structure with country and blues inflections; a strong beat and moderate-to-fast tempo; a wild, yelping, often stuttering vocal style, together with plenty of echo on the recordings are the main ingredients of rockabilly.

The rockabilly style was an eclectic hybrid of R&B, hillbilly music and country-boogie that emerged during the mid-1950s, and again owed much to Sam Phillips and his Sun Records label.

"I can hear rockabilly in the music that they play today ... bluegrass and the cotton-patch blues. They're still coppin' from that today."
Charlie Feathers

While country-boogie had drawn on jazz boogie-woogie rhythms during the previous decade, and been popularized by acts such as The Delmore Brothers, Webb Pierce, Red Foley and Moon Mullican, the acoustic bass and steel guitar prevalent in the hillbilly sound of Hank Williams exerted just as much influence on the likes of Bill Haley and, a little later on, Carl Perkins.

When Perkins arrived at Sun, he was performing hillbilly honky-tonk infused with the rhythm of black blues music. With Phillips' guidance he then added some R&B touches by way of scatting his vocal phrases and completing them on guitar, resulting in cuts such as 'Gone, Gone, Gone', which appeared on the flip side of his first Sun single, and the seminal self-penned 'Blue Suede Shoes'. Perkins sold two million copies of 'Blue Suede Shoes' before Elvis's cover version was released. A true country boy, Perkins originally wrote the song on a potato sack.

Sam Phillips, owner of Sun Records and creator of the rockabilly style. Hearing Elvis Presley fooling around in the studio with Scotty Moore and Bill Black, Phillips recognized potential in the new sound.

A More Commercial *Sound*

Complemented by Phillips' trademark use of slap-back echo and over-amplification, songs such as 'Gone, Gone, Gone' and 'Blue Suede Shoes' were quintessential rockabilly (or "hillbilly bop", as they were sometimes described), a style that the producer had largely concocted in collaboration with Elvis Presley. The B-side of Elvis's first single ('That's All Right (Mama)', issued in July 1954) was a total revamping of Bill Monroe's 1947 bluegrass waltz, 'Blue Moon Of Kentucky'.

Searching for a more commercial sound that might appeal to a widespread audience, Phillips tried to encourage the young singer, as well as guitarist Scotty Moore and bass player Bill Black, to find a comfortable uptempo groove. This began to take shape over the course of several takes, until what finally emerged was a jumped-up, freewheeling, echo-bathed version, the feel of which was light years away from that of the Monroe original.

The process continued through subsequent Presley recordings such as 'I Don't Care If The Sun Don't Shine', 'Milkcow Blues Boogie' and, most supremely, an electrifying cover of Junior Parker's 'Mystery Train', which borrowed a guitar riff from Parker's earlier 'Love My Baby' to bridge the gap between country and R&B. Still, it was Carl Perkins' 1956 recording of the self-penned 'Blue Suede Shoes' that gained rockabilly worldwide recognition, encouraging major labels such as Capitol, Columbia, Decca, Mercury and RCA to jump on the bandwagon and exploit the genre.

Key Artists:

Charlie Feathers
Carl Perkins
Elvis Presley
Billy Lee Riley

For its part, Sun served as the main rockabilly hub, and a number of other artists signed to the label did make some notable recordings. Prime among them was Charlie Feathers, who co-wrote 'I Forgot To Remember To Forget' before moving to other labels and recording classics such as 'Tongue-Tied Jill' and 'Get With It'. At a time when rock'n'roll was breaking big on both sides of the Atlantic, Feathers felt that he never got the record company support he deserved – a view shared by Billy Lee Riley.

Carl Perkins, one of rockabilly's finest.

Limited Chart *Success*

Billy Lee Riley's more memorable recordings at Sun included 'Rock With Me Baby' and 'Red Hot', but none made the chart inroads he hoped for and expected. A similar fate befell the efforts of, among others, Sonny Burgess, Ray Harris, Hayden Thompson and Warren Smith.

Rockabilly's place in the spotlight was limited and its time was short-lived; its performers came from a very specific background, too. Indeed, because only a handful of the artists were black, Sam Phillips wasn't even comfortable with the genre's name.

"I've always thought 'rock'n'roll' was the best term," he'd comment more than four decades later, "because it became all-inclusive of white, black and the whole thing, whereas 'rockabilly' tended to just want to lend itself so specifically to white. It also promoted the feeling that maybe we were stealing something from the blacks and wanted to put it in a white form, so I never did like 'rockabilly'."

Key Tracks:

'Blue Suede Shoes' Carl Perkins
'Gone, Gone, Gone' Elvis Presley
'Mystery Train' Elvis Presley
'Rock With Me Baby' Billy Lee Riley
'Tongue-Tied Jill' Charlie Feathers

Still, numerous people consider the golden era of rockabilly, which burned out towards the end of the 1950s, to be a shining period in the annals of popular music; a time when often basic instrumentation and primitive recording equipment combined with uninhibited energy to produce rough-edged music that was vital, honest and, to many minds, the purest form of rock'n'roll. It was also a musical form that encapsulated the feelgood party spirit of the mid-1950s: as Carl Perkins once said, "We shook the devil loose! We bopped those blues!" In the 1970s and 1980s rockabilly enjoyed a revival with bands such as the Stray Cats playing down-home 1950s-style music with a punk-rock edge. There were also purist rockabilly revival bands who followed the original style more closely.

The Stray Cats, one of the bands who led the rockabilly revival in the 1970s and 1980s.

Doo-*Wop*

While many hit doo-wop records featured full instrumental accompaniment, the groups themselves had usually started out singing a cappella. It was, in short, a music that required collaborative effort but no instrumental outlay or expertise, to be performed on street corners as a means of escape, public entertainment, personal fulfilment and professional ambition.

Deriving its name from the nonsense backing vocals that often provided its rhythm, R&B-flavoured doo-wop was one of the most popular veins of music to attach itself to rock'n'roll during the second half of the 1950s. The most prominent characteristic of the emotive romantic ballads and jaunty, uptempo, sometimes comical numbers was their interweaving harmonies, whose roots lay not only in gospel but also in black American vocal outfits of the 1940s such as the Mills Brothers and the Ink Spots.

"We sang on the beaches, or on rooftops, or in hallways of tenement buildings. We must have been sensitive artists, even back then, because we always looked for the hallway that had the best sound."
Dion Di Mucci

Arguably, the first doo-wop hit was the Orioles' 'It's Too Soon To Know' in 1948. Thereafter, a number of similar, bird-named groups emerged throughout the early 1950s, including the Cardinals, the Crows, the Larks, the Ravens, the Robins, the Wrens and the Penguins; the latter's 1954 hit, 'Earth Angel (Will You Be Mine)', was latched onto by white kids who could readily identify with lyrics concerning youthful romance. Consequently, a form of music that had initially been aimed at a predominantly adult, African-American audience began to cross over to a multiracial teenage market. In turn, this led to integrated doo-wop groups such as the Impalas and the Del-Vikings – whose 1957 hit 'Come Go With Me' was the first song that the adolescent Paul McCartney ever saw John Lennon perform – as well as all-white outfits such as Dion & the Belmonts, the Mystics and the Skyliners.

Doo-wop usually suggests sweet harmonies and tender ballads, but this was not always the case. This compilation contains a selection of more up-tempo doo-wop songs.

The Doo-Wop *Bandwagon*

Doo-wop had made vast strides within a very short time, and many of the teens who were buying the records were also inspired to form their own a cappella groups.

As singles by the Dominoes and Hank Ballard & the Midnighters made the transition from the R&B charts to the mainstream pop market, and as acts such as the Jewels, the Cadillacs, the Chords, the El Dorados and the Five Satins enjoyed short-lived success, so many of the record companies jumped on the doo-wop bandwagon and hundreds of "new discoveries" were rushed into studios all over the US. Cities such as Los Angeles and Philadelphia produced a fair number of the acts, but the main hub was New York, where both African-Americans and Italian-Americans with little cash in their pockets, but with melody in their hearts, harmonized on teen-oriented songs that conveyed the innocence of a now long-gone era.

Key Artists:

The Coasters
The Clovers
Little Anthony & the Imperials
The Moonglows
The Platters

Thanks to the exploitative, cut-throat practices of the record industry at that time, many of the relatively small percentage of performers who did manage to have their efforts released still emerged without cash in their pockets. Still, some did profit from their endeavours, and others did enjoy an extended stay in the charts. These included the Clovers, the Moonglows, Little Anthony & the Imperials, and Frankie Lymon & the Teenagers, while the plateau was occupied by the Platters and the Coasters.

Hank Ballard brought a mixture of gospel influences and raunchy R&B to the Midnighters the vocal group that he joined in 1953. Their big hit, 'Work With Me Annie', inspired answer records from various musical spheres.

Crossover *Success*

One of the most pop-oriented of all the doo-wop groups, the Platters achieved crossover success in several regards, attracting not only a multiracial audience but also a worldwide, multigenerational one courtesy of such smash-hit ballads as 'Only You (And You Alone)' in 1955 and 'The Great Pretender', whose chart success peaked the following year, both composed by manager Buck Ram.

While 'The Great Pretender' made the Platters the first black act of the rock era to top the pop charts, 'Twilight Time' and 'Smoke Gets In Your Eyes' also occupied pole position and helped the group defy the convention of white artists enjoying greater success with covers of R&B songs.

Meanwhile, the other massive doo-wop favourites of the late-1950s were the Coasters, whose wild, comedy-filled songs contrasted sharply with the Platters' plaintive, soul-stirring ballads. Thanks to the input of legendary composer-producers Jerry Leiber and Mike Stoller, as well as manager Lester Sill, the Coasters turned out a string of million-sellers such as 'Young Blood', 'Searchin' ', 'Yakety Yak', 'Charlie Brown' and 'Poison Ivy' that, in the case of the first two numbers, capitalized on the vocal and improvisational talents of bass lead Bobby Nunn and lead tenor Carl Gardner. Tenor Leon Hughes and baritone Billy Guy completed the quartet. 'Young Blood' and 'Searchin'' were, in fact, released as a double-A-sided single, but by the time 'Yakety Yak' and 'Charlie Brown' were recorded for Atlantic's new Atco label, the group had relocated from Los Angeles to New York with a revamped line-up. This saw Nunn and Hughes replaced by bass lead Will "Dub" Jones and tenor Cornell Gunter, with Adolph Jacobs added on guitar, while among the choice session musicians were the likes of saxophone virtuoso King Curtis.

Key Tracks:

'Earth Angel (Will You Be Mine)' The Penguins
'Only You (And You Alone)' The Platters
'Searchin'' The Coasters
'The Great Pretender' The Platters
'Young Blood' The Coasters

Thanks to the Coasters and their brilliant songwriting/ production team, doo-wop was accorded an all-around brassier treatment in the form of strident sax solos and raucous vocal interplay. However, this only fuelled many people's tendency to not take the genre too seriously, and by the end of the decade it had run out of steam.

The winning combination of the Coasters' vocal talents, Leiber & Stoller's humorous lyrics and King Curtis's stonking saxophone solos led to a string of hits that reflected the light-hearted side of doo-wop.

Skiffle

A cheap acoustic guitar, a washboard, some thimbles, a tea chest, a broom handle and a length of string, together, with a modicum of musical talent – these were all that was required for skiffle, an amalgam of American jazz, blues and folk that caught on with Britain's cash-strapped teenagers in 1956 and 1957, temporarily challenging the supremacy of rock'n'roll.

"It was a simple way into music because a lot of the songs had just two chords, and the maximum was three.... Everyone was in a skiffle group." George Harrison

Rhythmic and decidedly upbeat, skiffle was a white, Anglicized extension of the black music that, drawing on blues, jazz, rag and traditional country, had originated in America during the late nineteenth century and been performed all over the South during the 1920s and 1930s by what were variously known as skiffle, skuffle, spasm, hamfat, washboard, jook and, most popularly, jug bands.

These makeshift outfits usually consisted of a fiddle, a banjo, a kazoo and, sometimes, a guitar, mandolin and/or harmonica, together with percussive, rhythmic household items such as spoons, tin cans and washboards (upon which thimbled fingers and thumbs would be run up and down). Nevertheless, whereas the bass line was provided by at least one band member blowing into or across the top of a jug, when the 1950s skiffle revival took place in England, said jug was supplanted by a crude imitation of an upright bass in the form of a broom handle poked through a hole in an upturned tea chest, with a cord attached between the two.

The 6.5 Special TV programme, launched by the BBC in 1957, featured live music including traditional folk and the latest craze, skiffle. Popular at first, the show went into decline when producer Jack Good defected to rival channel ITV.

A Raw, American-Accented *Style*

The king of British skiffle – and the only one of the artists to earn international recognition – was Lonnie Donegan, who introduced the music to concert audiences during the early 1950s when he performed his versions of blues, country and folk standards in between sets by Ken Colyer's Jazzmen.

Playing banjo or acoustic guitar while backed by an upright bass and drums, Donegan delivered the vocals in a raw, American-accented style that quickly made him more popular than the star attraction. When Colyer's outfit evolved into Chris Barber's Jazz Band in 1954, Donegan took the lead on what turned out to be a seminal track on the group's debut album, *New Orleans Joys*. Featuring Barber on bass and Beryl Bryden on washboard, Lonnie Donegan's rendition of the old Huddie "Leadbelly" Ledbetter blues standard, 'Rock Island Line', was released as a single and sold a staggering three million copies, spending 22 weeks on the UK charts, where it peaked at number eight, while also making the American Top 10.

Key Artists:

Lonnie Donegan
Johnny Duncan
The Vipers Skiffle Group
The Chas McDevitt Skiffle Group
 featuring Nancy Whiskey

Still, although the sales figures were more than a little impressive, what made 'Rock Island Line' unique in the annals of British pop at that time was the fact that most of the people who bought the record were teenagers. Suddenly, like an oasis in a desert of staid formality, here was a raucous, bluesy, homegrown sound that not only caught the kids' attention but also inspired them to form their own bands in an attempt to duplicate the Lonnie Donegan formula. By the time Donegan's single 'Lost John' climbed to number two on the UK chart in early 1956, there was a full-scale skiffle boom taking place in Britain, with anywhere up to half a million teens forming their own bands while their idol was appearing on stage and nationwide television in America.

Lonnie Donegan, 'The King Of Skiffle', became a more homogeneous UK equivalent to Elvis Presley than Tommy Steele. His first album, The Golden Age of Donegan, *reached number three during a 23-week stay in the music charts.*

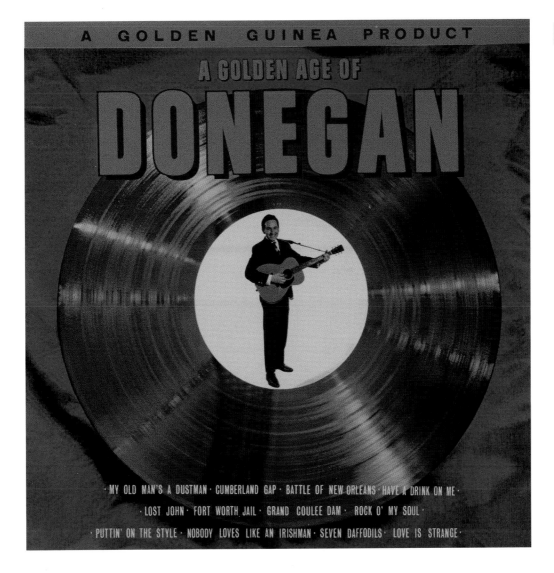

An Enduring *Effect*

Donegan's first album, *Showcase*, sold in the hundreds of thousands, and he continued to make the Top 10 on the British singles chart with tracks such as 'Bring A Little Water Sylvie', 'Don't You Rock Me Daddy-O', 'Cumberland Gap' and 'Putting On The Style'.

Meanwhile, a number of other acts were appearing on the scene. The Vipers Skiffle Group, whose sound was rougher than Donegan's, and more firmly steeped in folk and the blues, also enjoyed a Top 10 hit with 'Don't You Rock Me Daddy-O' (penned by Vipers singer/guitarist Wally Whyton). Courtesy of several subsequent releases, the Vipers were second only to Donegan in terms of their success. That of certain others, however, was altogether more brief: the Chas McDevitt Skiffle Group featuring Nancy Whiskey charted with 'Freight Train', and an American by the name of Johnny Duncan climbed to number two in the UK with 'Last Train To San Fernando'. Even Britain's first true rock'n'roll star, Tommy Steele, started out playing skiffle.

It was, of course, rock'n'roll that, by the end of 1957, put an end to the skiffle boom. However, although its time in the sun was short-lived, skiffle's invaluable contribution to popular music was the enduring effect that it had on a generation of teenagers who would be at the vanguard of the British – and subsequently international – rock scene of the 1960s: the Who, the Hollies, the Kinks, the Moody Blues, the Searchers, Procol Harum.... These and many more all had band members who cut their musical teeth on a skiffle-inspired acoustic guitar, washboard or tea-chest basis.

Key Tracks:

'Don't You Rock Me Daddy-O' The Vipers Skiffle Band
'Freight Train' The Chas McDevitt Skiffle Group featuring
  Nancy Whiskey
'Last Train To San Fernando' Johnny Duncan
'Lost John' Lonnie Donegan
'Rock Island Line' Lonnie Donegan

In fact, Lonnie Donegan's 'Putting On The Style' was sitting at the top of the UK chart when an outfit by the name of the Quarry Men performed the song at a church fête in Liverpool on 6 July 1957. The lead vocalist that day was a 16-year-old John Lennon; in the audience to see him for the first time was a 15-year-old Paul McCartney. Skiffle's role doesn't come any bigger than that.

The Vipers grew from the vibrant music scene that converged at the 2I's Coffee Bar in Soho, London, along with countless other performers, including Tommy Steele, Joe Brown, Hank Marvin and Adam Faith.

The Nashville *Sound*

The Nashville sound has been both praised and maligned. Occasionally called "crossover country", "easy listening country" or "countrypolitan", it was a trend more than an innovation. As such, it arose as much from commercial considerations as it did from personal artistry.

All through the decades there have been periodic cross-pollinations between the country world and the wider pop audience. From the 1930s well into the 1950s *Grand Ole Opry* star Red Foley charmed both country folk and urbanites alike with his smooth voice and mellow musical sensibilities. In the 1950s and early 1960s Patti Page, an Oklahoman who started out singing western swing music, had a few best-selling pop hits with covers of country tunes. Her 1950 recording of Pee Wee King's 'Tennessee Waltz' sold nearly five million copies. Crooner Bing Crosby even got in on the act with a cover of Ernest Tubb's 'Walkin' The Floor Over You'.

An Antidote to Rock'n'Roll

Oddly enough, it was the advent of rock'n'roll that really spurred the late-1950s and early 1960s Nashville crossover era. The emergence of the rock'n'rollers unleashed a national craze that for a while seriously impacted on country record sales. The negative impact on the country record market was such that even hardcore country artists like George Jones responded by trying their hands at rockabilly and rock'n'roll. Others, like Sonny James, Marty Robbins and Don Gibson, broke through the late-1950s crossover market with mellow teen ballads like 'Young Love' and 'A White Sport Coat (And A Pink Carnation)'. The success of such records was not lost upon Nashville producers Chet Atkins and Owen Bradley, the widely acknowledged pioneers of the Nashville sound. They, along with any number of other Music Row producers, had been trying to figure out for a long time how to make country records that could jump the fence into the far more lucrative pop crossover market.

Their appetites were further whetted by the success of Nashville-based artists like the Everly Brothers, Roy Orbison and Brenda Lee, who managed to achieve longevity in the 1950s and 1960s as teen pop idols with hits that were written by Nashville-based songwriters and recorded and produced in Nashville studios.

Nashville, Tennessee, the "Music City", in 1933. Home to the Grand Ole Opry *and country music's top producers, Nashville was the destination of many a hopeful hillbilly dreaming of a recording contract.*

From Nashville to *"Cashville"*

What distinguished the Nashville sound was the way it aggressively dressed up mainstream country music for pop radio airplay. Producers like Atkins and Bradley found tasteful ways of toning down the clatter and clang of country music's raw edges and nudging it in a more uptown direction. They eased up on – or eliminated altogether – the vocal twang and replaced raucous fiddles and steel guitars with lush vocal arrangements, bright, sparkling slip-note piano embellishments and laid-back string and horn arrangements.

The term "Nashville sound" also refers to the increasingly regimented, almost factory-like approach to hit-making that producers like Atkins and Bradley. By the early 1960s, the Music Row studio system had become dominated by a relatively small, tight-knit group of "A Team" studio musicians who played on hundreds of recording sessions, conducted with the precision and efficiency of a factory time clock.

Many fans of traditional and honky tonk-style country music took such Nashville sound refinements as an affront to the music's integrity. They found it even more irritating when a few premier honky tonk singers such as Ray Price blithely segued into a mellow, easy listening pop cushiness with hits like 'Danny Boy' and 'For The Good Times' that seemed the very antithesis of hard country.

Some artists most closely associated with the Nashville sound, like crooner Eddy Arnold, *Grand Ole Opry* star George Morgan and Virginia-born songstress Patsy Cline flourished and found their natural voices in the Nashville sound setting. So did others like Marty Robbins, Ferlin Husky and former honky tonkers Don Gibson and Faron Young. Ironically, practically all of these singers had begun their careers in a much more traditional spirit. Crossing over from a slightly different angle were artists like Bobby Bare, George Hamilton IV and Johnny Cash, who enjoyed some success in the country charts and at least some in the pop charts, with a subgenre often referred to as folk country. Roger Miller managed to cross over in his own quirky way and won 11 Grammy Awards with hip, scat-sung novelty tunes like 'King Of The Road' and 'Dang Me'.

Key Artists:

Eddy Arnold
Patsy Cline
George Morgan
Charlie Rich
Tammy Wynette

Patsy Cline, whose song 'Crazy' received three standing ovations when first performed at the Grand Ole Opry in 1961.

The Sherrillization of *Nashville*

The producer who inherited the Nashville sound mantle in the 1970s was Billy Sherrill, a talented and somewhat enigmatic former Alabama rhythm & blues saxophone player. Sherrill would earn both kudos and scorn for upping the Nashville sound ante even further by adapting the "wall of sound" approach pioneered by legendary rock producer Phil Spector on pop hits by artists like the Righteous Brothers.

Sherrill applied his own heavily layered wall of sound to hits he produced for stars of the day like Tammy Wynette (who, despite the overblown arrangements on hits like 'Stand By Your Man', usually avoided the Nashville sound tag simply because her voice was so countrified), David Houston ('Almost Persuaded') and Charlie Rich.

Rich, a gifted former white R&B and supper-club jazz singer who made it big with slick crossover chart-toppers in the 1970s like 'Behind Closed Doors', became a particular embodiment of what has been both praised and damned as the "Sherrillization" of country music. Love it or hate it, many of the Billy Sherrill-produced records by Rich and Wynette, like 'Stand By Your Man' were runaway best-sellers.

Key Tracks:

'Behind Closed Doors' Charlie Rich
'Crazy' Patsy Cline
'Stand By Your Man' Tammy Wynette
'The Most Beautiful Girl In The World' Charlie Rich
'What's He Doing In My World' Eddy Arnold

Permutations of the Nashville sound have persisted right up into the present era. But by the early 1970s, its refinements had begun to lapse into predictability and stagnation. The trend reached its embarrassing nadir in 1975 when the Country Music Association saw fit to bestow its highest honour, the "Entertainer of the Year" award, on pop star John Denver, to the chagrin of innumerable country music performers and enthusiasts. Although the Nashville sound remains a factor in mainstream country to this day, it fell upon a handful of strong-willed mavericks, popularly known as the outlaws, to rise from the late-1960s and 1970s Nashville sound morass and revitalize country's mainstream by swinging it back toward its rustic roots.

Chet Atkins, together with Merle Travis and Doc Watson, is considered one of the "holy trinity" of country guitarists. But as a producer, his countrypolitan style was the precursor to Billy Sherrill's "wall of sound" productions.

Sixties *Pop*

As the 1960s approached, the controversy associated with rock'n'roll was superseded by an array of inoffensive smoothies on both sides of the atlantic. However, the ongoing popularity of artists such as Elvis Presley, Bobby Darin, Ricky Nelson, Sam Cooke, and, in the UK, Lonnie Donegan, Billy Fury and Cliff Richard, ensured a degree of continuity in the music scene.

Likewise the success of singers such as Roy Orbison endured into the 1960s, and the trend for pop instrumentals grew, courtesy of groups such as the Shadows in Britain and the Ventures in America, where Dick Dale & His Del-Tones were purveyors of the "surf guitar". The remains of white doo-wop could be heard in recordings by the Four Seasons and Dion (both with and without the Belmonts); and the last vestiges of Gene Vincent-style rock'n'roll was performed in Britain by Johnny Kidd & the Pirates.

"This generation is producing poets who write songs, and never before in the sixty-year history of American popular music has this been true."
Ralph J. Gleason

Still, while the controversy associated with rock'n'roll had also been superseded by an array of parent-friendly smoothies on both sides of the Atlantic, there is little truth in the often-expressed notion that the US pop scene was uniformly bland before the Beatles came along. On the contrary, from 1960 to the end of 1963, there was a prevalence of material that epitomized the art of the perfectly crafted three-minute pop song.

The 1960s vibrant college art scene spawned the inimitable Bonzo Dog Doo Dah Band, whose legendary stage shows earned them a slot in the Beatles' 1967 film Magical Mystery Tour.

The Leading *Lights*

Among the most successful exponents in this regard were Chubby Checker, whose renditions of 'The Twist' and 'Let's Twist Again' incited a new international dance craze and the teams of young composer/ producers such as Gerry Goffin & Carole King and Jeff Barry & Ellie Greenwich housed inside New York City's Brill Building, who turned out hit after classic hit for artists such as the Shirelles, the Shangri-Las, the Chiffons, the Drifters, Little Eva, Connie Francis, the Crystals and the Ronettes.

Elswhere were Phil Spector, whose echo-bathed "Wall of Sound" creations added an entirely new dimension to record production; the in-house roster of songwriters, producers and artists assigned to Detroit's Motown label, whose dynamic soul- and R&B-based numbers were just starting to create waves; and the surf-and-hot-rod bands led by the Beach Boys were setting new pop standards by distinguishing fairly basic three- or four-chord songs with intricate four- and five-part harmonies.

In essence, although rock'n'roll had rebelled against the overt professionalism and sterility of the popular music that preceded it, the logical progression that took place during the early 1960s consisted of the aforementioned exponents, drawing on Tin Pan Alley's skilled and methodical approach towards songwriting in order to raise pop to the next level. What's more, while the likes of Brian Wilson helped set the precedent for artists writing and even producing their own songs, there was an increasing emphasis placed on the record's sound as well as its musical content.

5 Top 1960s UK Artists:	*5 Top 1960s US Artists:*
1 Cliff Richard	1 The Beatles
2 The Beatles	2 Simon And Garfunkel
3 Rolling Stones	3 Bob Dylan
4 Roy Orbison	4 The Doors
5 The Everly Brothers	5 The Beach Boys

Rock'n'roll had shaken things up by displacing most of the old brigade of artists at the top end of the charts. The early 1960s marked an end to the era of innocent lyrics prevailing in mainstream pop, as well as black acts feeling obliged to "dress white" in order to broaden their appeal. Conformity had taken a temporary vacation when rock'n'roll was at its height; at this point it was about to disappear for good.

Chubby Checker, whose cover version of Hank Ballard & the Midnighters' 'The Twist' was so close to the original that Ballard, upon hearing it, thought that it was his own recording.

Changing *Times*

Cynicism replaced optimism following Kennedy's assassination in 1963, and people began to look for a change. In musical terms, this need was answered by the glut of homegrown "beat groups" who swamped the UK charts throughout 1963 and invaded America the following year, sweeping away most of the previously established acts like so much dust.

Outfits such as the Beatles, Gerry & the Pacemakers, the Searchers, Freddie & the Dreamers, Billy J. Kramer & the Dakotas, Herman's Hermits and the Dave Clark Five exuded youthful cheer and vitality by way of their vivacious guitar-and-drums-based music and well-groomed appearances. These, however, were counterbalanced by the relatively unkempt looks, surly demeanour and harsher, R&B-tinged sounds of fellow Brits such as the Rolling Stones and the Animals, not to mention the proto-heavy-metal riffs of the Kinks and, by 1965, the guitar-and-drums pyrotechnics of the Who.

Attitude had returned with a vengeance, and hereafter would remain the predominant characteristic of rock music as it branched away from the mainstream pop performed by American "answers to the Beatles" such as the Buckinghams, the Beau Brummels and even the Monkees. At a time when Western youth was becoming more concerned with the war in Vietnam than with carefree, fun-in-the-sun beach parties, popular music was suddenly shaping public opinion and inspiring social change instead of simply reflecting it. Amid this acid-drenched, peace-and-love climate, the idea of young girls screaming hysterically during concerts was passé – and so, in an age of increasingly elaborate album projects, was the heyday of the three-minute single. Pop music would continue to evolve, but in many respects its halcyon years were now behind it.

5 Top 1960s UK Tracks:
1. 'She Loves You' The Beatles
2. 'I Want To Hold Your Hand' The Beatles
3. 'Tears' Ken Dodd
4. 'Can't Buy Me Love' The Beatles
5. 'I Feel Fine' The Beatles

5 Top 1960s US Tracks:
1. 'Hey Jude' The Beatles
2. The Theme From 'A Summer Place' Percy Faith
3. 'Tossin' And Turnin'' Bobby Lewis
4. 'I Want To Hold Your Hand' The Beatles
5. 'I'm A Believer' The Monkees

This photograph, staged by a national newspaper in the early 1960s, shows a selection of the myriad of Merseybeat bands that sprung up across Liverpool in the wake of the Beatles' phenomenal success.

Lounge *Music*

Following on from the lush bombast of the swing era, and established by a colourful group of American artists in the 1950s and 1960s, lounge was easy listening's quirky kid brother. It was more playful than its more populist relative and, when viewed retrospectively, had a high camp factor.

Although ostensibly laid-back and mellow, lounge artists like Les Baxter and Esquivel were not afraid to experiment with tempo and style and helped lounge mutate into new forms. Space-age pop made use of futuristic new instruments and exotica stole influences from Latin America, Africa and beyond with a magpie's zeal. This music was dilettantish rather than authentic, presenting snapshots of far-off countries or future worlds for an audience hungry for luxurious escapism.

"It seems that most of my life I have had inclinations towards ... different, interesting music. I never like to do prosaic." Les Baxter

Lounge music was later re-branded as cocktail music, martini music and lounge-core by the trendsetters who rediscovered it in the 1990s. To them, it evoked kitsch 1960s lifestyles pursued in bachelor pads stuffed with lava lamps and leopard- skin sofas. Whether this image was accurate or not was irrelevant: retro freaks descended in droves on second-hand record shops to unearth vintage LPs like *Equinox* (1967), by the Brazilian Sergio Mendes, and the entire back catalogue of the mighty Burt Bacharach.

(Right) Prolific exotica pioneer Les Baxter also created the music for over 250 films and shows for television and radio, as well as composing and arranging pieces for the top swing bands of the 1940s and 1950s. (Above) Baxter's legendary album Music Out Of The Moon.

A Musical Trip Around the *World*

One of the foremost lounge artists was Les Baxter, a pianist from Detroit who worked with some of the biggest bands of the swing era, but is best remembered as the most important pioneer of exotica, which gained considerable popularity in America during the 1950s. His compositions retained the backbone of strings and brass that characterized most popular music of the time.

But he also assimilated everything from the striking, four-octave range of the legendary Peruvian vocalist Yma Sumac to the steel guitars of Polynesia and Hawaii, whose tiki bars and hula dancing permeated American pop culture in the post-war years. African percussion was another influence: in 1951, Baxter recorded his seminal *Ritual of the Savage* LP, a musical travelogue replete with recorded jungle noises and bird calls. The album remains a classic of exotica – its lead track, 'Quiet Village', was covered with great success by another renowned lounger, Martin Denny, in 1959, and it also inspired Denny's bandmate Arthur Lyman, who had a hit with 'Yellow Bird' in 1961.

Key Artists:

Les Baxter
Esquivel
Burt Bacharach
Sergio Mendes

A prime mover in both space-age pop and exotica was Esquivel, a bona fide lounge eccentric who created some of the strangest music of the late-1950s and 1960s. Much of the Mexican's output was based on the big band format and shot through with exaggerated Latin American rhythms, from cha-cha to mambo, but he also employed the theremin and an arsenal of other outlandish instruments, including Chinese bells, early electronic keyboards and the ondioline, a vacuum tube instrument that emits a reedy, vibrato sound. His surreal sense of humour extended to having his vocalists sing comic-book injections like "Pow!" and "Boink!".

His most infamous recording was 1962's *Latin-Esque*, the first album recorded with full stereo separation: two orchestras performing in separate studios whom he conducted using headphones. He divided opinions during the 1950s and 1960s: some critics were turned off by his wild clashing of styles and tempos and occasional disregard for tonal beauty. Others became great fans, and Esquivel ended his career as a stalwart of the Las Vegas circuit and a favourite with Frank Sinatra and REM.

Esquivel's bizarre use of instrumentation and innovative arrangements were designed to exploit the new stereo equipment. Futuristic as the music sounded, it dated quickly, but became a kitsch favourite in the 1970s.

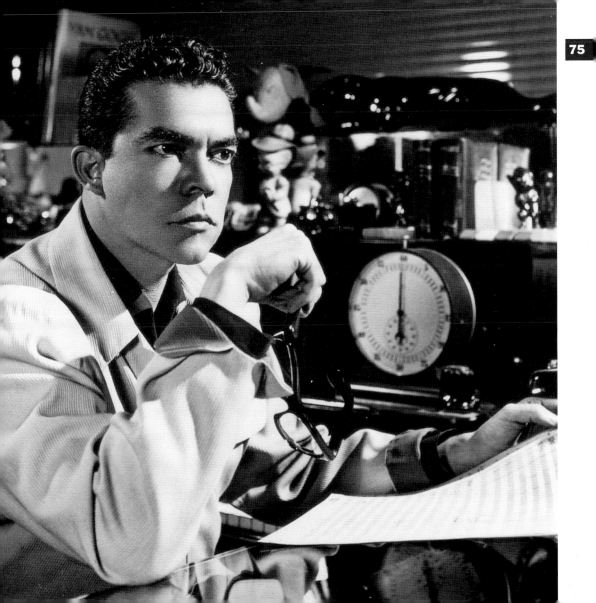

Revival of a Master *Songwriter*

The popularity of Esquivel and his cohorts declined after the 1970s, but enjoyed a revival in the 1990s, inspiring British electronic artists such as Funki Porcini and receiving a more tongue-in-cheek reworking by Mike Flowers, who achieved UK chart success with a lounge-style cover of Oasis's 'Wonderwall' in 1996.

It was this exposure, along with appearances in the Austin Powers films, that helped to renew interest in another 1960s star – Burt Bacharach – who would come to embody lounge for a new generation of listeners. Back in 1948, Baxter also experimented with a theremin, one of the world's first electronic instruments, combining its eerie, otherwordly sound with a choir, rhythm section, cello and French horn. The result, an LP titled *Music Out Of The Moon*, was the progenitor of space-age pop, a future-fixated relation of lounge that exploited the possibilities afforded by the stereo format and nascent electronic instrumentation.

Key Albums:

Equinox Sergio Mendes
Latin-Esque Esquivel
Music Out Of The Moon Les Baxter
Ritual Of The Savage Les Baxter

Of course, it would be an injustice to one of the twentieth century's greatest musicians to describe the Kansas City-born Bacharach as solely a lounge artist. Since the early 1950s he has written hits for the Carpenters, toured with cabaret star Marlene Dietrich, composed Oscar-winning music for Butch Cassidy & The Sundance Kid and released a string of classic collaborations with Dionne Warwick.

Bacharach's sophisticated yet light melodies have something in common with those of easy listening titans like Henry Mancini. But his twinkling versatility, which has taken in jazz, bossa nova, soul, Brazilian grooves and pure pop, is even truer to the playful eclecticism of lounge. Today, such tracks as 1965's 'Make It Easy On Yourself', which he wrote for the Walker Brothers, exude a breezy, kitsch panache that makes Bacharach, among many other things, a quintessential lounge hero.

Burt Bacharach, with guest stars Mireille Mathieu, Juliet Prowse and Dusty Springfield, on a 1970 television show. Springfield is considered to be one of the best interpreters of Bacharach's songs, along with Dionne Warwick.

The Wall of *Sound*

No one had ever produced records like Phil Spector. There had been lavish orchestrations and raucous sounds, but until the early 1960s, the elements were clearly defined in recordings with a fair amount of separation allotted to a limited number of rhythm and percussion instruments within the confines of a mainly monaural medium. Spector changed all that.

Applying copious amounts of live and tape-delayed echo to layers of percussion, strings, brass, vocals and an R&B-derived rhythm section, comprising drums and multiple basses, keyboards and guitars, Spector, together with arranger Jack Nitzsche and engineer Larry Levine, fused the individual components into a unified "Wall of Sound", which, despite being monolithic, enriched the material to create timeless works of three-minute art.

"That's gold. That's solid gold coming out of that speaker."
Phil Spector to Sonny Bono after listening to the final playback of 'Da Doo Ron Ron'.

Some of what Spector described as "little symphonies for the kiddies" made him more famous than the semi-anonymous artists – for example, although she was not a member of the Crystals, Darlene Love filled in for their regular lead singer, La La Brooks, on the group's US-chart-topping 1962 single, 'He's A Rebel'. Spector owned the band's name, so he could do as he pleased. However, rather than overwhelming the passionate lead vocals, his productions invariably glorified them. To this end, he employed the very best songwriters, as well as a wide array of the industry's foremost session musicians.

Phil Spector infiltrated the LA music scene in the late 1950s and recorded his own composition 'To Know Him Is To Love Him', which was inspired by the inscription on his father's gravestone.

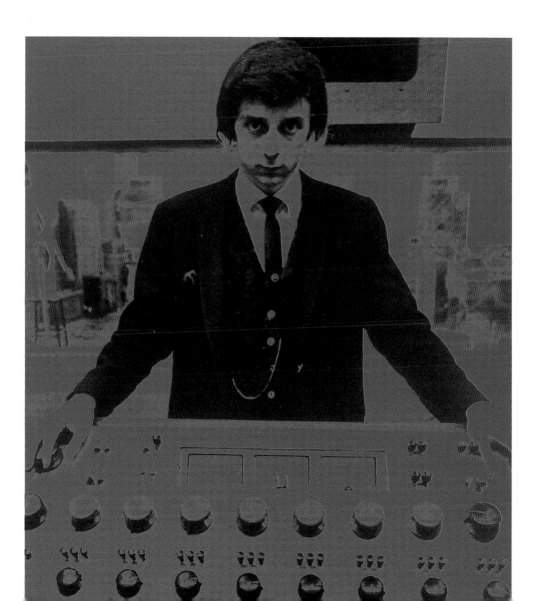

The Wrecking *Crew*

Working in LA's Goldstar Studios, Spector's "Wrecking Crew", as it came to be known, comprised a solid core of luminaries, including drummer Hal Blaine; bass player Carol Kaye; guitarists Glen Campbell, Barney Kessel, Tommy Tedesco and Billy Strange; keyboard players Larry Knechtel and Leon Russell; saxophonist Jay Migliori; and multi-instrumentalists Sonny Bono and Nino Tempo.

Many, many others also contributed to the sessions, ranging from King Curtis, Herb Alpert, Harry Nilsson and Lenny Bruce to Brian Wilson, Billy Preston, Cher and Dr. John. After running the musicians through each of their parts and rehearsing them incessantly, Spector would record countless takes until the sound approximated what he envisaged in his head; he would then complete the picture by way of the mixing process.

Key Artists:

The Crystals
Darlene Love
The Righteous Brothers
The Ronettes
Ike & Tina Turner

"Phil was notorious for never giving the band five because he didn't want anybody to move," recalled Bones Howe, who engineered a couple of Ike & Tina Turner and Ronnie Spector sessions. "He knew exactly where he wanted the instruments positioned, and it would take him such a long time to get the balance exactly the way he wanted. There'd be, say, a mandolin mixed in with the guitar section. ... He had the band play the chart over and over and over again, like a tape loop. You know, the minute they reached the end they'd play it again, and he would go out and change people's parts. It would sometimes only be zillionths of an inch of change to make the difference that Phil wanted, but he'd know when it all fell into place. The amazing thing about it was, when that happened it did have an incredible sound, and I'm not sure that some of that wasn't just down to the musicians getting beat by playing it over and over and over again, so that the sound began to all melt together."

The rich arrangement of Ike & Tina Turner's Spector-produced single 'River Deep, Mountain High' seems to echo the landscape of the title, alternating flowing bassline passages and screeching climaxes.

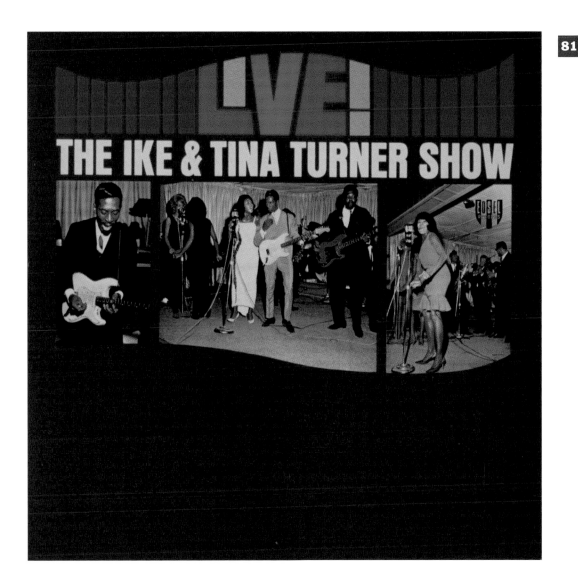

Multitalented and *Autocratic*

Whatever the formula, it certainly worked, as proven by a startling series of recordings between 1962 and 1966 including: 'He's A Rebel' and 'Then He Kissed Me' by the Crystals; the Ronettes' 'Be My Baby' and 'Walking In The Rain'; Darlene Love's '(Today I Met) The Boy I'm Gonna Marry'; 'Zip-a-Dee Doo-Dah' by Bob B. Soxx & the Blue Jeans; the 1963 all-star Christmas album, which included Darlene Love's majestic 'Christmas (Baby Please Come Home)'; 'You've Lost That Lovin' Feelin'' and 'Unchained Melody' by the Righteous Brothers; and Ike & Tina Turner's 'River Deep, Mountain High'.

Multitalented and autocratic, Spector contributed to these and other recordings in numerous ways. Not only did he produce them; in many instances, he was also a co-composer. In addition, he played session guitar and owned the Philles label, which he launched in late 1961 with Lester Sill. Not for nothing did the writer Tom Wolfe label him "The First Tycoon of Teen".

Suddenly out of Step

While girl-group classics such as 'Da Doo Ron Ron' and 'Be My Baby' stand as shining examples of pop perfection many cite 'You've Lost That Lovin' Feelin'' and 'River Deep, Mountain High' as the apotheosis of the "Wall of Sound". Even so, and despite being a number three hit in the UK, 'River Deep' was a flop in the US upon its release in 1966. A dispirited Spector folded his label and withdrew from a rapidly changing scene, one that was suddenly out of step with both his working methods and his preoccupation with producing singles instead of albums.

Spector resurfaced in the late 1960s but worked only sporadically during the next decade, bringing his "Wall of Sound" to many records. Eccentric, egotistical and volatile, Spector enjoyed a relatively short halcyon period. And yet, during that time, he demonstrated a depth of artistic vision that forever changed the course of popular music.

Key Tracks:

'Be My Baby' The Ronettes
'Da Doo Ron Ron' The Crystals
'River Deep, Mountain High' Ike & Tina Turner
'(Today I Met) The Boy I'm Gonna Marry' Darlene Love
'You've Lost That Lovin' Feeling' The Righteous Brothers

Spector was smitten with Veronica "Ronnie" Bennett, lead singer of the Ronettes, and reserved some of his best songs for the group, including 'Be My Baby' and 'Baby I Love You'. They later married.

The Classic Soul *Era*

The story of soul's golden age is linked with the story of two American record labels: Berry Gordy's Motown and Jim Stewart & Estelle Axton's Stax. They discovered artists, wrote songs and developed recording and marketing methods that would irrevocably change popular music, and have a profound effect on the perception of race all over world.

Motown's base in Detroit and Stax's in Memphis symbolized the Afro-American migration from south to north, and the differences in style and aspirations between those who left and those who stayed. Berry Gordy came from a Georgian farming family who had relocated to Detroit. He began writing songs in the mid-1950s, after stints as a boxer, soldier, jazz record shop assistant and car worker, and hit big with songs for former sparring partner Jackie Wilson, including big band R&B classic 'Reet Petite'. Gordy was persuaded to form his own record company in 1959 by singer/songwriter protégé Smokey Robinson, making his big breakthrough in 1961 with 'Shop Around', performed by Robinson's vocal group the Miracles. Gordy's tightly controlled methods were considered both revolutionary and controversial in later years. Artists were signed on salaries and ordered to perform the material that Gordy insisted upon. The house producers and composers – Robinson, Holland/Dozier/Holland, Ashford/Simpson, Whitfield/Strong – were all-important. The in-house band the Funk Brothers (pianist Joe Hunter, guitarist Dave Hamilton, drummer Benny Benjamin and the legendary James Jamerson on the most influential bass guitar in pop history) pioneered the all-important Motown sound but saw little in the way of financial recompense (a complaint subsequently echoed by many Motown artists) or recognition. Motown package tours were tightly choreographed and chaperoned, with the young stars given lessons in deportment and etiquette by Motown staffers.

"The Temptations could have come from Central Casting. . . five great-looking men, all over six foot tall, and they did it all."
Shelly Berger, manager

Originally just the Miracles, in 1967 the group became known as Smokey Robinson & the Miracles. They had a total of 25 Top 40 hits during the 1960s.

The Hit *Factory*

Whatever the rights or wrongs of the set-up, the inexhaustible supply of Motown hits dominated the 1960s, in Europe as well as America. The unmistakable Motown blend of powerful R&B rhythm, highly sophisticated orchestral arrangements and poetic lyricism came to define the language of pop.

The peerless parade of charismatic virtuoso gospel-derived vocal groups and solo artists beguiled white fans as much as black, and raised the level of artistry that pop could attain. The likes of Robinson, Diana Ross & the Supremes, Marvin Gaye, the Four Tops, the Temptations and Stevie Wonder fronted hit after hit, rising from pop ingénues to era-defining artists within the ten years of Motown's peak period. Although they may have signed to Motown in 1968, after its peak, the Jackson Five's debut single 'I Want You Back' was the label's fastest-selling record ever, and three of their subsequent five singles reached the number one spot in the US.

The Southern Melting Pot

1960 saw the formation of Stax, a label that, by signing a distribution deal with powerful New York jazz and R&B company Atlantic, would see their completely contrasting style of soul cross over to the rapidly growing rock audience. The Stax/Atlantic phenomenon was based upon a complete racial mix: raucous and untamed black gospel-raised vocalists such as the Stax label's Otis Redding, Sam & Dave, and Carla Thomas; plus Atlantic's Aretha Franklin, Ben E. King, Solomon Burke and Wilson Pickett, worked with multi-racial R&B bands Booker T & the MG's and the Muscle Shoals rhythm section, performing the songs and sounds of racially integrated backroom geniuses. If Stax/Atlantic's true reflection of the young southerners' rebuffal of segregation was challenging, then the music was incendiary: power-packed testimonies of love, sex, spiritual freedom and political protest matched with horn-driven proto-funk that gave a feeling of earthy, spontaneous, almost live authenticity, and contrasted perfectly with Motown's highly sophisticated studio symphonies.

Key Artists:

Smokey Robinson & the Miracles
Aretha Franklin
Diana Ross & the Supremes
Marvin Gaye
Dionne Warwick

Berry Gordy, the owner of Motown records, with Diana Ross. Following the defection of producers Holland/ Dozier/Holland in 1970, Gordy concentrated on promoting the solo career of the singer who was also his lover.

Soul's Full *Circle*

While Motown and Stax/Atlantic dominated, the market inevitably became saturated with soul artists and records pouring from labels both major and independent. Many magnificent singles became lost amidst the deluge, but some non-Motown/Stax/Atlantic artists emerged to comparable acclaim and impact.

James Brown continued to be known as "Soul Brother Number One", remaining soul's greatest live performer and developing the rhythmic innovation known as funk. Ohio singer/songwriter/ guitarist Bobby Womack who was discovered in the early 1960s by Sam Cooke, saw his 'It's All Over Now' covered by the Rolling Stones, and had a slew of tough and bluesy R&B hits based around his rough, gruff vocals and hard rocking blues guitar. In complete contrast, New Jersey's Dionne Warwick forged the template for the perennial sophisticated soul diva in the mid-1960s, with her subtle and beautiful recordings of songs by Burt Bacharach & Hal David, most famously on the sweeping romantic dramas of 1964's 'Anyone Who Had A Heart' and 'Walk On By'.

Key Tracks:
'Baby Love' Diana Ross & the Supremes
'I Heard It Through The Grapevine' Marvin Gaye
'I Never Loved A Man (The Way I Loved You)' Aretha Franklin
'Shop Around' Smokey Robinson & the Miracles
'Walk On By' Dionne Warwick

As the integrationist hope of the 1960s faded into the pessimistic 1970s, Motown and Stax struggled to come to terms with changing trends and a loss of identity. Amidst the coming dominance of funk and disco, the death of Otis Redding in a 1967 plane crash and the reinvention of Marvin Gaye and Stevie Wonder as social comment singer/songwriters, one last great soulman emerged. Arkansas vocalist Al Green, working out of Willie Mitchell's Hi studio label in Memphis, brought a new sexual intensity to romantic soul with his astonishing falsetto voice and a string of sensual hits produced between 1971 and 1974. In October of that year, a horrifying incident, in which a girlfriend poured boiling grits over the singer before shooting herself, prompted Green to reject his sex-symbol stardom and the promiscuous lifestyle it had led to. He reverted to gospel music and became the pastor of his own church, symbolizing a full circle for the Golden Age of soul.

Otis Redding recorded 'Sittin' On the Dock Of The Bay' just three days before he died in a plane crash near Madison, Wisconsin, in 1967. It was number one for four weeks in 1968.

Sixties Pop *Singer/Songwriters*

The term "singer/songwriter" tends to be applied to the kind of introspective, socially conscious artist who – in the wake of the folk-inspired movement that was kick-started by Bob Dylan in the early 1960s before peaking in the next decade – performs in a direct yet reflective manner, emphasizing the song's message over style or calibre of presentation.

This is hardly an all-encompassing description, however. Following in the footsteps of 1950s luminaries ranging from Chuck Berry to Paul Anka, there have also been legions of more pop-oriented singer/songwriters whose chief aim is to entertain rather than advocate ideas or indulge in self-analysis. Throughout the 1950s, singer/songwriters ranging from Paul Anka to Buddy Holly produced music whose primary aim was to entertain, and even if there was social commentary in the songs of Chuck Berry, self-analysis and radical ideas were never on the agenda. Accordingly, the early 1960s heralded yet another wave of pop-oriented singer/songwriters.

Having made the switch from writing 'Stupid Cupid' for Connie Francis to experiencing success in his own right with 'Oh Carol', Neil Sedaka started the decade with a string of solo hits, co-composed with lyricist Howard Greenfield: 'Stairway To Heaven', 'Calendar Girl', 'Little Devil', 'King Of Clowns', 'Happy Birthday Sweet Sixteen' and 'Breaking Up Is Hard To Do'. Among the most saccharine material created by the teams of young composers housed inside New York City's Brill Building, Sedaka's songs consisted of memorably catchy melodies constructed around lyrics relating to the ups and downs of teenage love. Such concerns were perfectly suited to the pop market of the era, as proven by smooth, self-penned numbers such as Sam Cooke's 'Cupid', 'Wonderful World', 'Another Saturday Night', 'Having A Party', 'Good Times', 'Twistin' The Night Away' and 'Shake', as well as the more melodramatic work of another 1950s carry-over, Roy Orbison.

> *"To be a singer-songwriter you must, first and foremost, be too sensitive to live, too vain to die."*
> David Dennum

The intensity of Bob Dylan's early songs introduced politics and social commentary to the pop charts, bombarding the saccharine music of the time with an explosion of words and sneering attitude.

Carefully Crafted Numbers

In 1960, when the Orbison/Melson composition 'Only The Lonely' was rejected by Elvis Presley and the Everly Brothers (who had scored a hit with their rendition of 'Claudette', written by Orbison for his wife), the singer/guitarist who had struggled as a rockabilly artist decided to record the song himself.

The result was a chart-topping single in the UK, which narrowly missed out on matching that feat in the US. Thereafter, "The Big O" demonstrated his remarkable vocal range in a succession of heavily produced, often doom-laden ballads and mid-tempo numbers, which were carefully crafted to suit his powerful voice and mysterious image. Distinguished by sweeping strings and striking crescendos at a time when much pop music was fairly lightweight, songs such as 'Running Scared', 'Crying', 'Blue Bayou', 'It's Over' and 'Oh, Pretty Woman' were Orbison co-writes, while 'Leah', 'Workin' For The Man' and 'In Dreams' were his own solo compositions.

In 1963, Roy Orbison toured Britain with the Beatles, whose self-contained writing team of John Lennon and Paul McCartney subsequently made the transition from the boy-loves-girl/boy-loses-girl innocence of 'Please Please Me', 'From Me To You', 'She Loves You' and 'I Want To Hold Your Hand' to the personally, socially and politically conscious numbers that would characterize rock music in the second half of the decade. Indeed, Lennon was composing introspective numbers such as 'There's A Place' as early as 1962; within a couple of years, too, he was taking a leaf out of Bob Dylan's book with 'I'm A Loser' and, in 1965, 'You've Got To Hide Your Love Away'.

Key Artists:

Sam Cooke
Barry, Maurice and Robin Gibb
John Lennon and Paul McCartney
Roy Orbison
Neil Sedaka

Roy Orbison, "The Big O", was a hugely influential singer/songwriter and a pioneer of rock'n'roll.

Metaphors and Obscure *Imagery*

One of the great lyrical communicators of all time, John Lennon publicly acknowledged the influence of Bob Dylan on his writing. The incredibly talented and prolific team of Lennon and McCartney covered many musical styles, and inspired contemporaries such as the Kinks' Ray Davies and the Rolling Stones' Mick Jagger and Keith Richards to compose their own songs.

Dylan's impact was to encourage a generation of artists whose roots were in folk, country, blues or rock'n'roll to infuse the pop canon with material that examined personal and social issues. As Dylan kicked open the musical doors to protest social issues via the pop/rock scene, so he was joined by other folk contemporaries such as Joan Baez, Judy Collins, Joni Mitchell, Pete Seeger, Phil Ochs and Donovan. To an increasing extent, songs' poetic lyrics were steeped in metaphors and obscure imagery, while original material also began to take precedence over the time-honoured use of cover songs. Today, the savvy folk-pop numbers of Paul Simon; tomorrow, the darker, more rock-oriented compositions of Jim Morrison.

The Bee Gees' Barry Gibb was 19 years old and his twin brothers Maurice and Robin Gibb just 17, when, in 1967, they wrote and recorded timeless numbers such as 'New York Mining Disaster, 1941', 'To Love Somebody' and 'Massachusetts'. Not that Brian Wilson was any older than Barry Gibb when he began turning out hits for the Beach Boys in 1961. By the middle of the decade, Wilson was composing and arranging intricately structured music, while working with lyricists whose introspective themes were aeons away from those of the band's surf and hot-rod songs, written just a few years before.

Key Tracks:

'Cupid' Sam Cooke
'Only The Lonely' Roy Orbison
'Stairway To Heaven' Neil Sedaka
'To Love Somebody' Barry, Maurice and Robin Gibb
'I Want To Hold Your Hand' John Lennon and Paul McCartney

The singer/songwriters were a rapidly expanding breed within the burgeoning rock field, and they would be far less the exception than the norm in years to come. In mainstream pop, on the other hand, the trend would not be quite so pronounced. Performing your own songs may have been cool, but for now it was not obligatory.

Together with Art Garfunkel, Paul Simon wrote some of the most enduring folk-based songs of the decade. The duo had little success until producer Tom Wilson added electric instrumentation to the acoustic 'Sound of Silence'.

The Folk *Revival*

Mention of the folk revival is generally applied to the late-1950s and early 1960s, when a new generation of enthusiasts earnestly set about exploring the history of folk music and recreating its passionate, social ideals.

There had been other folk revivals throughout history, but they tended to stem from the middle classes in search of a purer identity, resulting in the tendency to patronize real folk music. The folk revival of the 1950s and 1960s, however, was a naturally organic affair generated by the musicians themselves, rather than the academic view of social culture that had been at the heart of previous revivals.

Its American roots began with groups such as the Kingston Trio, the Weavers and the New Christy Minstrels bringing folk, blues and country songs to the masses. Their arrangements may have been trite and sanitized, but the Weavers had massive hits with Woody Guthrie's 'So Long (It's Been Good To Know You)' and Leadbelly's 'Goodnight Irene'. They also opened the commercial door to a roots music that had previously been confined to its rural locality, be it the Appalachian mountains, Mississippi cotton fields or Texas bars. It was enough to inflame the curiosity of a new, young generation of guitarists and singers researching those roots, who were further spurred on by the political implications of the McCarthy witch-hunt and the refusal of Pete Seeger and others to bow to establishment values. Their guru was Oklahoma-born Woody Guthrie, whose own songs vehemently addressed issues close to him, including the human agony caused by the dust storms, or were created at singalongs for his own children.

Woody's legacy was a new generation of acolytes who were inspired by his simple tunes and abrasive lyrics and sought to embody his maverick lifestyle. Most famously, Bob Dylan visited Woody at his bedside and wrote his first song as a tribute to his hero, but a closer embodiment of the Guthrie spirit was represented by his friend Ramblin' Jack Elliot, who travelled extensively with Woody, aped his voice and attitude and performed many of his songs. Yet Guthrie's legend was best perpetuated by his own son Arlo, who went on to achieve a commercial breakthrough that obliterated anything his father had done, with the long, autobiographical singing blues tome 'Alice's Restaurant', which captured the anti-Vietnam War mood of the times so acutely it was made into a film.

Woody Guthrie's refusal to profit from any of his music during his lifetime did not prevent him from reaching legendary status after his death.

A Lasting *Legacy*

Woody Guthrie's legacy flowered in Greenwich Village, where a new breed of singer/songwriter with attitude, wordy songs and idealistic values descended to energize a new scene. With his sharp lyrics and revolutionary message, Bob Dylan was the most visible and successful of the new breed of folk star.

There were many others, too, including Dylan's then-partner, Joan Baez. She was a highly rated singer of ballads, stridently political and often to be found on the front line of various anti-war demonstrations and marches. An explosion of singer/songwriters with acoustic guitars followed, with Paul Simon, Joni Mitchell, James Taylor, Phil Ochs, Tom Paxton, Tim Hardin, Gordon Lightfoot, Dave Van Ronk, Judy Collins and Buffy Sainte-Marie among them. Despite their mix of styles and backgrounds, they were all associated with the folk revival.

Key Artists:

Bob Dylan
The Weavers
Woody Guthrie
Joan Baez

The growing popularity of the scene also refocused attention on the lesser-known artists providing inspiration – and often material – for the main attraction. The likes of Doc Watson, the Carter Family, Sonny Terry & Brownie McGhee, Muddy Waters and Mississippi John Hurt thus came to prominence, the focus on the latter accelerated by the emergence of British bands such as the Rolling Stones and the Yardbirds, with a rock take on the blues tradition. Odetta, a black folk-blues singer from Alabama who worked early on with Harry Belafonte and Pete Seeger, also achieved an important international breakthrough. A network of clubs, coffeehouses and informal "hootenannies" emerged, along with famous festivals, such as the Newport Folk Festival in Rhode Island, to give the music a high profile. The revival achieved widespread commercial success for a while, too, with Peter, Paul & Mary playing huge concerts all over the world.

With shifts in her folk music to country and pop, Joan Baez remains one of the most influential artists on the folk scene. This image shows a performance in a typical Greenwich Village folk venue in the 1960s; note the artist in the audience, busy sketching Baez.

An Abiding Interest in Folk *Blues*

The UK folk revival had similar roots, and it occurred at about the same time. But it emerged in a very different form. Those Kingston Trio and Weavers hits caught the imagination of young British fans and musicians, too, but interest in the roots of this music manifested itself in an unexpected way.

Lonnie Donegan was playing banjo with Ken Colyer's jazz band and started playing primitive American folk blues. Donegan broke through with 'Rock Island Line' in 1956 and the following year went to number one with 'Cumberland Gap'. This gave licence to young hopefuls to form groups whether or not they had talent, instruments or places to play, and in 1958 skiffle was everywhere. Although it did not last, its legacy was an abiding interest in the folk blues songs that had driven it. Many of those who had started in skiffle bands shifted gear, reshaped their musical policy and became folk groups.

While several of them, such as the Ian Campbell Folk Group, homed in on the songs of Dylan and the rest coming across the Atlantic, a network of clubs with different values was also emerging. Ewan MacColl opened one of the first dedicated folk music venues – the Ballad & Blues Club – in London and caused great debate when he declared that musicians would only be permitted to perform music of their own culture at his club. It may have seemed bizarre, but MacColl's aim was to force young British musicians to research their own tradition for material rather than slavishly copy songs off Kingston Trio albums. It was controversial, but it worked, as artists such as the Watersons, Martin Carthy, Shirley Collins, Young Tradition, Anne Briggs and Louis Killen quickly developed into popular performers, playing a rapidly growing network of folk clubs throughout the country.

Key Tracks:
'A Hard Rain's A Gonna Fall' Bob Dylan
'Alice's Restaurant' Arlo Guthrie
'Cumberland Gap' Lonnie Donegan
'So Long (It's Been Good To Know You)' The Weavers

The momentum of those early days of the revival lasted into the 1970s, when other musical forces came into play and folk music splintered into different sub-genres. Folk clubs are not as plentiful now, but the music is still there and it generally wields the same values. That is its own tribute to the work of the folk revival pioneers.

Lonnie Donegan's mix of folk, jazz, gospel and blues continues to influence British folk music today.

The British *Invasion*

On 1 February 1964, The Beatles' 'I Want To Hold Your Hand' topped America's *Cashbox* singles chart. Six days later, they arrived in New York for their first US visit, and on 9 February an audience of around 73 million people tuned in to see them on *The Ed Sullivan Show*, which had been booked the previous November. The timing could not have been better.

Accustomed to leading the way in terms of pop culture but reeling from the recent assassination of President Kennedy, America was ready for change and in need of an uplifting diversion. With their infectious music, charismatic personalities and unconventional "moptop" appearance, the Beatles were able to deliver the goods. The group's reputation in the US was already established prior to their arrival, largely due to the support shown to them by influential New York DJ Murray "The K".

Even more remarkable than the Fab Four achieving the previously unimaginable feat of taking America by storm was the manner in which – with the doors to the States kicked wide open – a slew of other acts from across the Atlantic swamped the US charts. The shake-up quickly consumed all facets of American popular culture. In just less than 200 years after the War of Independence, a "British Invasion" was under way.

"Middle-aged America at that time thought everyone with long hair and English was a Beatle."
Peter Asher

Finally recovering from the ravages of the Second World War, Britain was in the thick of a particularly rich and creative period in all areas of the arts. With London about to "swing", it was in a prime condition to export its musicians, actors, writers and fashions to Americans who were, to an extraordinary and unprecedented degree, receptive to anyone with a Liverpudlian – make that English – accent.

The Beatles arrive in New York in 1964.

Supposed *Rivalry*

In 1963, while the UK pop charts were swamped by so-called Mersey sound acts such as the Beatles, Gerry & the Pacemakers, the Searchers, the Swinging Blue Jeans and Billy J. Kramer with the Dakotas, only three British singles managed to crack the US Top 40.

In 1964, this paltry number rose to an astonishing 65. Previously, just two British singles – the 1962 instrumentals 'Stranger On The Shore' by Acker Bilk and 'Telstar' by the Tornados, written, produced and mixed by the legendary British producer Joe Meek – had topped *Billboard's* Hot 100. In 1964, nine of the 23 *Billboard* chart-toppers (for 26 out of 52 weeks) were by British acts.

Admittedly, six of those records were by the Beatles, who on 4 April held the top five positions on the Hot 100 and another seven spots lower down the chart. However, others were following fast behind them, and not only many of their aforementioned Liverpudlian compatriots. There was also the Animals from Newcastle, the Hollies from Manchester and the Dave Clark Five from Tottenham, North London. The DC5 had visited the US a month before the Beatles, having ended the six-week reign of 'I Want To Hold Your Hand' at the top of the British charts with 'Glad All Over' (composed by Clark and keyboardist/ vocalist Mike Smith), prompting a national newspaper headline to ask, "Has The Five Jive Crushed The Beatles' Beat?" To help promote a supposed rivalry with the Beatles, the press described the combination of Smith's raw vocals and the band's loud, thumping beat as "The Tottenham Sound".

However, despite making more appearances on *The Ed Sullivan Show* than anyone else, and scoring 17 *Billboard* Top 40 hits with numbers such as 'Bits And Pieces', 'Can't You See That She's Mine', 'Because','I Like It Like That', 'Catch Us If You Can' and 'Over And Over' (their sole US number 1), the DC5 were not a serious challenge to the Beatles' supremacy. No one was, although the Rolling Stones were the strongest contenders in that regard.

Ironically, many young Americans were introduced to their own country's blues heritage through England's Rolling Stones.

Benefiting Both *Sides*

Throughout 1964, while the aforementioned British acts – in addition to newcomers such as Peter & Gordon, Herman's Hermits, Manfred Mann and the Kinks – all enjoyed Stateside success, the Stones struggled to establish themselves there. However, in the summer of 1965 their efforts finally paid off when '(I Can't Get No) Satisfaction' topped the *Billboard* Hot 100, followed that November by 'Get Off Of My Cloud'.

The Stones' breakthrough coincided with the second half of the British Invasion, which, in addition to lightweight acts such as Wayne Fontana & the Mindbenders, Freddie & the Dreamers (whose star had already faded in their home country) and Chad & Jeremy (who few people had even heard of in Britain), also included the folk singer Donovan ("Britain's answer to Bob Dylan") and the harder-edged sounds of the Who, the Yardbirds, the Zombies and the Moody Blues. In 1965, a total of 68 British singles cracked the US Top 40, with 11 of them again spending a combined 26 weeks at number one. And yet, although a number of American acts felt obliged to adopt English-sounding names and even put on English-sounding accents, by 1966 the hysterical, all-encompassing Anglophilia was clearly on the slide, as evidenced by the abundance of home-grown artists who were redressing the balance on the pop charts.

Key Tracks:

'(I Can't Get No) Satisfaction' The Rolling Stones
'I Want To Hold Your Hand' The Beatles
'Over And Over' The Dave Clark Five

After a two-year onslaught, the "Invasion" started to come to an end. Yet aside from casting a number of previously successful American artists into the proverbial wilderness, it had served to benefit both sides. After struggling to come to terms with the virtual end of their Empire, the British had regained their self-esteem, while obliterating the invisible barrier that had traditionally prevented their pop acts from succeeding in the most prosperous market of all. The Americans, on the other hand, had not only been stirred out of their post-Kennedy blues; in addition, by being forced to respond, their own music scene had been greatly invigorated. There would be plenty of musical cross-pollination from here on, and the entire scene would be all the richer because of it.

The songs of the Kinks paired Ray Davies' quick-witted, observant lyrics with his brother Dave's powerful guitar style.

Surf *Music*

Characterized by twangy, reverberation-soaked guitars; percussive instrumentals designed to simulate the effect of crashing waves; vocal harmonies underscored by a soaring falsetto – surf music was perfectly suited to an early 1960s pop scene of escapism and innocent fun and was to have a profound and lasting influence on the sound of the rock guitar.

Whereas chart-friendly instrumental recordings by bands such as the Ventures in the US and the Shadows in the UK helped to sustain the guitar's popularity in the period between the demise of rock'n'roll and the British Invasion, surf rock often featured the raunchiest and most expressive solos.

Leading the way in that regard was the justifiably self-proclaimed "King of the Surf Guitar", Dick Dale. A keen surfer, his musical endeavour to convey the excitement of the sport resulted in a rapid-fire style of single-note picking, coupled with an innovative use of portable reverb effects to help recreate the feel of the oceanic cascades. His aggressive playing style led to the destruction of so many speakers that Fender was obliged to develop its existing amplifiers.

"Hey, surfing's getting really big. You guys ought to write a song about it."
Dennis Wilson to brother Brian and Mike Love, 1961

Born Richard Monsour to a Polish mother and Lebanese father, Dale further distinguished his music by infusing it with Eastern European and Middle Eastern melodies, all of which came to bear when Del-Tone released the first-ever surf instrumental, 'Let's Go Trippin' ', as a single in September 1961. This was only a regional hit in Southern California, but it single-handedly ignited a musical craze that saw the quick formation of dozens of local bands. Among the first of these were the Beach Boys, whose debut single, 'Surfin', was recorded the same month that 'Let's Go Trippin' ' was issued, prior to its own release on the tiny Candix label that December.

Dedicated surfer and influential musician Dick Dale was an inspiration to man.

A Flamboyant *Performer*

Dick Dale's influence was enormous. The 1962 *Surfer's Choice* was his and surf music's first album (released on Del-Tone before Capitol distributed it nationally). During the course of recording three further albums in 1965, he also helped develop, road test and popularize an array of equipment manufactured by the Fender Musical Instrument Company: amplifiers, reverb units and a custom-designed, left-handed, gold metalflake Stratocaster guitar.

An accomplished musician and flamboyant performer, Dale played his guitars left-handed and upside-down in a style that made a significant impression on Jimi Hendrix, as well as on a subsequent generation of axe-wielding heavy-metal merchants.

Key Artists:

The Beach Boys
The Chantays
Dick Dale
The Pyramids
The Surfaris

In the meantime, while only a handful of surf instrumentals (such as the major 1963 chart hits 'Wipe Out' by the Surfaris and 'Pipeline' by the Chantays) enjoyed national success, the Beach Boys were bringing a new dimension to the genre. Under the guidance of songwriter/producer/ arranger/musician Brian Wilson, the group blended Four Freshmen-inspired vocal harmonies, which conveyed a fun-in-the-sun California lifestyle, with lyrics describing the thrill of waxing down your surfboard, "loading up the Woody" and "walking the nose". After 'Surfin' ' led to a contract with Capitol Records, the title track of the band's 1962 debut album, *Surfin' Safari*, made the national Top 20. That of its early 1963 follow-up, *Surfin' USA*, adapted pertinent lyrics to the tune of Chuck Berry's 'Sweet Little Sixteen' and catapulted the group into the Top 10, earning it nationwide recognition. Nevertheless, since surfing itself was still a growing fad, the first album's liner notes included a paragraph describing the activity. The notes to *Surfin' USA* then explained the meaning of expressions such as "a good set of heavies" and "toes-on-the-nose".

The only surf act to graduate to the mainstream, the Beach Boys (and more specifically creative genius Brian Wilson) went on to record Pet Sounds in 1967, which many consider to be the most important album of all time.

Tiring of the Surfing *Association*

Later in 1963, the beautifully harmonized title ballad of the Beach Boys' third album, *Surfer Girl*, displayed a growing sophistication on the part of composer/producer Brian Wilson, who was already tiring of the surfing association. Although one of the record's other cuts, 'Surfers Rule', contained the competitive challenge "Four Seasons, you better believe it!" during the fade-out, following this album – and after Wilson handed Jan & Dean a chart-topper in the form of 'Surf City' – the band steered clear of the theme with which its name would remain synonymous.

The surf guitar and high harmonies would be adapted increasingly to songs about hot rods and drag racing, before Wilson would rethink his approach in the wake of the Beatles, borrow from the production techniques of Phil Spector and, with the aid of mind-bending chemicals and new lyrical collaborators, focus on far more obscure topics. Landmark numbers such as 'Good Vibrations' and 'Heroes and Villains' would usher in a new era of increasingly sophisticated west coast music, even though drug abuse and emotional problems would subsequently force the chief Beach Boy to withdraw almost totally from the scene.

Surf music was another casualty of the British invasion, as was, eventually, the cycle of beach party movies that often featured cameo appearances and/or musical performances from luminaries of the genre: Brian Wilson in *Beach Party*, Dick Dale in *Muscle Beach Party*, the Surfaris in *The Lively Set*, the Astronauts in *Surf Party* and *Wild On The Beach* and the Beach Boys in *The Girls On The Beach*. The surfing craze would continue to flourish, but the music that popularized it was on the way out.

Key Tracks:

'Good Vibrations' The Beach Boys
'Let's Go Trippin'' Dick Dale
'Pipeline' The Chantays
'Surfin' The Beach Boys
'Wipe Out' The Surfaris

In early 1964, 'Surfin' Bird' by the Trashmen (who hailed from landlocked Minneapolis) was kept off the top of the charts by the Beatles, while the Pyramids' 'Penetration' would prove to be the last major instrumental surf hit. The following year, even Dick Dale was dropped by Capitol. Still, though its time in the sun was relatively short, the sound and influence of surf music lived on.

Teen pop duo Jan & Dean were introduced to surf music when they shared a stage with the Beach Boys in 1963. Brian Wilson gave them the partially written 'Surf City' to record, to which he contributed guest vocals.

Merseybeat

A basic line-up of drums, bass and two guitars, sometimes augmented by a piano or a saxophone – this was the blueprint for the 500 or so bands who, staying faithful to the spirit and material of classic rock'n'roll, and to many obscure R&B songs, invigorated the pop scene in and around Liverpool between 1958 and 1964.

Taking its name from the river that runs through the city, what came to be known as "Merseybeat", or the "Mersey Sound" was often built around guitars backed by a solid beat and fronted by an energetic lead vocal. However, because these characteristics weren't always shared or necessarily unique, it is debatable whether Merseybeat was anything other than a convenient, press-contrived pigeonhole assigned to bands hailing from the north-west of England.

Performed onstage at "jive hives" such as the Aintree Institute, Grosvenor Ballroom, Hambleton Hall, Litherland Town Hall, Knotty Ash Village Hall, New Clubmoor Hall and, most famously, the Cavern Club, the bright and melodic music was, largely, a throwback to the days of leather-clad rockers, both in terms of the material covered and, during an ultra-slick pop era, the groups' rough-and-ready appearances. Smart attire and smoother attitudes would only be adopted once the scene became known beyond Merseyside, for while British acts were virtual nonentities on the American pop charts throughout the early 1960s,

"Beat City? A sprawling area of murky slums and muddy seas ... eighty thousand crumbling houses and 30,000 on the dole. And yet, at the moment, there's money to be made in Liverpool if you sing or play with an accent."
Tom Spence, the Daily Worker, 7 September 1963

much the same could be said about the UK recording scene for artists based anywhere but in London. All of the major British record labels and studios were located in the capital, and if the artists and/or their managers were not able to audition for them, it was equally unlikely that the A&R (Artiste & Repertoire) people would venture north of Watford in search of new talent.

The Swinging Blue Jeans perform on Ready Steady Go!. *The popular TV show, with its slogan "The weekend starts here!", ran from 1963 to 1966 and featured a wide variety of music, with musicians performing live or miming to their hits.*

Ripe for *Exploitation*

All of that changed in 1963, however, after the manager Brian Epstein's tireless efforts to secure a recording contract for the Beatles reaped dividends in the form of their smash-hit singles 'Please Please Me' and 'From Me To You'. The latter's seven-week stay at number one was sandwiched between fellow Liverpudlians and Epstein stablemates Gerry & the Pacemakers' chart-topping 'How Do You Do It?' and 'I Like It'.

As a result, it didn't take long for the record industry honchos to break with tradition and check out who else might be ripe for exploitation "up north". Liverpool was suddenly overrun with talent scouts, managers and booking agents, resulting in success for a few notable and not-so-notable acts. However, it also eluded many who, despite being highly popular on the local scene, fell between the cracks due to a fateful lack of luck and talent.

Key Artists:

The Beatles
Gerry & the Pacemakers
Billy J. Kramer with the Dakotas
The Searchers

Rory Storm & the Hurricanes, whose line-up formerly included Ringo Starr on drums; Kingsize Taylor & the Dominoes, who claimed to have been Liverpool's first beat group; Derry Wilkie & the Seniors, who were the first Merseysiders to play a residency in the German rock'n'roll stomping ground of Hamburg; Faron's Flamingos – the raw-edged sounds and stage performances of these and other favourites may have excited the fans, but they did not translate well onto vinyl. Conversely, among the major local acts who did succeed in this respect, the band that best epitomized Merseybeat was, perhaps, the Searchers. Their well-arranged recordings of 'Sweets For My Sweet', 'Sugar And Spice' and 'Don't Throw Your Love Away' established the group as early rivals to the Beatles in the top region of the British charts, while the jangling guitar sound distinguished both the superb 'Needles And Pins' (the band's US breakthrough, composed by Phil Spector associates Jack Nitzsche and Sonny Bono) and a cover of Jackie DeShannon's 'When You Walk In The Room'.

Meet the Searchers had a rather hurried release in order to cash in on the success of the band's number one single 'Sweets for my Sweet'. The remaining eleven album tracks were recorded in the space of a day.

MEET THE SEARCHERS

SWEETS FOR MY SWEET

TWIST AND SHOUT

AINT GONNA KISS YA

DA DOO RON RON

SINCE YOU BROKE MY HEART

MONEY

STAND BY ME

WHERE HAVE
ALL THE
FLOWERS GONE

TRICKY DICKY •

AND OTHERS

Blessed with Good *Fortune*

At the same time, certain lesser lights that were blessed with good fortune made a name for themselves on the domestic and international scenes. Having previously been backed by fellow Liverpudlians the Coasters, Billy J. Kramer was teamed with the Manchester-based Dakotas upon signing with Beatles manager Brian Epstein.

Despite his vocal limitations, which the producer George Martin concealed by way of heavy double-tracking, Kramer scored a string of 1963 hits with songs penned by the prolific team of John Lennon and Paul McCartney: 'Do You Want To Know A Secret?' as well as the previously unrecorded 'Bad To Me' and 'I'll Keep You Satisfied'. In 1964, he released 'From a Window' and then 'Little Children', written by the Americans Mort Shuman and John McFarland. The latter track became Kramer's third UK number one and first Top 10 hit in the States, where he was part of the British invasion. After a 1965 cover of the Bacharach-David composition 'Trains And Boats And Planes', however, the hits dried up.

The same applied to the equally clean-cut, lightweight and consequently outmoded Gerry & the Pacemakers, who, thanks to the compositional efforts of singer/guitarist Gerry Marsden, enjoyed international chart success until the tail end of 1965 with songs such as 'It's Gonna Be All Right', 'I'm The One', 'Don't Let The Sun Catch You Cryin' ' and 'Ferry Aross The Mersey' (the title of the group's only film). By then, with the Beatles having long since moved on to more progressive musical pastures, the Merseybeat explosion was over and, worse still for Liverpool, its incredible live scene had been decimated. Not only had most of the major acts been lured away by the prospect – real or imagined – of stardom elsewhere; so had many of the up-and-coming musicians who would have comprised the next generation. The city was now world-famous, but its musical glory days were at an end.

Key Tracks:

'Do You Want To Know A Secret' Billy J. Kramer with the Dakotas
'From Me To You' The Beatles
'How Do You Do It' Gerry & the Pacemakers
'Please Please Me' The Beatles
'Sweets For My Sweet' The Searchers

Gerry & the Pacemakers' cheerful, chirpy sound embodied the more upbeat side of Merseybeat. The Ferry Cross the Mersey film showcased the band, among other Liverpool acts, in the guise of a music contest.

Mod

"Are you a mod or a rocker?" a reporter asked Ringo Starr in *A Hard Day's Night*. **"Uh, no,"** he answered, **"I'm a mocker."** The question was a pertinent one. On 18 May 1964, just over three weeks after the film was completed, the English seaside town of Margate saw a violent showdown between packs of fashion-conscious mods and leather-jacketed rockers.

Throughout that and the following year, there were further clashes at resorts such as Brighton, Hastings, Southend, Clacton and Bournemouth, resulting in chaos, destruction and plenty of arrests.

Little was resolved between the motorcycle gangs, who were still championing 1950s rock'n'roll, and the hedonistic "modernists" who lapped up American soul and R&B in addition to Jamaican ska. Indeed, up until the start of 1965, the mods belonged to a movement that was yet to spawn its own music. Even when that did take place, it was limited to just a couple of domestically well-known exponents and a handful of nearly-rans. Melding R&B with rock guitar and an idiosyncratic, British edge, they nevertheless defined a short-lived sub-genre that bridged the gap between the beat boom and psychedelia.

"We were still a bunch of rotten, dirty-boy rock'n'rollers, but kids began identifying with our short hair and Ivy League clothes, and it just took off from there." Roger Daltrey

It was in 1963 that the working-class, male-dominated mod lifestyle really took off in Britain. Based in and around London, which was increasingly turning into a hub of high fashion and pop culture, this embraced a colourful, "New Dandy" dress-code of button-down shirts, narrow trousers, and sharp-looking mohair and two-tone suits, as well as the more casual parka, which was *de rigueur* for riding about town on economical Italian motor-scooters manufactured by Vespa and Lambretta. Attending any number of parties and clubs that catered to their musical tastes, the mods bolstered their nightlife by way of amphetamines, anxiety suppressants and other drugs such as Dexedrine, "Black Bombers", "Purple Hearts" and "French Blues". It was this scene that gave rise to the Who.

The mod movement was carefully contrived and the style guidelines set by the mods were as sharp as the suits they wore. As well as clothes and hairstyles, mods had their own music, drugs and modes of transport.

Performances with *Aggression*

The Who started out as the Detours in the west London neighbourhood of Shepherd's Bush in 1963. The band's name was changed to the High Numbers by manager/publicist Peter Meaden, who dressed the quartet in mod attire and rewrote Slim Harpo's 'Got Live If You Want It' as 'I'm The Face'. (In mod slang, a "face" was a fashion leader.) The single flopped, but its target audience began attending the group's pub performances, featuring a set that consisted entirely of soul, Motown and R&B.

Taking note of this growing fan following, the aspiring film directors Kit Lambert and Chris Stamp assumed the management reins, switched the band's name back to the Who, and encouraged the singer Roger Daltrey, composer/ guitarist Pete Townshend, bass player John Entwistle and drummer Keith Moon to lace their performances with an aggression that would match that of the mods in their battles with the rockers.

So while Entwistle remained stoic onstage, Daltrey assumed the air of a brash thug, Townshend leaped into the air with his guitar while spinning his right hand in a windmill motion, and Moon played his drums like a crazy man. Echoing the painter Gustav Metzke's auto-destructive art, Townshend soon took to smashing his guitars against floors and amplifiers, prompting Moon to respond by virtually destroying his kit. It was this style of display that turned 'I Can't Explain' into the Who's first British Top 10 hit, after they performed the song on the landmark television pop show *Ready Steady Go!*.

Key Artists:

The Small Faces
The Who
The Action
The Creation
The Smoke

Taking their lead from the Rolling Stones, the group had already courted publicity by way of a mod-friendly, anti-social attitude. This discouraged the major labels from signing them, despite a highly successful residency at London's Marquee Club. But on the strength of the Townshend-penned 'I Can't Explain', which clearly borrowed from the Kinks' 'You Really Got Me', the band secured a deal through Kinks producer Shel Talmy with American Decca (sub-contracted through Brunswick in the UK).

Although they later moved into rock territory, the Who were originally marketed as a mod band. Their status as mods was amplified by Pete Townshend's irreverent attitude and Keith Moon's diet of Purple Hearts.

Adolescent *Defiance*

Sporting their target T-shirts and Union Jack blazers, the Who were the perfect embodiment of the mod movement and its affiliations to the whole "Swinging London", Carnaby Street fashion scene. Furthermore, although 'I Can't Explain' did not convey the band's more explosive attributes, this was rectified by its follow-up singles, 'Anyway, Anyhow, Anywhere' and 'My Generation'.

The latter, a study in adolescent defiance armed with amphetamine-fuelled power-guitar chords and a stuttering lead vocal, was not only the mod anthem but also a pivotal number that helped turn pop into rock. At the end of 1965, the energy-pumped *My Generation* album further delineated the mod lifestyle, courtesy of Townshend originals such as 'Out In The Street' and 'The Kids Are Alright'. Before long, however, he and the band were looking towards other themes.

In August of that year, Decca issued 'What'cha Gonna Do About It', the debut single by the Who's East London contemporaries the Small Faces. A stylish, R&B-oriented group fronted by the singer/guitarist Steve Marriott alongside bassist Ronnie Lane, keyboard player Jimmy Winston and drummer Kenney Jones, this was the only other major act to emerge from the mod scene. Soon after 'What'cha Gonna Do About It' climbed to number 14 on the British charts, Winston was replaced by Ian McLagan, and during 1966 the band enjoyed Top 10 UK hits with 'Sha-La-La-La-Lee', 'Hey Girl' and 'All Or Nothing'. The last of these, a powerful slice of Anglo white soul, went all the way to number one, but although its cheery follow-up, 'My Mind's Eye', nearly matched that success, it also signalled a departure in style.

By the start of 1967, on the cusp of the peace-and-love "flower power" era, the mod scene was finished. At that point, neither the Who nor the Small Faces had broken through in the States, although that would subsequently change. The whole fad, then, remained an exclusively British phenomenon, to be revived by a new generation of musicians and fashionistas in the late 1970s.

Key Tracks:
'All Or Nothing' The Small Faces
'I Can't Explain' The Who
'My Generation' The Who
'What 'Cha Gonna Do About It' The Small Faces

The Small Faces released some of the most commercially successful and durable music of the mod movement. They went on to fuse their cockney-mod style with psychedelia, resulting in their UK number one album Ogden's Nut Gone Flake.

Folk *Pop*

Folk pop is often looked down on by connoisseurs of the music who believe that in its purest form it should have nothing in common with the charts and the commercial world. Yet folk has punctured the mainstream more often than most would imagine, and in many ways its popularity has been reliant on those who've broadened the market by taking it into the pop era.

Part of the cachet of folk music is its alternative status. It has drifted in and out of fashion through the years, but the purity of the music and its ideals means that it could never co-exist naturally in a commercial environment. Yet every genre needs a visible face to fire the imagination as well as attract new audiences and musicians, and folk is no different. The early folk boom was built on the back of hits by the Weavers, the Kingston Trio and Harry Belafonte, and the vision of Bob Dylan inspired a whole generation of singer/songwriters.

"It was amazing when we got our first hit single... everyone came out to applaud us. Then we went into our dad's pub and he made us work behind the bar. Folk music keeps you grounded."
Máire Brennan, Clannad

Succeeding generations have accessed traditional music as an important source, but the fusion of folk music with other musical genres has increasingly provided interest for a less specialized audience.

The advent of folk rock certainly rejuvenated the fading folk revival, led by bands such as the Byrds and Flying Burrito Brothers in America and, in the UK, Fairport Convention and Steeleye Span. The Byrds enjoyed several hits – most spectacularly with Bob Dylan's 'Mr Tambourine Man' and 'All I Really Want To Do' and Pete Seeger's adaptation of the biblical passage 'Turn Turn Turn' – and there have been sporadic UK folk hits, too. One of the earliest came from the Irish folk pioneers the Dubliners, who took the risqué traditional song 'Seven Drunken Nights' into the Top 10 in 1967, following it up with 'Black Velvet Band'. It was 20 years before they made the charts again, in a collaboration with one of the bands they helped inspire, the Pogues, on a raucous treatment of the popular pub song 'Irish Rover'. The Pogues themselves scored one of the most memorable folk-inspired hits of all with their classic, bittersweet Christmas song 'Fairytale Of New York', which reached number two in the UK in 1987.

Melding elements of the British Invasion with psychedelic pop and folk, American group the Byrds became a powerful force in music, influencing artists such as the Beatles and the Rolling Stones.

Celtic *Overtones*

The Irish have a good track record of giving folk music populist appeal. In 1973, Thin Lizzy enjoyed its first Top 10 hit with a rocking cover of another old pub classic, 'Whiskey In The Jar'. In 1982, Donegal's Clannad had a massive hit with 'Harry's Game', the atmospheric, haunting theme of a TV drama.

Clannad went on to enjoy several more hits in the same style, and inspired a new genre of highly produced, richly layered Celtic music of tranquil overtones. In fact, Enya, a member of the same Donegal family as Clannad, has enjoyed the greatest crossover success of all in this sphere; her 'Orinoco Flow' went to number one in the UK in 1988 and her various albums have sold in the millions. The lead singer of Clannad, Máire Brennan, even enjoyed a pop hit dueting with Bono of U2. In the 1990s, the family group the Corrs gave their pop sensibility an enticing dose of their traditional Irish background, scoring a series of major hits. Even more oddly, the Scots band Capercaillie had a hit with the ancient walking song 'Coisich A Ruin', the first Gaelic-language record ever to make the charts.

Fairport Convention had a novelty hit in 1969 with a bizarre version of Bob Dylan's 'If You've Gotta Go, Go Now', which the band translated into French and performed as 'Si Tu Dois Partir'. And yet they did not have as much pop success as their folk rock cousins Steeleye Span, who first hit the charts with the Latin hymn 'Gaudete' in 1973, and scored an even bigger hit two years later with an upbeat version of the traditional song 'All Around My Hat'. But even Steeleye could not match Fiddler's Dram, who later metamorphosed into Oysterband and had a Top Three smash with the singalong anthem 'Day Trip To Bangor' in 1979.

Key Artists:

Enya
Sinéad O'Connor
The Byrds
The Corrs
Ladysmith Black Mambazo

One of the most influential names in British folk music, Ewan MacColl scored a huge, unexpected hit when one of his self-written songs 'The First Time Ever I Saw Your Face', was covered by Roberta Flack. Written in a matter of hours, this song has had more cover versions than most, and MacColl was highly amused when he heard Elvis Presley's version.

Having undergone numerous member changes throughout its existence, Capercaillie has evolved from playing strictly traditional Scottish music to incorporating modern influences to create something that is very much the band's own.

Folk Pop

Folk Pop of a Certain *Type*

Paul Simon has had a variety of pop folk hits through the years, but his most significant crossover contribution was the Graceland album. Although it was, controversially, recorded in South Africa at the time of a cultural boycott, it effectively sparked interest in African music throughout the world.

Launched to fame on the back of it, Ladysmith Black Mambazo subsequently enjoyed a series of crossover hits. Not that this was the first time music of African origin had hit the charts. Miriam Makeba's Xhosa music brought her international acclaim as far back as the 1950s, while Harry Belafonte's various calypso hits, including 'Banana Boat Song' and 'Island In The Sun', might be considered folk pop of a certain type.

Key Albums:

I Do Not Want What I Haven't Got Sinéad O'Connor
Mr Tambourine Man The Byrds
Shaka Zulu Ladysmith Black Mambazo
Watermark Enya

As musical boundaries fall, folk music is increasingly integrated into other musical forms. Sinéad O'Connor won acclaim for her traditional Irish album *Sean-Nòs Nua* in 2002, and it could be argued that the Seattle grunge band Nirvana touched on folk roots with its *MTV Unplugged* show, which included a powerful acoustic version of Leadbelly's 'Black Girl'. The techno dance world, too, has occasionally used folk samples, proving that, no matter how ancient it is, folk music can still make its impact felt on contemporary music.

Paul Simon, one half of the successful duo Simon & Garfunkel, wrote many folk pop hits. His best contribution to the genre was his Graceland *album.*

Funk *Soul*

Since the dawn of the jazz era, the appeal of pop music had become increasingly intertwined with the demands of the dancefloor. As 1960s rock and soul became ever tougher and more orientated towards youth and hedonism it was only a matter of time before someone would come up with the ultimate dance groove.

That someone was soul's greatest innovator, James Brown, who pioneered a music so orientated towards pure, African-derived rhythm that melody would finally be forced to take a back seat as backbeat took the wheel.

Funk as a term had been around since the turn of the twentieth century, when it applied specifically to the odours produced by the human body during and after sex. By the 1930s it was used to describe music with a dirty, lowdown feel, and by the 1950s it was an alternative name for hard bop, the post-bebop jazz with a straight-ahead, gospel- and swing-influenced rhythm, as typified by Milt Jackson and Horace Silver. But it was 1964 before funk formally twinned with soul, on James Brown's minor American hit single 'Out Of Sight'. The track had a familiar blues structure, but the hard-but-swinging rhythm dominated, and was further developed by Brown on 1965's world-changing 'Papa's Got A Brand New Bag' and 1966's 'I Got You (I Feel Good)', by which time the entire JB band was surrendering melody to beat with a power and vibe as much African as Afro-American. Somewhat surprisingly however, Brown didn't apply the term funk to his new sound until 1967's flop single, the instrumental 'Funky Soul No. 1'.

"He was the true representative of the dream of the crossover between rock and soul and funk and psychedelia." Jim Irvin on Sly Stone

As Brown's career progressed, funk began to dominate his oeuvre. As well as making his own genre-defining classics including 'Say It Loud – I'm Black And I'm Proud', 'Sex Machine' (arguably the first disco record) and 'Funky Drummer', Brown co-wrote, arranged and produced an enormous catalogue of funk classics for his "Funk Family". In some cases, tunes by the likes of Fred Wesley & the JB's, Maceo & the Macks, Lyn Collins and Marva Whitney are more treasured than Brown's own by the funk connoisseur.

James Brown, soul's greatest innovator, pioneered funk soul.

Soul Greats Get *Funky*

Of course, other soul greats applied the same kind of rolling, undulating rhythms to their work. Atlantic Records soul singer Wilson "The Wicked" Pickett's 1965 anthem 'In The Midnight Hour' is a blueprint for strutting downtempo funk, and arguably the greatest soul singer of all, Memphis's Aretha Franklin, essayed a more subtle, gospel-edged funk sound on 1967 classics 'Respect' and 'Chain Of Fools' and 1971's 'Rock Steady'.

Funk/R&B crossovers like Eddie Floyd's 1966 'Knock On Wood' and Bob & Earl's 1969 'Harlem Shuffle' (originally recorded in 1964 and arranged by Barry White) also added to the burgeoning funk wave. The most sophisticated funk soul sounds came, predictably, from Motown and Stax alumni. Motown backroom boys Norman Whitfield and Barrett Strong began constructing tracks for the Temptations that blended funky wah-wah guitars, widescreen orchestration and tough counter-cultural lyrical themes. From 1969's 'Cloud Nine' to 1973's 'Papa Was A Rollin' Stone', the formerly poppy vocal group became an object lesson in funk as artistically ambitious social commentary. Fellow Motown vocal group and R&B veterans the Isley Brothers left the Detroit label and released defiant funk tracks such as 'It's Your Thing' and 'Work To Do', as they built up to their funk/rock crossover peak.

Key Artists:

James Brown
Wilson Pickett
Aretha Franklin
The Temptations/Whitfield/Strong
Isaac Hayes

The same late-1960s/early 1970s period saw Stax writer/producer Isaac Hayes step into the limelight. His 1969 *Hot Buttered Soul* album invented a new seductive soul, transforming standards like 'Walk On By' into groaning, heavy breathing orchestral funk epics that inspired the likes of Barry White and Teddy Pendergrass. Of course, Hayes's 1971 soundtrack for the blaxploitation movie *Shaft*, with its intro of twitching hi-hats and chattering wah-wah guitar, is one of funk's most instantly recognizable motifs.

By 1976 the Temptations had seen so many line-up changes that only two of the original five members remained. In this year they recorded their final album for Motown – The Temptations Do The Temptations.

A Sly *One*

Meanwhile, Texan Sylvester Stewart – better known as Sly Stone – was approaching funky soul from a different angle. He was already a 24-year-old veteran artist, producer and DJ on the San Francisco hippy rock scene before his inter-racial, multi-gender big band Sly & the Family Stone grabbed their first US hit with the exuberant 'Dance To The Music' in 1968.

Sly & co. mixed funk, soul, big-band jazz, pop and psychedelic rock with brave abandon, making a string of era-defining US hits until 1971's extraordinary *There's A Riot Goin' On* album marked both his peak and his downfall. A dark, rambling yet powerful funk comment on the disillusion of the times, the album reached number one but also highlighted Stone's increasing emotional decline through drug addiction. Subsequent records became weaker until addiction, rehab and prison stretches rendered one of pop's greatest talents missing in action.

Key Tracks:

'I Got You (I Feel Good)' James Brown
'In The Midnight Hour' Wilson Pickett
'Papa Was A Rollin' Stone' The Temptations/Whitfield/Strong
'Respect' Aretha Franklin
'Walk On By' Isaac Hayes

Swamp Funk

New Orleans, the birthplace of so much jazz and R&B, had its own unique take on the new sound. Dr. John (originally Malcolm Rebennack) was a white piano prodigy already steeped in bayou jazz and blues when he made 1968's *Gris Gris*, a unique mélange of voodoo mysticism, woozy psychedelia and laid-back funk virtuosity. His friends the Meters, led by Art Neville, responded with their 1969 self-titled instrumental album, which boiled funk down to subtly insistent syncopated beats and infectious "chicken scratch" guitar, a uniquely live-sounding style that reached its height on 1974's vocal *Rejuvenation* album.

Sly & the Family Stone formed in 1967 and, unusually for the time, included male and female and black and white members.

Mainstream *Country*

The names of this array of landmark artists whose music either straddled or transcended specific genres, – Johnny Cash, Dolly Parton, Tammy Wynette, Loretta Lynn, George Jones, Conway Twitty, Charley Pride and Buck Owens among others – have become synonymous with country music.

During the 1950s, 1960s and 1970s, country's popularity penetrated deeper into the American psyche and even won an international following. In 1953 there was only one full-time country music station in the US; by the late-1950s there was still only a handful, but by 1969 the scope of the "country explosion" was such that the number of full-time country stations had risen to 606. Country music also found a handy vehicle in popular network musical variety TV shows like *Hee Haw* and *The Johnny Cash Show*.

The Top Dog of Country

Foremost among this era's artists was Johnny Cash. Cash first emerged from the Memphis/Sun Records 1950s rockabilly stable with songs like 'I Walk The Line', but by the early 1960s he had embarked on an amazing four-decade country career, releasing such classics as 'Ring Of Fire' and 'Folsom Prison Blues'.

"Back when you're trying to make a living, you've got to do everything you can to get a record played to make enough money, to be accepted on the charts. I joke that I had to get rich in order to sing like I'm poor again."
Dolly Parton

With his unmistakably gruff, sonorous voice and his incredible breadth as a writer and interpreter of songs, Cash delved masterfully into everything from historic Americana ballads to gut-bucket prison songs and politically charged, folk-style ballads.

The "Man In Black", Johnny Cash. Cash had a huge fan base from a wide range of musical spheres and found receptive audiences in prisons and at mainstream pop festivals, as well as on the country circuit.

Country's Leading *Lights*

Nearly as formidable a figure was Merle Haggard. He first emerged from the Bakersfield, California music scene as a Buck Owens protégé, but by the early 1970s, Haggard manifested nearly unparalleled creative and stylistic ambition.

With his vivid songwriting, rich, fluid Lefty Frizzell-style baritone, accomplished lead guitar work and finesse as a country-jazz bandleader, Haggard became a dominant figure throughout the 1970s and 1980s. As a revivalist, he had a profound influence on the next generation of artists, with his masterful reprises of music by greats like Jimmie Rodgers, Lefty Frizzell and western swing king Bob Wills, as well as original material such as 'The Fugitive', 'Okie From Muskogee' and 'I Think I'll Just Stay Here And Drink'.

Key Artists:

Johnny Cash
Loretta Lynn
Tammy Wynette
Dolly Parton
Conway Twitty

Willie Nelson had a similarly pervasive impact. By the mid-1970s the vastly talented and musically adventurous singer-songwriter-guitarist transcended his spearhead role of the early 1970s outlaw movement to forge a remarkable career that has covered a panoply of styles – from hardcore honky tonk and country rock to pop balladry and even inspired excursions into soft jazz and 1930s and 1940s show tunes.

Straddling these two extremes was Conway Twitty ('Hello Darlin'', 'You've Never Been This Far Before', 'I'd Love To Lay You Down'). Though his instincts were more unerringly commercial than Cash's or Haggard's, Twitty (another Sun Records alumnus) would consistently top the charts from the late 1960s into the 1990s with everything from hardcore honky tonk ballads to syrupy countrified remakes of pop and rock ballads. Other country stars, such as Ferlin Husky, Mac Davis, Ronnie Milsap, Glen Campbell, Kenny Rogers and Barbara Mandrell, would thrive with more low-key and refined styles connected to the 1960s Nashville sound – which remained alive and well in one form or another even during the 1970s and 1980s.

Dolly Parton, for many people the epitome of country music, performs onstage with country-pop crooner Kenny Rogers. The duo had a smash hit in 1983 with the Bee Gees-penned 'Islands In The Stream'.

The Rise of the *Cowgirls*

The 1960s through to the 1980s also saw the rise of women as a dominant force in country. Central to the countrified "women's movement" was Kentucky-born coal-miner's daughter Loretta Lynn. With a singing style and songwriter's sensibility that was resolutely twangy, rustic and sassy, Lynn, like Johnny Cash, would ultimately achieve the stature of folk hero.

Nearly as emblematic for millions of "unliberated" American women was Mississippi-born former hairdresser Tammy Wynette, best remembered for anthems like 'Stand By Your Man' and 'D-I-V-O-R-C-E'. Though she would later segue into a more pop-oriented sound, Dolly Parton first gained prominence in the early and mid-1970s with unadorned yet eloquent original songs that celebrated her east Tennessee Smoky Mountain heritage.

Other Country Chart Sounds

The 1950s and 1960s also saw the rise of prototypical singer-songwriters like Don Gibson and Roger who enriched the music with eloquent and often idiosyncratic compositional styles. A few, like Don Williams, brought a laconic, introspective folk influence to the country field. Others, like the Statler Brothers, drew upon a gospel vocal quartet flavour to popularize sentimental story-songs like 'Countin' Flowers On The Wall'. Still others, like Vern Gosdin and Stonewall Jackson, found passing chart success by revitalizing the honky tonk sound. Brother harmony groups like the Louvin Brothers and the Wilburn Brothers also had occasional hits. Their sibling vocal sounds in turn inspired the Everly Brothers, who had a string of early Nashville-produced rock-pop classics like 'Wake Up, Little Susie' in the 1960s. The Kendalls, a talented father-and-daughter vocal duo, also hit big around 1980 with the song 'Heaven's Just A Sin Away'. It is artists like these who forged the template for most of the country music recorded over the years since. And perhaps more than any other generation of musicians, they have had an indelible influence on the younger artists who followed them.

> *Key Tracks:*
> 'D-I-V-O-R-C-E' Tammy Wynette
> 'Hello Darlin'' Conway Twitty
> 'Jolene' Dolly Parton
> 'Ring Of Fire' Johnny Cash
> 'Stand By Your Man' Tammy Wynette

Tammy Wynette, whose unmistakable country twang graced the charts as a solo artist, in duets with her one-time husband George Jones and as a trio with Dolly Parton and Loretta Lynn.

Reggae *Pop*

Jamaican music has never been that far away from mainstream British music since Millie Small stormed the charts in 1964 with the galloping ska of 'My Boy Lollipop', but it was not until the end of that decade that reggae became a bona fide part of pop.

Heralded by Desmond Dekker's incredible success in 1969 with 'It Mek' and 'The Israelites', hardly a week went by until the end of 1972 when the Top 40 didn't feature at least one reggae record. With bouncy, upbeat tunes, Max Romeo ('Wet Dream'), Bob & Marcia ('Young, Gifted And Black'), Jimmy Cliff ('Wonderful World, Beautiful People'), Nicky Thomas ('Love Of The Common People'), Dave & Ansell Collins ('Double Barrel'), and the Pioneers ('Long Shot Kick The Bucket') all became an integral part of the British Saturday night soundtrack.

Right Atmosphere for Success

One of the reasons reggae did so well in Britain as the 1960s rolled into the 1970s was the sorry state of the singles charts. Bands like Marmalade, Herman's Hermits and the Tremeloes still clung on but were clearly part of a bygone era, prog rock was not exactly the most dancefloor-friendly music and glam hadn't really kicked off. Soul and Motown were all over the pop charts and dominating the dancehalls, and reggae fitted alongside perfectly. Such was the demand for the music in the UK during this period that more reggae was sold in Britain than in Jamaica.

"I never believed the English people could love reggae so much...."
Dave "Dave & Ansell Collins" Barker

Desmond Dekker's Jamaican accent presented a problem for some western fans of 'The Israelites'; the opening line "Wake up in the morning, slaving for bread sir" was often misheard, one common example being the somewhat less evocative "Wake up in the morning, baked beans for breakfast".

Reggae Goes *Pop*

Kingston record producers reacted to this new marketplace with alacrity, and pretty soon men like Joe Gibbs, Bunny Lee, Derrick Harriot and Lee Perry were adapting their output to accommodate it. They would up the tempo, and lyrics and accents were adjusted accordingly.

The big change came about in response to BBC radio's reluctance to give reggae airplay because, it claimed, the music was "unsophisticated". Producers began to record vocals and rhythm tracks in Kingston, then send the tapes over to the UK to have lush string arrangements added, meaning songs like 'Young Gifted And Black' or 'Black Pearl' were as glossy as any other pop music and, consequently, became massive hits.

Of course, reggae did not disappear from the pop charts in the early 1970s, but it became a much less frequent visitor as tastes were changing on both sides of the Atlantic. In the UK, glam rock was taking over from soul and reggae as the dance music of choice, while in Jamaica the onset of roots meant fewer producers and artists were concerning themselves with an overseas pop market. But reggae that has been recorded in the UK or mixed with that market in mind has always maintained a presence, with artists including Matumbi, Maxi Priest, Shaggy, Apache Indian, Musical Youth and hardy perennials UB40, who continue to bring reggae to a mainstream audience.

Key Artists:

Nicky Thomas
Desmond Dekker
Bob & Marcia
Dave & Ansell Collins
The Pioneers

Jamaican music has had a great influence on the pop scene on both sides of the Atlantic. Beyond 10cc and the Police are the British 2-Tone bands – the Selector, the Specials, the Beat and Madness, all punkified ska revivalists – while in the US ska bands like Bim Skala Bim, Dancehall Crashers and the Toasters have taken 2-Tone as their model, moving it one stage further. And reggae hasn't been completely ignored by American pop fans – Eric Clapton covered Bob Marley's 'I Shot The Sheriff' to chart-topping effect, and Johnny Nash also made number one for four weeks in 1972 with his own composition 'I Can See Clearly Now', later covered by Jimmy Cliff.

Reggae pop star Jimmy Cliff starred in the 1973 film The Harder They Come. *The movie is seen through the eyes of a country boy who is lured from his home by the bright lights and promise of the big city.*

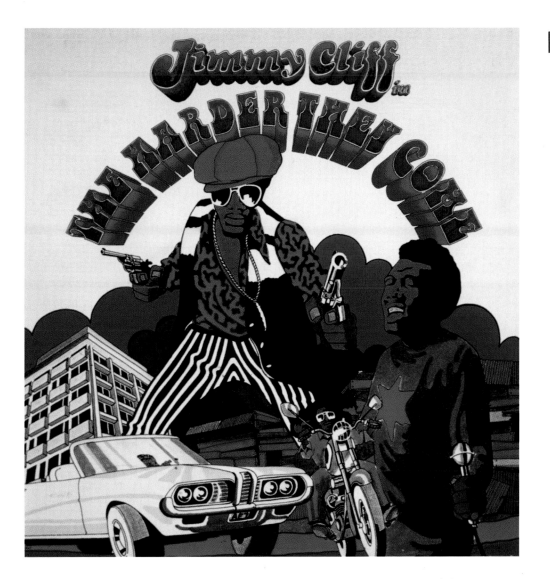

Northern *Soul*

This enduring British cult dance scene takes its name from the post-mod discos in the north-west of England where it developed, rather than the geographical location of the music-makers. Legendary disco venues like Manchester's Twisted Wheel, Blackpool's Mecca and The Wigan Casino are still spoken about in reverential tones by soul and dance connoisseurs.

The reason northern soul exists is because of the extraordinary amount of quality soul produced – and often initially ignored – in the Motown- and Stax-dominated 1960s soul Golden Age.

From Levi's Genes

The immediately recognizable northern soul sound derives directly from Motown, and specifically from one key record: the Four Tops' 1965 hit 'I Can't Help Myself (Sugar Pie, Honey Bunch)'. With its circular piano/guitar riff, pounding rhythm, dramatic orchestral arrangement, and masochistic, lovelorn lyric howled like a sermon by lead vocalist Levi Stubbs, this track saw Motown composer/ producers Eddie and Brian Holland and Lamont Dozier taking jazz and classical complexity and making it into totally accessible dancefloor R&B, with hooklines to match. As one of Motown's defining peak moments, it had an immediate influence on fledgling soul artists and small labels all over America. But, with Motown so commercially dominant, the majority of these more modest and derivative soul recordings failed to get radio airplay and slipped into obscurity.

"...until you've been there I don't think any mere written word can fully convey to you that special and unique vibration that generates amongst the brothers and sisters there."

Dave Godin, soul guru and first to use the phrase "northern soul" in Blues and Soul magazine in 1971

The Four Tops formed in 1953 after an impromptu performance at a friend's birthday party. Band member Lawrence Payton died in 1997, and the Tops split after an amazing 44 years of performing together.

No-Hit *Wonders*

Meanwhile, England's loyal late-1960s mods, who had made Motown and melodic soul their dance music of choice, were demanding something more from DJs than the familiar big hits. Those DJs began to take more chances on obscure US imports, and the competition to find the most upfront, unheard new tunes took off, particularly around the north-west of England, in and around Manchester.

But by 1968, soul was changing, taking on influences from funk, the blues and roots revival, and psychedelic rock, as typified by Norman Whitfield and Barrett Strong's productions for the Temptations including 'Cloud Nine' and 'Just My Imagination'. As they entered the 1970s the serious Twisted Wheel and Mecca dancers, who were now developing a post-mod dress code of longer hair, tight T-shirts or sweaters, and voluminous "Oxford Bag" pants, wanted their DJs to stick with light, uptempo grooves despite their increasing rarity. DJs like future Hi-NRG pioneer Ian Levine began to make trips to the US, often tracking down entire warehouses full of mid- to late-1960s soul singles that no one had bought. Played in the northern clubs, they sent the dancers wild and began a self-contained scene based not around artists or albums but particular singles. This also meant that northern soul discovered a non-dancefloor foundation built around collecting rare records, with "failed" singles often fetching hundreds of pounds on the collectors' market.

Key Artists:

The Four Tops
Edwin Starr
Jackie Wilson
The Impressions
Ramsey Lewis Trio

The northern soul cult spread throughout Britain, to Scotland, the Midlands, and eventually London, reaching its peak in 1975 when two novelty groups, Ovation and Chosen Few, both from Wigan, reached the UK singles chart with records designed to exploit the hitherto underground scene. This caused a split between the 1960s diehards and those – particularly the DJs and patrons of the Wigan Casino – who put crossover pop such as 'A Lover's Concerto' by Toys and 'Love On A Mountain Top' and 'Everlasting Love' by Robert Knight into the mix.

A class northern soul act, Geno Washington achieved chart success with the Ram Jam Band during the 1960s. His album Geno's Back *in 1976 took him back on the road and he continued to tour into the 2000s.*

Anthems and *Tributes*

By the late-1970s, the Casino, Mecca and Twisted Wheel had closed down, and northern DJs such as Levine and Pete Waterman began mixing light soul with Europop, creating the gay disco of Hi-NRG and having a profound influence over all subsequent forms of British manufactured pop.

Nevertheless, northern soul refused (and still refuses) to die, and new generations of DJs and followers continue to emerge, sustaining regular clubs and one-off "all-nighters", fanzines, a plethora of CD compilations and digital radio shows.

Inevitably, the music associated with northern soul has gone on to encompass an ever-widening range of styles; aficionados are still arguing over what is or isn't true northern soul. Scene anthems range from the pure soul stomp of Edwin Starr's 'S.O.S. (Stop Her On Sight)' and the great Jackie Wilson's 'The Sweetest Feeling' to the plaintive orchestral social conscience ballads of Curtis Mayfield and his 1960s vocal group the Impressions; to the girl-group pop of the Velvelettes and the Chiffons; to the R&B of Sugar Pie De Santo and the Capitols; to the soul-jazz instrumentals as 'The In Crowd' by Ramsey Lewis; to records such as Evelyn King's 'Shame' and the O'Jays' 'I Love Music', which typify the northern soul/disco crossover of the scene-splitting late-1970s.

Key Tracks:
'Everlasting Love' Robert Knight
'I Can't Help Myself (Sugar Pie, Honey Bunch)' The Four Tops
'In The Crowd' Ramsey Lewis Trio
'S.O.S. (Stop Her On Sight)' Edwin Starr
'The Sweetest Feeling' Jackie Wilson

Apart from the obvious influence on gay disco and manufactured pop, northern soul directly inspired various 1980s British acts. Electro pop duo Soft Cell covered northern classics 'Tainted Love' and 'What'. Dexy's Midnight Runners scored their first UK number one with 'Geno', a tribute to club performer Geno Washington. Joboxers had a short shot at fame with northern-inspired hits 'Boxer Beat' and 'Just Got Lucky'. And the 2-Tone bands took a little from the genre too, as is especially obvious on 'Embarrassment' by Madness.

Gloria Jones recorded 'Tainted Love' (the song made famous by Soft Cell's cover version) in the mid-1960s, but moved to Britain to find work amid the northern soul craze. She joined the rock band T Rex in 1974 and became the girlfriend of singer Marc Bolan.

Seventies *Pop*

The early 1970s music scene saw rock and pop continue to separate, with the latter usually aiming for not only an ever-younger audience, but also an increasingly middle-aged one. Three major strands of new pop defined both this process and pop's increased preoccupation with different forms of escapism.

Glam rock was a peculiarly English phenomenon, signalling a return to Beatlemania-style scenes of teen hysteria after the late-1960s move towards the seriousness of roots revivals and rock opera. Its two inventors were both "swinging London" veterans in their early twenties who had enjoyed minor success, firstly as psych-mod pin-ups and then as hippy-folk troubadours.

Glamour Boys

Marc Bolan became an overnight Britpop sensation at the tail end of 1970. His extraordinary blend of stomping rhythms, a pre-grunge guitar style, abstract sex lyrics, reverberant sound, flamboyant glitter clothes and make-up, as well as androgynous beauty introduced British teenagers to the delights of both adolescent sexual confusion and joyously daft rock'n'roll fun. An inability to develop this trademark sound precipitated a fall from pop grace before the Electric Warrior died, tragically, at the age of 30.

"From '72 to '76 I was the ultimate rock star. I couldn't have been more a rock star. Anything that had to do with being a rock'n'roll singer was what I was going for."
David Bowie

As Bolan hit big in 1970-71, his south London friend and rival David Jones looked on in interest. Having already changed his name to David Bowie, the art-loving dance student transformed into an even more beautiful and sexually ambiguous figure than Bolan, teamed up with hard-rock guitarist Mick Ronson, and invented an iconic glam-rock character. His 1972 concept album, *The Rise And Fall Of Ziggy Stardust And The Spiders From Mars*, established Bowie as the pop phenomenon of the age. Of course, unlike Bolan, Bowie became a master of pop reinvention, switching from nihilistic rock to blue-eyed soul, to electronic introspection and mainstream pop, all the while remaining one of both pop and rock's most iconic and influential figures.

David Bowie's foray into glam rock came in the form of his extraterrestrial alter ego, Ziggy Stardust. Bowie took the name Ziggy from a clothing boutique, while Stardust came from the inimitable Legendary Stardust Cowboy (a.k.a. Norman Carl Odam).

Glam *Thrives*

For the first four years of the 1970s, glam was the dominant language of UK pop. While Roxy Music further represented the intelligent side of this gender-bending exuberance, the likes of Gary Glitter, the Sweet, Mud and Suzi Quatro offered pure, infectious bubblegum and knowing slapstick.

The genre had less impact in the US, although satirical horror-rockers Alice Cooper and Kiss forged a more overtly theatrical connection. As the 1970s moved on, Scotland's Bay City Rollers took glam's three-minute anthems and sartorial madness (feather cuts and tartan flares, in this case) into the early boy-band genre, causing hysteria among teenage girls on both sides of the Atlantic. Meanwhile, Freddie Mercury's Queen fused the flamboyant androgyny of glam with the musical excesses of progressive rock. The epic meaninglessness of their 1975 number one hit, 'Bohemian Rhapsody' effectively brought a fitting end to glam's glorious mix of the daring and the deliciously daft.

Totty for Tots

Throughout all of this, a form of pop emerged for those too young and/or sensitive to deal with all this queerness and clowning. Teenybop struck with a three-pronged attack from America. The Osmonds, a family of Mormons from Ohio, purveyed a squeaky-clean kind of romantic schmaltz, centred on the toothy grin of their youngest member, Donny. The Osmonds' biggest competitors were the last great product of the Motown hit factory. Led by the sensational child prodigy Michael, Indiana's Jackson 5 were cooler and funkier – and, of course, blessed with a lead singer who would go on to change the course of pop history. Finally, the star of Monkees-lite US TV show *The Partridge Family*, the dreamily pretty David Cassidy, slayed a generation of pre-pubescent girls with a succession of sophisticated, breathy ballads. These three acts proved, once and for all, that you could market pop to small children without having to descend to novelty. Every subsequent manufactured pop act is sprinkled with a little of their stardust.

5 Top 1970s UK Artists:	5 Top 1970s US Artists:
1 Elton John	1 Elton John
2 Rod Stewart	2 Fleetwood Mac
3 Marc Bolan	3 Neil Diamond
4 David Bowie	4 Bee Gees
5 Sweet	5 Barry Manilow

Marc Bolan's love for rock'n'roll music was allegedly born out of a fortuitous mistake in which his father, trying to purchase a Bill Hayes record for Marc, accidentally picked up a Bill Haley single.

Be My Baby *Boomer*

But few of the aforementioned acts catered for the most significant new market. For those who were old enough to experience the cultural upheavals of the 1960s, but wanted a mellower pop soundtrack for their inevitable settling down, a classy and smooth kind of adult pop emerged.

Rod Stewart moved from raucous roots-rock to a flashy yet restrained everyman style of pop, applying his white soul rasp to dramatic ballads and hilariously crass, disco-rock sexual come-ons. The Carpenters – again family, but this time the Californian duo Richard and Karen – produced the embodiment of anti-rock. Their Bacharach ballads and jolly versions of country classics appeared frothy and cynical, until you listened closely to the well of eerily detached sadness in Karen's voice. She died of heart failure, brought on by a lifelong struggle with anorexia nervosa, in 1983, aged just 32.

Elsewhere, former 1960s rockers created a pop-rock hybrid based on high production values and lush, ambitious albums. 1977's *Rumours* marked Brit/US band Fleetwood Mac's transformation from blues-rock renegades to inventors of "divorce pop" – a smooth sound smuggling bitter tales into the all-ages mainstream. California's Eagles used mellow country rock to detail the pain of growing old and the death of the hippy dream. But sly disillusion was not all there was. The Electric Light Orchestra, from Birmingham, England, took the Beatles' more pseudo-classical moments and carved an entire career out of them. Meat Loaf teamed up in 1978 with producer/composer Jim Steinman for the magnificently overblown and massively successful *Bat Out Of Hell*, a loving pop pastiche of every teen-rock dream. The decade ended with 1960s pop auteurs the Bee Gees applying their mastery of harmony pop to disco's dancefloor hedonism, the all-conquering soundtrack of Saturday Night Fever reinventing them as pioneers of the coming dance-pop crossover.

---

5 Top 1970s UK Tracks:
1. 'Bohemian Rhapsody' Queen
2. 'Mull Of Kintyre' Wings
3. 'Rivers Of Babylon' Boney M
4. 'You're The One That I Want' John Travolta and Olivia Newton John
5. 'Mary's Boy Child, Oh My Lord' Boney M

5 Top 1970s US Tracks:
1. 'You Light Up My Life' Debby Boone
2. 'Night Fever' The Bee Gees
3. 'Tonight's The Night (Gonna Be Alright)' Rod Stewart
4. 'Shadow Dancing' Andy Gibb
5. 'Le Freak' Chic

In the early 1960s, the Bee Gees were child stars in Brisbane, Australia, where they released their first single. Their return to England set them on course for greater success.

Seventies Pop *Singer/Songwriters*

The 1970s remains the era most closely associated with the artistic and commercial triumph of the singer/songwriter. Mature introspection was the order of the day, though a yearning for songs that pondered both youthful nostalgia and the concerns of adult lives led to the emergence of two distinct camps of singer/songwriters.

While rock singer/songwriters dismissed hit singles and revealed their own state of mind through their art, pop singer/songwriters were more romantic and radio-friendly, less specific and challenging, and crossed over into what some sceptical critics labelled "hip easy listening". Although Carole King, the maker of the definitive 1970s pop singer/songwriter album, had only a short-lived superstardom, her biggest success neatly defines the key elements of the genre.

A Rich Tapestry

Formerly Carole Klein, New Yorker Carole King had formed one of the most successful songwriting partnerships of all time at the turn of the 1960s. Working out of the legendary New York hit factory The Brill Building, King and her future husband, Gerry Goffin, composed a host of pop anthems ('Will You Love Me Tomorrow' for the Shirelles, 'The Locomotion' for Little Eva and 'Pleasant Valley Sunday' for the Monkees, among many others) throughout the decade. Although King had a fitful career as an artist during the period – her only major success was 'It Might As Well Rain Until September' in 1962 – she suddenly re-emerged in early 1971 with *Tapestry*, a complete break from tremulous teen pop. The album's deft blend of classic, Golden Age pop melody, white soul vocals and arrangements, combined with lyrics of sincere yet world-weary romance, made it the biggest-selling album ever at that point. King's subsequent career of typically Los Angeles adult pop never quite reached the same heights, but the former backroom girl had forged the template for all pop singer/songwriters to come.

"Good songs should last. A good one should last forever. 'Just the Way You Are', by Billy Joel, is that sort of great song." Elton John.

Carole King's 1971 album, Tapestry proved that she was not only capable of writing successful hit songs but also of singing them in a gentle, emotive style that led the way for many others.

Three Piano *Men*

A trio of ivory ticklers developed this budding pop tradition, and became commercial kings of the mainstream. The most unlikely was one Reg Dwight, a plump, bespectacled Englishman who changed his name to the more poetic Elton John and looked set for a journeyman career through British pop's backwaters until his second, self-titled album scored a surprise transatlantic hit in 1970.

Although Elton never wrote his own lyrics (he forged a career-long partnership with wordsmith Bernie Taupin), and also gleefully embraced the comic end of glam rock's onstage sartorial flamboyance, his 30-years-and-counting success was, and is, based squarely upon classic singer/songwriterly values. Emotive, piano-led melodies, sad and introspective lyrical themes and an ever-present nostalgia for pop's past combine to make him the genre's most enduring superstar.

His American mirror figure was another plump and unprepossessing troubadour – Long Island's Billy Joel. Again, from his 1975 breakthrough album, *Piano Man*, to his eventual commercial slump in the 1990s, Joel's ability to blend lonely introspection with the nostalgia kick of, say, 1983's 'Uptown Girl' proved the key to him becoming one of the biggest-selling pop artists of all time. Joel was melancholy and musically articulate, but an ordinary guy – a description you couldn't apply to the third piano man, Stevie Wonder.

Key Artists:

Carole King
Elton John
Billy Joel
Stevie Wonder
Paul Simon

The blind former Motown child prodigy Steveland Judkins broke away from his label's formula pop-soul with 1972's *Music Of My Mind*, embarking on a run of classic albums (through to 1980's *Hotter Than July*) that broke the R&B and pop mould with their blend of rock, funk, jazz, soul, romantic introspection and political protest. Black music was changed forever by the depth and breadth of Wonder's artistic vision.

Stevie Wonder's expressive style is perhaps linked to his being blind for almost all his life.

The 1960s *Revisited*

Two particular artists refused to let hippy ideals lie – at least, within their music and for a short but significant period. Paul Simon split from Art Garfunkel and ploughed his own singular furrow of innocent 1960s pop, mature melodicism, wistful nostalgia and wry New York cynicism. His polished, post-graduate pop theorems threw everything from gospel and doo-wop to jazz and reggae into the mix. In 1986, he delivered a unit-shifting fusion with African pop in *Graceland*, drawing praise and criticism when his insistence on recording and performing in South Africa broke the anti-apartheid cultural boycott.

Cat Stevens – a British/Greek/Swedish minor 1960s pop star – also went on to create controversy in later years. Having scored major success in the early 1970s with a folky brand of peace-loving acoustic pop, Stevens converted to Islam in 1979, changed his name to Yusuf Islam and retired from music. The controversy arrived when he allegedly announced his support for the persecution of author Salman Rushdie in the 1980s.

MOR to Come

Elsewhere, various artists tugged the singer/songwriter impulse into increasingly shallow waters. In America, Tin Pan Alley veteran Neil Diamond, housewives' favourite Barry Manilow, 'Vincent' and 'American Pie' nostalgist Don McLean, died-young faux-country minstrel Jim Croce and one-man love-song factory David Gates (who hid behind the band name Bread) provided a mellow respite from rock's cultural domination. In the UK, even the MOR ("middle of the road") types needed a gimmick; hence Gilbert O'Sullivan's flat cap and Leo Sayer's clown suit in their early careers. Nevertheless, the sound was unmistakable: easy, catchy, introspective and nostalgic, with the guitars turned down to one. Both faded from view when they became typical, bouncy pop singers. But the singer/songwriter wave they were part of has never retreated and almost certainly never will.

Key Tracks:

'Piano Man' Billy Joel
'Rocket Man' Elton John
'Will You Love Me Tomorrow' Carole King
'You Are The Sunshine Of My Life' Stevie Wonder

The Carpenters had a beautiful clarity of sound – a combination of Karen's clear soprano, Richard's piano arrangements and beautifully smooth studio production techniques. They defined the MOR mood of popular seventies music.

Roots *Reggae*

Roots reggae is probably the best-known genre of Jamaican music. Thanks to artists such as Bob Marley and Burning Spear, it achieved genuine worldwide success. Through these artists and their carefully articulated political dissent, social commentaries and praises to Jah Rastafari, it has been accepted across the world as one of the most potent protest musics.

Roots reggae grew up in Kingston's slums in the early 1970s, as the ghetto dwellers – or "sufferahs" as they called themselves – wanted to express their dissatisfaction at a government that, almost a decade after independence, had failed to deliver on its promises for a better life. If anything, ordinary people were worse off. Many were turning to Rastafarianism, if not going so far as to grow dreadlocks then at least following its principles as a way of surviving the harsh times as Jamaica's underclass.

"Roots and culture was a necessity, the times called for a positive stance...."
Jimmy Cliff

Rasta is a faith inspired by Marcus Garvey (1870–1940) who believed that black Caribbeans were the lost tribes of Israel, and that they should rid themselves of the oppressions of the west and return to the promised land, Africa. Rasta espoused black self-help and self-respect, and struck a particular chord with a people less than a century removed from the slave ships. And this being Jamaica, popular feeling soon found its way into popular song.

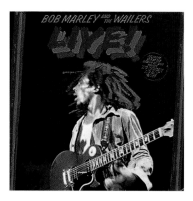

(Right) Bob Marley quickly became the biggest artist Jamaica has ever produced. (Above) Bob Marley and the Wailers' Live album, recorded in London, is regarded as one of the best live albums ever.

Finding a *Voice*

It was on the sound systems that the voices of protest first made themselves heard, as people could simply pick up the mic and chat about anything they wanted to, provided it was on the beat. This was a new breed of deejays, who felt the same pressures as their audiences and gave voice to them in a way the people could identify with.

It was then that Big Youth, Prince Jazzbo, I-Roy and Prince Far-I built up huge followings and went on to have hits with tunes like 'Under Heavy Manners' (Prince Far-I), 'Natty Cultural Dread' (Big Youth) and 'Natty Passing Thru' (Prince Jazzbo). It did not take long for a new wave of producers to sit up and take notice, seeing this new attitude as their chance to make an impact: Gussie Clarke, Augustus Pablo, Keith Hudson, Niney, Jack Ruby, Lee Perry and Yabby U all made their names producing roots reggae's first records.

Key Artists:
Burning Spear
The Mighty Diamonds
Bob Marley
Big Youth
Culture

Once it became obvious that there was a market for protest music, it broadened out and as Michael Manley's People's National Party, voted into office in 1972, was far more tolerant of Rastafari, reggae's whole tone changed. As part of the shift towards Rasta's ganja-fuelled spirituality, rhythms slowed, basslines became more pronounced, east-Africanisms began to creep in, dub versions sought to intimidate with the very weight of their presence, and lyrics pulled few punches as they told of society's ills and preached revolution.

The deejay Prince Far-I was known for his gruff voice and critiques aimed at the government of the time. His 'Under Heavy Manners' took a lyrical stance against new measures initiated towards violent crime.

The Main *Man*

Vocal groups like Culture ('Two Sevens Clash'), the Mighty Diamonds ('Right Time'), the Abyssinians ('Satta Massa Gana'), Max Romeo ('War Inna Babylon') and the Congos ('Heart Of The Congos') made sure the roots era took Jamaican music all over the world, but none made a bigger impact than Bob Marley.

First with Peter Tosh and Bunny Wailer as part of the Wailers, releasing albums like *Catch A Fire* and *Burnin'*, Marley showed he had all the sensibilities and charisma to take roots reggae to rock-star levels. In 1974 his vocal partners split, going on to pursue international solo careers. Tosh's *Legalise It* remains a dope-smoker's anthem, and Wailer's *Blackheart Man* is one of roots reggae's best albums. Bob Marley's star burned brightest, though, and through albums such as *Exodus*, *Natty Dread* and *Kaya* he quickly became the biggest artist Jamaica has ever produced. He was an easily understood figurehead, and through his depth of purpose, virtuoso musicianship and close associations with high-grade marijuana, roots reggae found a place for itself in mainstream rock that Jamaican music had not achieved before or has since.

Roots Lives On

Roots'n'culture seemed to fade out at the end of the 1970s, as so many in Jamaica believed that 10 years of sufferation had made no difference at all and that it was time to have some fun. In the wider world, once Bob Marley died in 1981, the mainstream record industry seemed to lose interest as it couldn't see another obviously rock-friendly leader. However, during the 1990s, as reggae's pendulum swung the other way towards glorifying violence, misogyny, homophobia and general unpleasantness, the roots movement has undergone something of a revival through deeply spiritual artists like Luciano ('Where There Is Life'), Bushman ('Nyah Man Chant'), Tony Rebel ('If Jah'), Cocoa Tea ('One Way'), Morgan Heritage ('Protect Us Jah') and the Bobo deejays Sizzla ('Black Woman And Child'), Capleton ('More Fire') and Anthony B ('Real Revolutionary').

Key Tracks:
'Jammin'' Bob Marley
'Natty Cultural Dread' Big Youth
'No Woman No Cry' Bob Marley
'Right Time' Burning Spear
'Two Sevens Clash' Culture

Legendary roots reggae producer Lee Perry became an important part of the roots'n'culture movement. His single 'People Funny Boy' used a lazy, bass-driven beat, the first Jamaican pop record to signal the shift from upbeat ska to the languor of roots.

Urban *Soul*

Although the 1960s golden age established soul as the foundation of Afro-American pop, the 1970s and 1980s saw soul's supremacy challenged and ultimately ended by, in turn, funk, disco, electro, dance-rock, hip hop and house. In hindsight, the soul music of the 1980s went into a form of stasis, waiting for a new style of soul to revive the genre.

Nevertheless, soul, like rock'n'roll, will never die, and a few true soul voices continued to survive and adapt to the new market. Before looking at these 1980s urban soul artists, it's necessary to acknowledge the important performers who kept soul breathing during the funk- and disco-deluged 1970s.

Sweet Soul

Producer Thom Bell and songwriters Kenny Gamble and Leon Huff set up the Philadelphia International label in the late-1960s. By the mid-1970s, the trio had established the "Philly sound", a massively successful blend of gospel- or doo-wop-influenced vocals and heavily orchestrated black pop that heavily informed disco through the music of the O' Jays, Harold Melvin & the Blue Notes, the Three Degrees and the cast-of-thousands house band MFSB. Bell also co-wrote and produced for the three vocal groups who defined the mellifluous sound of sweet soul: the Delfonics, the Stylistics and the Spinners, who all produced a string of much-loved romantic hits in the early 1970s. Bell had no hand in Chicago's Chi-Lites, who mined an identical seam, reaching a peak of tear-stained male masochism on 1972's gorgeous 'Have You Seen Her?'

"If you got the feeling, you can sing soul. You just sing from the heart."
Otis Redding

An altogether more defiant gospel-derived take on sweet soul came from Atlanta's Gladys Knight & the Pips who fronted the first and funkier version of 'I Heard It Through The Grapevine' in 1967, and scored their biggest Motown hit in 1972 with country composer Kris Kristofferson's 'Help Me Make It Through The Night'. The group became part of the Motown talent drain the following year, when they signed for Buddah and made the extraordinary 'Midnight Train To Georgia', a weepy ballad that showcased one of the toughest and most expressive voices in soul history.

Roberta Flack and Donny Hathaway studied music together at Howard University. Hathaway's 1973 urban soul recording of 'Killing Me Softly' was a huge success and spent five weeks at the top of the charts.

Solo *Superstars*

The first solo sweet soul superstar arrived when Teddy Pendergrass, lead singer of Harold Melvin's Blue Notes, went solo in 1976. His definitive take on boudoir soul seduction produced a string of US hit albums before a car crash in 1982 paralyzed him from the neck down. Undaunted, Pendergrass continued to record throughout the 1980s, duetting on 'Hold Me' with a pre-stardom Whitney Houston in 1984.

An even more tragic story concerns critically acclaimed Chicago vocalist Donny Hathaway. His virtuoso blends of soul balladry, subtle jazz and Latin grooves brought admiration but little commercial impact, aside from hit duets with former classmate Roberta Flack. In 1979 he fell to his death: a suicide brought about by depression over his faltering career, which seemed to symbolize the demise of soul in the disco era.

In the early 1970s, Marvin Gaye made music that stands among the greatest in any genre, defining soul's conscience on 1971's *What's Going On* and soul's sensuality on 1973's *Let's Get It On*. After a bitter break from Motown Gaye returned in 1982 with the extraordinary *Midnight Love*, featuring a single, 'Sexual Healing', that proved that deep soul and the new technology could co-exist perfectly – as long as you happened to be one of the best singers on Earth. The glorious comeback was ended forever when the tortured Gaye was shot dead by his father in April 1984.

Key Artists:
Marvin Gaye
The Chi-Lites
The Stylistics
Luther Vandross
Anita Baker

The King & Queen of Sophisto-Soul

As disco and its beat-led offshoots dominated, it became obvious that the soul alternative lay in ignoring the dancefloor completely and producing a new kind of sweet soul for an adult audience. Cue chubby New Yorker Luther Vandross, who began his career as a session singer before taking centre stage by blending a voice like melting chocolate shot through with a subtle vulnerability, and clean, synthetic backdrops constructed by jazz bassist Marcus Miller. It was masochistic romantic yearning all the way for Luther, hitting heights on 1986's *Give Me The Reason*. The same year saw jazzy soul siren Anita Baker seduce the world with the smoky sensuality of her *Rapture* album, which took adult soul into a level of glossy sophistication.

A seminal album of the early 1970s, What's Going On addresses many political issues troubling America at the time, and captures the frustration and concern felt by Marvin Gaye and many of his fellow countrymen.

The Minneapolis *Sound*

Flip back to the turn of the 1980s, and a Minneapolis all-singing, dancing, composing, arranging and instrument-playing prodigy called Prince Rogers Nelson. His backing band, the Time, includes in its number Jimmy Jam and Terry Lewis, who eventually left Prince to his approaching superstardom and became writer/producers.

While their former leader was effortlessly mixing soul with funk, rock, jazz and pop (and creating, along with Michael Jackson, the ultimate soul/pop crossover.) Jam and Lewis opened their Flyte Tyme studios and explored ways to fit their beloved soul and gospel with the electro-funk, groove-based opportunities that new synthesizer technology offered. The emphatic, funky and soulful 1980s hits they went on to create for Janet Jackson, The S.O.S Band, Alexander O'Neal, Change (whose former lead singer was Luther Vandross) and gospel choir Sounds Of Blackness built a bridge between the funk era and the swingbeat/R&B future.

The Coming of Brit-Soul

Negotiating the same river from the direction of London, two new black British acts also sought ways to blend electro with soul melodicism. Carl McIntosh's Loose Ends fused 'Sexual Healing'-type synthetic soul with a tougher hip hop feel, hitting a commercial peak with the lovely 'Hangin' On A String', a transatlantic hit in 1985. This proved to be the harbinger of a sound that will be forever associated with loved-up London at the turn of the 1990s. Jazzie B (originally Beresford Romeo) and his Soul II Soul collective took the Loose Ends sound and doubled it, adding deep, much-imitated hip hop beats, bittersweet optimism and a sense of space borrowed from dub reggae. The 1989 hits 'Keep On Movin'' and 'Back To Life' effectively reminded America what it was missing by rejecting soul, and inspired R&B's self-consciously retro cousin, nu soul.

Key Tracks:

'Have You Seen Her?' The Chi-Lites
'Never Too Much' Luther Vandross
'Sexual Healing' Marvin Gaye
'Sweet Love' Anita Baker

Anita Baker followed her Grammy Award-winning album Rapture *with a world tour. She went on to win two further Grammys in 1988 for her follow-up album* Giving You The Best That I Got.

Europop

Camp. Trashy. Lightweight. Throwaway. Exploitative. Fraudulent. Europop has drawn all those insults and more, and remains, after 30 years, most popular among those with a love of kitsch. Nevertheless, the danceable pop of early 1970s mainland Europe has had an enormous influence on manufactured pop, as well as all house and disco-derived dance music.

Throughout the 1950s and 1960s, America and Britain dominated global pop trends. Although Europe had already delivered some uniquely indigenous pop artists – most notably, the sophisticated pop suites of France's Serge Gainsbourg and Françoise Hardy – Europop as a universally recognized pop language was created in the mid-1970s by two very different artistic teams. One prioritized the song, while the other pioneered a new sound. All subsequent Europop blended the two on some level, but never with such artistry and impact.

Swede Soul Music

ABBA formed in 1971, after the four members had already become folk-pop stars Sweden. It was 1974 before songwriters Benny Andersson and Björn Ulvaeus, and lead singers Agnetha Faltskog and Anni-Frid Lyngstad, achieved the international breakthrough they craved, winning the annual Euro trash-fest that is the Eurovision Song Contest with the arrestingly odd-but-irresistible 'Waterloo'. The two married couples (Björn and Agnetha, Benny and "Frida") went on to conquer the world with an unbroken string of million-selling albums and singles, purveying an increasingly perfect and increasingly lovelorn blend of sweeping melody, glistening production and Beach Boys-meets-Mamas & the Papas-influenced harmony pop. Yet the sometimes surreal imagery produced by the Swedes' second-language English, and Benny and Björn's singular MOR-tinged songwriting style, created a pop language that transcended their US and UK influences. The band fell apart in 1981 but, in seven short years, ABBA had become the biggest pop group since The Beatles, while simultaneously proving that you did not need a rock attitude – or good dress sense – to create affecting and original pop artistry.

ABBA's popularity has endured to such an extent that a smash hit musical, Mamma Mia!, uses their timeless songs as its basis and draws in huge audiences from a wide range of ages and cultures.

ABBA

ON TOUR

PRESS OUT BOOK

Sex and *Synths*

Meanwhile, in Italy, a veteran Italian producer and a Boston-born star of German stage musicals were inventing what we now know as dance music. In 1975, Giorgio Moroder and Donna Summer caused a sensation with the 17-minute epic 'Love To Love You Baby', whereby Ms Summer moaned her way to orgasm over a low-tempo synthesized version of Philadelphian orchestral disco-soul.

This was followed in 1977 by, arguably, the most influential dance record of the modern era, 'I Feel Love', a chugging, churning, futuristic disco machine based on one repetitious, but subtly developing, electronic drone-riff. It made Summer a superstar – the first and biggest disco diva.

> *Key Artists:*
> ABBA
> Donna Summer
> Giorgio Moroder
> Boney M
> Milli Vanilli

The pair went on to make hit after hit with synthetic takes on everything from hard rock ('Hot Stuff') to Spectoresque girl-group pop ('Love's Unkind'), all possessed of a camp sexual immediacy that somehow sounded entirely unique, entirely European. While Moroder was to enjoy even greater success as a soundtrack producer/composer (*American Gigolo* with Blondie, *Flashdance*, *Top Gun*), Summer headed towards a more overtly American kind of dance-pop, and then gospel as a born-again Christian.

Her star waned when she made insensitive comments about people with HIV/AIDS (which she later insisted were misquotes), appalling her huge gay following. None of this, however, changes Summer and Moroder's invention of Eurodisco, a key influence on house and techno, and a guiding presence in every Europop and female vocal dance hit of the last 25 years.

After contributing to the soundtrack of Top Gun *in 1986, Giorgio Moroder steered away from dance music and focused on rock, producing the album* Flaunt It *by the short-lived band Sigue Sigue Sputnik.*

Mime Doesn't *Pay*

The third great Europop progenitor was the German writer/producer Frank Farian, who formed a vocal quartet to front a string of strange novelty disco hit singles in the late 1970s.

Comprising West Indian session singers Marcia Barrett, Bobby Farrell, Liz Mitchell and Maizie Williams, Boney M turned up on every European pop show of the period performing comic, catchy singalongs based on everything from historical drama to Christmas carols to Jamaican nursery rhymes. It had all petered out by the turn of the 1980s, predictably, but Farian's brand of manufactured pop genius was to return and provide a bizarre twist to the tale.

Milli Vanilli comprised two aspiring models, Rob Pilatus and Fabrice Morvan, who became an overnight transatlantic pop sensation in 1989 with a parade of massive, Farian-produced hits. The problem was that their Grammy Award-winning songs had actually been recorded by singers Johnny Davis and Brad Howell, with rapper Charles Shaw. The pretty pair were simply mime artists. Farian eventually revealed the truth in 1990. An embarrassed Grammy committee stripped Milli Vanilli of their award, and everyone involved in MV became pop pariahs. It all reached a grisly end when, after failed attempts to forge a new pop career, Pilatus slid into drug addiction followed by a public suicide attempt, various crimes and, finally, his drugs- and alcohol-related death in 1998.

Key Tracks:
'Brown Girl In The Ring' Boney M
'Dancing Queen' ABBA
'I Feel Love' Donna Summer and Giorgio Moroder
'Love To Love You Baby' Donna Summer and Giorgio Moroder
'Waterloo' ABBA

Euro Currency

Despite Milli Vanilli's tragic tale, Europop has continued to serve up light pop to those put off by the pretensions of "serious" rock and pop. Usually based on disco beats (Black Box, Technotronic, 2 Unlimited, Sash!, Livin' Joy); often applying "cheese" to various forms of black music soul food, such as rap (Snap!, Bomfunk MCs) and reggae (Ace Of Base); never, especially in the cases of Aqua, Whigfield and Roxette, taking itself too seriously. Classic Euro's happy, gay-friendly mix of repetition and catchiness directly influenced the entire sweep of twenty-first-century boy- and girl-band pop.

Boney M's 1978 single, 'Rivers of Babylon'/'Brown Girl in the Ring', became the biggest-selling single in UK chart history.

Novelty *Songs*

Straddling genres from pop to rock, country to dance, novelty songs tell humorous stories using satire, wackiness or a topical link with television, film or a popular craze. Though often musically dubious, they have enjoyed massive, but generally fleeting, success in the modern era.

Music and comedy have been bedfellows since the days of music hall and vaudeville, when many singers doubled as comedians, incorporating burlesque and innuendo into their performances. The tradition was continued by Spike Jones' anarchic rock and classical parodies of the 1940s and 1950s (1942's 'Der Fuehrer's Face'), Tom Lehrer's twisted pop music satires of the 1950s and 1960s ('I Hold Your Hand In Mine' from 1953) and Ray Stevens' country crossovers in the 1960s and 1970s ('Bridget The Midget', 1971).

Sherman Conquers America

Perhaps the most successful musical humourist of the post-war years was Allan Sherman, a Jewish comedian who was the toast of America's radio waves during the early 1960s. Specializing in spot-on parodies of folk songs and popular hymns and classical works, his most famous hit was 'Hello Muddah, Hello Fadduh'. His first three LPs went to the top of the charts; legend has it that President Kennedy was overheard singing 'Sarah Jackman', Sherman's version of the French standard 'Frère Jacques'.

"A lot of people look at it as a badge of honour when they get a 'Weird Al' parody." "Weird Al" Yankovic

Since Sherman's star waned in the mid-1960s, there have been very few consistently successful novelty singers, but plenty of popular novelty songs. Some of these were light-hearted digressions by established American performers (Chuck Berry's 'My Ding-a-Ling' (1972) and Johnny Cash's 'A Boy Named Sue' (1979)) and unlikely celebrities (William Shatner's cover of 'Lucy In The Sky With Diamonds', 1968).

Rolf Harris (one of the world's best-loved novelty stars) leaves for a tour of Bermuda in 1963, together with some of the props for his stage act: a wobble board (Harris's own invention) and a false limb, for his character Jake the Peg (with the extra leg).

One-Hit *Wonders*

Britain has a particular thirst for silly one-offs: the comedian Benny Hill had a hit with 'Ernie (The Fastest Milkman In The West)' in 1971, as did actor Clive Dunn in the same year, with an eponymous spin-off from his *Grandad* series. The Tweets even coerced Britons into performing the actions to their 'Birdie Song' for much of 1981.

Links with non-musical popular culture often provided inspiration and publicity. Carl Douglas's 'Kung-Fu Fighting' ruthlessly exploited the 1970s enthusiasm for martial arts; The Firm topped the UK charts in 1987 with 'Star Trekkin'', which was based around the sci-fi show; and Eric Idle hit the number one spot in 1991 with 'Always Look on the Bright Side of Life', from the film Monty Python's Life Of Brian.

Two notable exceptions transcended one-hit wonder status: Rolf Harris and "Weird Al" Yankovic. The latter was the king of parodic pop on both sides of the Atlantic throughout the 1980s and 1990s. His favourite target was Michael Jackson, whose 'Beat It' and 'Bad' he reworked in food-fixated style as 'Eat It' and 'I'm Fat'.

Key Artists:
Allan Sherman
Johnny Cash
William Shatner
Carl Douglas
"Weird Al" Yankovic

Harris's popularity is largely a result of an ironic appetite for lovable cheesiness. The Australian artist and TV personality made his musical debut in 1963 and has remained popular in the UK ever since. Harris performs gentle digs at antipodean stereotypes, like his 'Tie Me Kangaroo Down Sport', and cover versions of songs like Led Zeppelin's 'Stairway To Heaven'.

Weird Al's recording career took off when he began to send his parodies to Dr. Demento, the host of a radio show with a cult following, which specialized in novelty material.

Disco

The Afro wig. The mirror ball. Platform heels. A pair of lurid flares. The enduring iconography of the mass-market disco era might seem laughable now, but to reduce such a revolutionary social force and creative musical explosion to a few items of fashion tat would be very short-sighted indeed.

As has happened with many other musical forms, the black (and, in this case, also gay) origins of disco have tended to be somewhat brushed over. Indeed, for many, disco is summed up by the movie *Saturday Night Fever* or disco latecomers like the Bee Gees. It may be true that the all-dancing John Travolta film took disco overground, and the previously washed-up Gibb brothers made disco more widely known in the late-1970s, but the first discotheque dates back to the 1940s.

Discothèque literally means "record library", derived from the French word *bibliothèque*. During their Second World War occupation of France, the Nazis banned dancing to, or playing, American-sounding music. The French Resistance took to playing the jazz records of black America furtively in the dark, makeshift cellar bars, and the term *discothèque* gained a more widespread parlance. When English speakers picked up on the concept of *discothèques*, their very Frenchness lent these early establishments a degree of sophistication.

"The disco scene is a classic case of spilled religion, of seeking to obtain the spiritual exaltation of the sacred world by intensifying the pleasures of the secular." Albert Goldman, 'Disco'

As New York DJs like Francis Grasso began mixing records together in late-night joints – keeping the beat going so that the music constantly flowed – revellers could begin to party harder and longer. Boundaries and prejudices were being broken down on the dance floors, and the cultural climate was heading towards a kind of post-civil rights inclusivity. Other DJs, such as David Mancuso, at his New York loft parties, would emphasize the spiritual journey a musical evening could take, while Nicky Siano realised that Mancuso's vibe could still work on a more commercial club level. By the mid-1970s, there were more than 100 nightclubs in NYC. The disco sound had genuinely begun to germinate.

The soundtrack to the 1977 film Saturday Night Fever *proved to be the biggest-selling soundtrack album in history, selling over 25 million copies.*

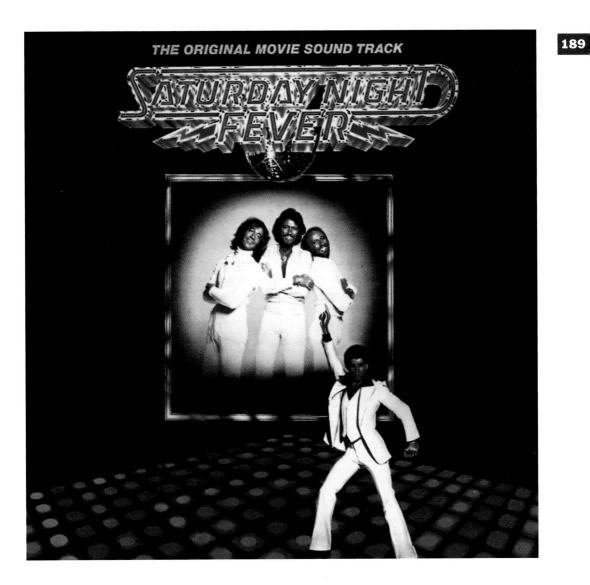

Soul, Sex and *Dancing*

In general, disco had a soulful feel about it, boosted by a quality, post-Spector production that incorporated uplifting, orchestral strings or brass. In addition, Giorgio Moroder's productions introduced a hi-NRG European influence, on classic cuts such as 'Love To Love You Baby' and 'I Feel Love', by Donna Summer.

The definition of disco remained quite open: essentially, it referred to what would work on the dance floor. Even non-disco songs would become disco tunes, such as the Sugar Hill Gang's hip-hop prototype 'Rapper's Delight', or Blondie's 'Heart Of Glass'. Some artists even seemed to become disco for one week only, and not simply to revive a flagging career – the list of opportunists included Kiss, Cher, Bryan Adams, Queen, Bay City Rollers, Burt Bacharach and Diana Ross.

Some key musical innovations went hand in hand with the rise of disco. DJs fuelled the demand for remixes or re-edits of records, many of which were, initially, done by Tom Moulton. By 1974, labels were releasing DJ-only vinyl pressings of remixes, and 12 percent of vinyl was cut to allow for more space between the grooves.

Key Artists:

The Bee Gees
Gloria Gaynor
Sister Sledge
Chic
Donna Summer

The results included such bona fide sex-and-dancing classics as 'Love Is The Message', 'Never Can Say Goodbye', 'Ring My Bell', 'Disco Inferno' and 'Funky Town', the big name artists including Gloria Gaynor, MFSB, Lipps Inc., Sister Sledge, Ottawan, Gamble & Huff, the O'Jays and the Temptations. With indie labels such as Salsoul and Prelude rising to challenge the majors, there was no shortage of tuneage with which DJs could provide the soundtrack for a night of hedonism.

Donna Summer combined her sultry vocals with Giorgio Moroder's songwriting and production talent to become the undoubted Queen of Disco.

How the Bubble *Burst*

By 1977 a New York celebrity haunt called Studio 54 was stealing the headlines. With its velvet-rope exclusivity, 54 was the sort of place where you could see Bianca Jagger riding in on a white horse – and indeed, the attending glitterati were probably more important than the music.

It was the sort of joint that Nile Rodgers and Bernard Edwards of Chic loved, but their exclusion one night prompted them to return to their studio and, enraged, pen one of disco's most enduring anthems. Originally called 'Fuck Off', its title was soon changed to 'Le Freak'.

By 1978, the USA boasted 20,000 nightclubs. Disco dominated a third of the singles chart and radio airwaves, and the industry's worth rose into the billions. The majors tried to make a fast buck, of course, but the bubble finally burst.

Key Tracks:
'I Will Survive' Gloria Gaynor
'Le Freak' Chic
'Love To Love You Baby' Donna Summer
'Stayin' Alive' The Bee Gees
'We Are Family' Sister Sledge

Disco soon fell out of favour, becoming unfashionable, kitsch and naff. The backlash was aided in part by US rock DJ Steve Dahl who called on disco-haters to demolish disco records at a Detroit Tigers baseball game in Comiskey Park. The fans rioted, causing the game to be cancelled, and chanted repeatedly "Disco sucks!". Punk rock by now was the new rock'n'roll, and disco for some was just fluff pop, becoming increasingly a watered-down version of black funk music stripped of its funk and blackness. Zipping up its boots, disco went back to its gay roots, already having laid the foundations for many more dance music genres to come.

The co-founder of the disco band, Chic, Nile Rodgers is known for his distinctive choppy style of guitar playing. Since Chic he has written and produced songs for David Bowie, Diana Ross and Eric Clapton.

Hip *Hop*

As the 1970s played out and disco took over, a new generation reacted against the commercial homogenization of black music by creating a completely new sound. This sound came from the streets and was accompanied by its own dress code, language, dance styles and attitude: Hip Hop was a way of life.

"I wanted to be the first black electronic group. Some funky mechanical crazy shit with no band, just electronic instruments."
Afrika Bambaataa

Whereas disco was symbolized by the swank Manhattan nightclubs, these new sounds swaggered out of the street corners and house parties of the Bronx, where the most plentiful resource was ingenuity. During the second half of the 1970s, young black America was literally cutting disco up as DJs made their sets more challenging by working two turntables with the same record on each, mixing between them to prolong the interesting bits at the expense of the banalities.

The DJ credited with starting this is Jamaican ex-pat DJ Kool Herc, who noticed, when operating his sound system, that it was the instrumental breaks in the extended 12-inch mixes that particularly moved the crowds, and began to mix two such sections together to create one seamless segment. It is from these extended instrumental breaks that the terms "break beats", "break-dancers", and "b-boys" (an abbreviation of "break boys") originated.

A teenage rapper in Harlem plays hip hop beats on a ghetto blaster.

Taking it *Further*

These impromptu remixes soon took on lives of their own and entirely different tunes were created out of parts of others as sections of vocals or melody were cut up and repeated to assume completely altered vibes.

An extra rhythmic thrust was provided by scratching, as a turntable's stylus was manipulated in a record's groove by moving the record itself backwards and forwards for beat-sized snatches. The burgeoning technology worked in tandem with this creativity as samplers and drum machines began to be used with increasingly sophisticated mixers and turntables allowing far more imaginative effects to be put into hip hop tunes. By the beginning of the 1980s, producers and mixers such as Arthur Baker, Grandmaster Flash and Afrika Bambaataa began to put this sound on record.

Key Artists:
Afrika Bambaataa
Arthur Baker
DJ Kool Herc

It also made stars of the slick-talking streetwise likes of the Furious Five, Spoonie Gee, the Cold Crush Brothers, the Sequence and Soul Sonic Force. Bringing a further, impromptu, anyone-can-join-in vibe to proceedings, DJs and MCs began rapping. Although such carryings-on are not unheard of in black American music – think of jazz's scat singing or jive-talking radio DJs – this was the first time it had been a sustained and featured part of proceedings instead of an optional extra. Essentially publicizing themselves, the club or the sound system, commenting on what was going on around them and just whooping with exuberance, the rappers were the glue that held the early hip hop scene together as they vibed it up and, more importantly, kept it exclusive.

Respectfully known as the "Godfather" and "Grandfather" of hip hop culture, Afrika Bambaataa was initially a gang warlord who went on to spread rap and hip hop culture around the world through his Zulu Nation.

Creative Spin-Offs

Break-dancing and graffiti were the physical manifestations of hip hop, each, like the music, representing a street expression that relied on little more than inventiveness and practised expertise. In the same way as the music, they also made use of their own environments to create something unique, energized and extraordinary out of not very much.

For these reasons dancing was at the very heart of hip hop; it gave anybody the chance to show off for the neighbourhood and excel at something. As dancers threw down increasingly audacious moves break-dancing competitions in clubs and parties echoed the dance floor cutting contests of the big band era. It was this healthy spirit of competition that former New York street-gang leader Afrika Bambaataa recognized as a far more viable and far less life-threatening alternative to fighting. Using his influence, gained from his notorious Black Spades gang, he set up dance competitions and created the Zulu Nation as a kind of umbrella organization for the city's growing number of hip hop crews.

It is understandable that graffiti art should grow up alongside rap and break-dancing as part of hip hop. Again, it is a spontaneous street expression and one that had the added bonus of being genuinely outlawed as it outgrew "tagging" (kids scrawling their customized initials, or tags, on any visible surface) to become "bombing" (painting detailed murals on subway trains in the stockyards). Graffiti became a political statement, inasmuch as its mere appearance represented a degree of anarchy, yet it blossomed into one of the most vibrant art forms of the late-twentieth century. Naturally, it ended up in smart uptown galleries. Fab Five Freddie, Futura and Phase II were hip hop's most influential graffiti artists, and were a vital part of its flourishing as a culture.

Key Tracks:
'Funk You Up' The Sequence
'King Tim III' The Fatback Band
'Rapper's Delight' Sugarhill Gang
'The Breaks' Kurtis Blow

Once hip hop went wide, marketing men became the decision makers rather than the kids themselves, which is why so much later hip hop does not have a sense of a "nation" in the way the old school used to. While hip hop has gained a great deal of logic, hip hop has also lost an equal amount of the raw, unpredictable spirit that originally served to unify it.

Break-dancing first emerged onto the New York street scene in the 1970s and competing gangs would regularly square up and seek to outdo each other with increasingly outrageous (and dangerous) moves.

Funk

By the 1970s, the new sound of funk dominated Afro-American music. Jazzers such as Miles Davis and Herbie Hancock scored their biggest commercial successes by incorporating its hip-grinding rhythms into what became known as fusion or jazz funk, while soul acts enjoyed a second wave of popularity as funk provided the bridge between the soul and disco eras.

Fuelled by Sly & the Family Stone's dark and druggy 1971 LP *There's A Riot Goin' On*, many of funk's themes were street-tough and angry, swapping soul's romance and hope for reportage on harsh ghetto realities. Other funk acts went in the opposite direction, using little more than chanted hooks and slogans to embellish their instrumental jams. Whichever way, the 1970s funk era remains one of the most vibrant periods in black music history, and those deep, dirty rhythms went on to provide sampling source material for hip hop's explosion in the late-1980s.

"James has more funk in his little finger than most people have in their life."
Saxophone player Pee Wee Ellis on James Brown

The Godfather of Soul

"The Godfather Of Soul", James Brown, continued to develop the funk he'd invented throughout the 1970s and 1980s. Although well-documented problems with drugs, women and the police led to an inevitable decline in his music's potency, classics such as 1975's 'Funky President' and 1976's disco-exploiting 'Get Up Offa That Thing' established him forever as the definitive funk artist. While Brown continued to throwdown, two other 1960s soul masters blended a mellower form of funk with socially concerned singer/songwriter elements. Former Motown child prodigy Stevie Wonder reached artistic peaks with the powerful fear-fuelled funk rock of 1973's 'Superstition' and the same year's *Innervisions*, an all-time-great LP mixing tough funk protest, sublime ballads and a jazzy spontaneity, despite Wonder playing almost everything himself.

The members of Funkadelic were initially part of George Clinton's funk band, Parliament. The 1978 album One Nation Under A Groove *proved their breakthrough and sold a million copies.*

Funky Soul *Men*

Meanwhile, Chicago's Curtis Mayfield broke away from his 1960s vocal group the Impressions and fashioned a unique music based upon his beautiful falsetto vocals and vivid lyrical pleas for social justice. This produced a funk masterpiece in 1972 with his soundtrack for blaxploitation movie *Superfly*.

All this Sly Stone-influenced funk politics was defined by a classic 1972 single by Ohio's O'Jays. This Philadelphia Sound vocal group produced, in the extraordinary 'Backstabbers', an expression of desperate pop paranoia that matched Marvin Gaye's legendary 'I Heard It Through The Grapevine' in intensity and dread.

The Coming of P-Funk

North Carolina's George Clinton had already been through 1950s doo-wop and 1960s soul with little success before his singular funk vision bore fruit in 1970. The debut album by his Funkadelic project took Sly Stone's psychedelic funk on an even weirder trip, mixing hard black rhythm with hallucinogenic guitar freak-outs and LSD-inspired sci-fi lyrics. By 1973, former James Brown cohorts Bootsy Collins (bass),

Maceo Parker (sax) and Fred Wesley (trombone) had joined Clinton in his two parallel groups, Funkadelic and Parliament. The two outfits mixed and matched up to 35 members and played the greatest freak-out live shows of their day. They swapped between pounding low-tempo big band grooves and maverick acid funk excursions, and became one of America's biggest bands. 1971's *Maggot Brain* (Funkadelic), 1976's *Mothership Connection* (Parliament) and 1978's *One Nation Under A Groove* (Funkadelic again) represent the high points of Clinton & co.'s catalogue, which took in equally influential sets by Bootsy Collins's Rubber Band and, in the 1980s, by Clinton as a solo artist. That influence is particularly evident in 1980s keepers of the funk faith – especially soul-pop and sex-funk genius Prince, his Motown label rival Rick James, electro-funk exhibitionists Cameo, and the Gap Band, who scored disco success by boiling Clinton's big beat excursions down into hook-laden pop singles such as 1980's infectious 'Oops Upside Your Head' – as well as hip hop's west coast G-Funk of the 1990s.

Key Artists:

James Brown
Stevie Wonder
Curtis Mayfield
Earth, Wind & Fire
Kool & the Gang

An all-round musical talent, Curtis Mayfield was a guitarist, singer, producer and songwriter. His movie soundtrack to Superfly *proved his greatest solo success, with the tracks 'Freddie's Dead' and 'Superfly' both selling millions in the US.*

Low Riders and High *Rollers*

Four remaining classic funk bands symbolize black American music's swift 1970s journey from rock and jazz-influenced bohemian innovation, through the much-parodied but well-loved period of sartorial flamboyance represented by Afro dos and outrageous flared jump-suits, to funk's eventual defeat and dilution at the hands of late-1970s disco crossover.

LA's War began as a back-up band for former Animal Eric Burdon before forging their own path with a heavily jazz- and rock-influenced form of funk complexity. Their finest moments veer from the dramatic protest of 1972's 'The World Is A Ghetto' to the irresistible street scene grooves of 1976's gravel-voiced 'Low Rider'. But by 1978 their attempts to ride the disco wave floundered and obscurity beckoned. Faring rather better were hardy perennials the Isley Brothers, who encouraged brother Ernie to unleash his coruscating post-Hendrix electric guitar licks. The result was the benchmark 3 + 3 album in 1973, and a prolific stream of small-band funk rock and ballad singles and albums. Again, the Isleys faltered over disco, but bounced back in 1983 with the 'Sexual Healing'-inspired boudoir soul of 'Between The Sheets'.

In the wake of P-Funk, horn-driven big bands from all over America mixed infectious chants with grooving jams. Two of those bands gradually changed tack and were among disco's big winners. Maurice White's Earth, Wind & Fire blended Clinton's cosmic vision with White's own jazz arrangement virtuosity and sophisticated pop songcraft. Between 1973's *Head To The Sky* and 1981's *Raise!* they were black America's most globally successful act. The 1980s advance of machine-driven dance music finally ended their triumphant run.

Key Tracks:

'Celebration' Kool & the Gang
'Get Down On It' Kool & the Gang
'Get Up Offa That Thing' James Brown
'Superfly' Curtis Mayfield
'Superstition' Stevie Wonder

The less flamboyant but similarly adaptable Ohio big band Kool & the Gang hit with a more modest form of funk-to-disco transition. After a string of jam'n'chant successes culminating in 1976's 'Open Sesame', they hired crooner James "J.T." Taylor and became disco pop hitmakers from 1979's 'Ladies Night' onwards, before those pesky machines rendered them unKool in the mid-1980s.

Kool & the Gang began life as a jazz quartet during the 1960s, but developed into an internationally successful funk band. Their enigmatic frontman, "J. T." Taylor stayed with the band until 1988, when he left to pursue a solo career.

Ambient

Ambient music has existed since the late-nineteenth century. Although Brian Eno was the first artist to use the term "ambient" to describe his music on his 1978 album *Music For Airports*, composers like Claude Debussy and Eric Satie, with their notion of composing pieces for listening surroundings, broke with musical conventions and expectations.

Frenchmen Erik Satie and Claude Debussy are often called the "fathers of modern music", and it's no idle claim. While Satie was writing musical pieces at the end of the 19th century that were based on the concept of setting a mood, his most significant works were composed around 1920. These were a series of pieces he called "furniture music", which Satie wanted both to be part of and include the surrounding noises. "Furniture music" laid the basis for what Brian Eno achieved with ambient music half a century later.

"It's exactly what you need if you have a busy and stressful life."
Mixmaster Morris

Similarly, Debussy's experiments with tone, texture and harmony in his orchestral works at the end of the 19th century and his early 20th century piano music would also play an important role in influencing the way composers – and later on, electronic producers – approached the composition of mood or ambient music.

By the middle of the 20th century, experimental composer John Cage questioned accepted notions of percussion, tone and texture with '4' 33" '. As its title suggested, the piece was exactly four minutes and thirty three seconds long and consisted of silence. Cage's message was clear: any musical expression, silence included, was valid. Cage was followed by composers like Karlheinz Stockhausen, whose tape-based audio collages laid the basis for modern-day sampling, and the acknowledged founders of minimalism: Terry Riley, Steve Reich and Philip Glass.

A contemporary of John Cage, Karlheinz Stockhausen was another pioneer of electronic music, with his tape-loop piece recordings amongst the first ever produced.

Early *Trendsetters*

By the late-1960s this freethinking approach, combined with a growing drug culture, had also produced some of rock's most adventurous forays as bands like Pink Floyd and Tangerine Dream soundtracked rock music's first tentative flirtations with electronic sounds.

Works like Pink Floyd's *Piper At The Gates Of Dawn* and Set *The Controls For The Heart Of The Sun*, released the same year man first walked on the moon, mapped out this new fusion, dubbed space rock. It heralded the beginning of synthesized sound's growing influence on contemporary music. It was only a matter of time before an artist made use of the technology in a mainstream manner, and Mike Oldfield's 1973 album, *Tubular Bells*, which did just that, was a huge success, selling millions worldwide.

Increased access to electronic equipment during the 1970s and 1980s allowed Brian Eno to fulfil his goal of making music that cultivated relaxation and "space to think". The advent of this technology also allowed German act Kraftwerk to pioneer their synth-based sound, a development that in turn influenced a whole range of 1980s synth producers and groups, including Trevor Horn, the Art Of Noise, the Human League and Ultravox.

Acid House Changes the Rules

However, by the mid- to late-1980s, electronic music took a radical new departure. As acid house and Ecstasy culture exploded in the UK and Europe, it was clear that there was a need for a more relaxed accompaniment to the high-octane beats. Even at early acid house clubs, DJs like Alex Paterson, from ambient dub act the Orb, were in charge of providing a soothing musical antidote in a second room. Consequently, the late-1980s saw the release of classic ambient albums including the Orb's dubby *Adventures Beyond The Ultraworld* and Mixmaster Morris's pastoral work as Irresistible Force, as well as pop situationists KLF's groundbreaking *Chill Out*.

Key Artists:

Brian Eno
The Orb
Air
Aphex Twin
Moby

Mike Oldfield's innovative Tubular Bells *release in 1973 on Virgin Records has sold over 16 million copies worldwide and is regarded as one of the finest pieces of ambient music to date.*

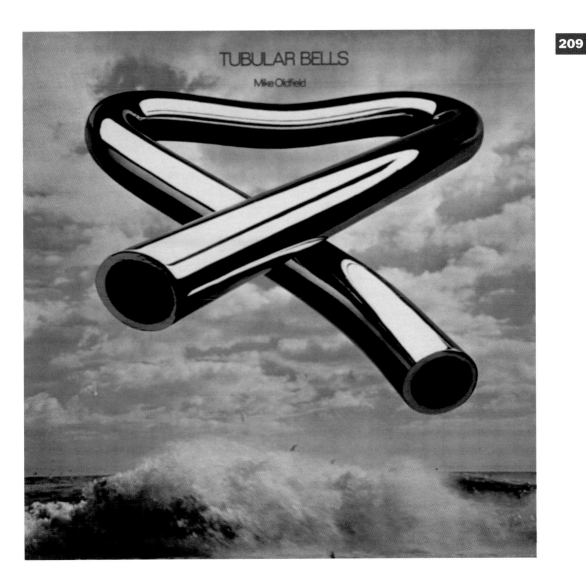

Ambient Branches *Out*

Rather than merely provide soft ear candy for tired ravers, ambient had spread its influence to house music and had taken on world and dub influences. These ethnic ingredients were evident in the mish-mash of musical textures that defined early 1990s London clubs Whirly-gig and Megadog, as well as in the work of Banco De Gaia and Bedouin Ascent.

Indeed, ambient's relevance to electronic music cannot be understated during the early to mid-1990s. It can be measured by the number of benchmark albums released during this period. In the electronic field, Aphex Twin released the hypnotic *Selected Ambient Works Volume 1*, while Sheffield label Warp started the *Artificial Intelligence* compilation series, introducing the subtle electronic nuances of Plaid, Autechre, Speedy J, Black Dog and B12 to a wide audience. Orbital's *Yellow* and *Brown* albums documented ambient's influence on dance floor techno and Tom Middleton's Global Communications project debuted with the haunting textures of the *76:14* album. Meanwhile, German producer Peter Namlook, along with Wagon Christ's Phat Lab Nightmare and the isolationist tones of Norway's Biosphere became the natural successor to John Cage and Steve Reich's minimalist legacy.

Key Tracks:
'Come To Daddy' Aphex Twin
'Little Fluffy Clouds' The Orb
'Sexy Boy' Air

Ibiza Chills Out

Although ambient music's increased profile and popularity meant major labels saturated the market with a succession of pale imitations, there was no danger it would succumb to commercial forces. Entwined in the original Balearic culture of Ibiza, pre- and post-club chill out sessions hosted by DJs like Lenny Ibizarre and Jon Sa Trincha had ensured tracks such as Sueño Latino's 'Sueño Latino', a version of 1970s German producer Manuel Gottsching's 'E2-E4', became as much the soundtrack to the White Island as high-octane house music. By the mid-1990s, Ibiza bars and beaches like Café Del Mar, Salinas, Bora Bora and Calla Llonga were playing host to UK chill DJs like Chris Coco and Phil Mison, who were playing diverse but universally chilled DJ sets.

Orbital's influential music has been remixed by such masters as Moby and gained them a spot at Woodstock 2 on the rave stage.

Chill Out on the *Rise*

Ambient had morphed into chill out and, although its name had changed, it still looked to the same concept of creating a mood to suit the listening environment. The other common bond between ambient and its mid- to late 1990s successor is that it still embraces a broad range of styles.

From the wispy electronica of Warp act Boards Of Canada to Nightmares On Wax's soulful hip hop, Bent and Lemon Jelly's lush compositions, Zero 7's cinematic productions and Royksopp's pop-informed atmospherics, chill out assimilates a wide range of diverse musical sources. Its increased popularity was bolstered by the release of French duo Air's *Moon Safari* album, which fused dreamy 1960s pop with blissed-out electronic textures and former techno producer Moby's *Play* album, which sampled the mournful outpourings of old blues songs and set them to haunting ambient backing tracks. To date, *Play* has sold over 10 million copies worldwide, its sales spurred on by the use of every track in a multitude of television commercials.

Chill out also enjoys an increased following due to sociological concerns: most people who started clubbing in the early 1990s have by now reached their early thirties and have either reduced the frequency with which they go out or are married and have children. In this scenario, chill out is the perfect soundtrack to staying in. At the same time, this shouldn't detract from the fact that chill out has its own dedicated series of festivals and events (for example, The Big Chill) every year in the UK.

Key Albums:

Adventures Beyond The Ultraworld The Orb
Discreet Music Brian Eno
Moon Safari Air
Play Moby
Tubular Bells Mike Oldfield

However, like ambient, chill has also attracted the attention of the corporate sector which has flooded the market with a succession of compilations; the Ministry Of Sound's chill out albums have sold hundreds of thousands of units. Like most electronic forms, chill out music hasn't been watered down by mainstream attention. Indeed, recent years have seen producers like Blue States, Susumu Yokota and John Beltran explore folk, organic and lush techno soundscapes. It seems that, to paraphrase ambient guru Mixmaster Morris, chill knows "it's time to lie down for its rights".

The Orb's 1992 UK chart-topping album, U. F. Orb, established the group as leading contributors to the growing interest in ambient electro.

Easy *Listening*

Until it was reclaimed with an ironic wink by 1990s hipsters, easy listening had been hugely popular, but rarely cool. While the teenagers of the 1950s and 1960s were getting off on dangerous rock'n'roll and subversive R&B, their parents were sweetly cocooned in the music of Mantovani and Percy Faith.

Easy listening music never launched any rebellions; no riots raged to its syrupy strains. It is unobtrusive, pacifying music built around pleasant, easily digestible melodies. Which is not to say it has no artistic value: within its wide borders can be found a rich spectrum of sounds. Though often dismissed as hollow and uninspired, the genre has been distinguished by the work of some lavishly talented musicians, including such immortals as Henry Mancini and Burt Bacharach.

A Birthplace in Business

Beautiful music, mood music, elevator music, background music, light music, adult contemporary, light classical; all fall in some way beneath the umbrella of easy listening. Since it was concerned with the subtle influencing of mood, it also had much in common with movie music; many easy listening stars doubled as soundtrack composers. But the genre's origins lie in commerce, and one of its fathers was not a musician but an American soldier. Brigadier General George Owen Squier patented the transmission of background music, which he named "Muzak", in the 1920s. Originally designed to soothe the nerves of workers making vertiginous journeys up the first skyscrapers, the modulated supply of watered-down classical, jazz and popular tunes soon became known as "elevator music".

Muzak became popular with company bosses, who believed it increased productivity and boosted morale. By the early 1970s, Muzak was played in shopping malls and airport departure lounges, used as telephone hold music, and was even piped into Polaris submarines. Muzak's ability to influence, or "tint", human moods fascinated musicians like Brian Eno, who explored it in his Discrete Music LP (1975), generally acknowledged as one of the earliest examples of ambient music. Detractors accused companies of using Muzak as an emotional sedative or a subliminal marketing tool. But the fact remains that it was popular with a large proportion of the millions of workers who were exposed to it from the 1920s onwards.

Easy listening pioneer Burt Bacharach, whose music has been praised for its distinctive melodies, sophisticated style and light classical feel.

The Maestro of Light *Classical*

In the 1920s, the British Broadcasting Corporation introduced a new genre, light classical, in order to attract listeners who could later be nudged towards more "highbrow" music. The most notable light classicist, and a name synonymous with easy listening, was Annunzio Paolo Mantovani. The classically trained violinist was a nationwide sensation in both America and Britain by the 1950s.

Mantovani reinvented classical music in a studio-produced style whose hallmarks were "cathedralized" strings, close harmonies and echo-laden, overlapping sound. His output was divided between lush waltzes based on familiar tunes like 'Greensleeves', and original compositions such as 'Charmaine', a dreamy extravaganza of fluttering violins and woodwinds, that was a big American radio hit in 1951. Mantovani topped the charts on both sides of the Atlantic and became the first musician to sell one million stereo records in the United States.

Key Artists:

Mantovani
Henry Mancini
Percy Faith
Liberace

From the Screen to the Airwaves

Many of Mantovani's albums revisited romantic film themes of the day, as did the mood music of Jackie Gleason, but the undisputed master of cinematic easy listening was Henry Mancini. After cutting his teeth on jazz and the big band sound of the 1940s, the Clevelander soon graduated to scoring soundtracks for film and television. He developed an inspired knack for creating songs that escaped the confines of the movie or show they were written for and became memorable classics in their own right. They varied enormously in tone, from the killer rhythms of his jazz-inflected theme for *The Peter Gunn Show* (1959) to the bittersweet refrains of his most celebrated song, 1961's 'Moon River'.

The musical centrepiece of *Breakfast At Tiffany's* was inspired by the film's elfin star, Audrey Hepburn, and boasted sublime, dreamy lyrics by Johnny Mercer. But it is the elegant simplicity of Mancini's melodies that make it one of the most perfectly realized pop songs of the past 50 years, and proves that easy listening can be brushed with genius. Mancini's peers heartily agreed: *Breakfast At Tiffany's* alone won him two Oscars and five Grammys.

Henry Mancini's 'Moon River' appears in various arrangements throughout Breakfast At Tiffany's. *Audrey Hepburn even sings the song herself at one point.*

A Bona Fide *Showman*

By the late-1960s, dedicated radio stations were pumping out what had then become known as "beautiful music", to devoted (mainly female) fans across America. The soft strings of conductor-composers like Mantovani, Mancini and Percy Faith dominated the schedules. But, in terms of charismatic showmanship, none of them could hold a candle to an incendiary pianist by the name of Wladziu Valentino Liberace.

A Polish-American from Milwaukee, Liberace was not just the most flamboyant figure in easy listening, but one of the biggest personalities in all of popular music. A child prodigy, he was playing solo piano with symphony orchestras by his teens, but by the 1950s, he was a star, performing a mixture of light classical, lounge jazz and show tunes while exuberantly clad in furs, sequins and gold lamé. Like many easy listening artists, he was never loved by the critics, but his audiences adored him.

Enter the Vocalists

Largely because a lack of vocals was more conducive to its original status as "background music", the genre had been dominated by instrumentals. But the laid-back vocal releases of Sinatra, Martin et al had always had plenty in common with the classic lounge and easy listening compositions and, in the 1970s, the beautiful music stations began to play more records by soft-edged pop acts like Barbra Streisand and the Carpenters. The latter, a brother-sister duo from Connecticut crafted a melodic, commercial sound that was as popular with easy listeners as it was with chart followers. Like Mancini and Mantovani before him, Richard Carpenter was fond of lush, emotive arrangements. But the focus was his sister Karen's clean, resonant voice, showcased to seminal effect on a cover of Burt Bacharach's '(They Long to Be) Close To You' that was a hit around the world. The Carpenters' gentle-on-the-ear approach remains one of easy listening's most familiar touchstones. And the genre lives on in the output of both the deeply uncool, like Barry Manilow, and the knowingly trendy, like the Mancini-inspired Stereolab. It seems our appetite for hassle-free melody will never be sated.

> *Key Tracks:*
> 'I'll Never Fall In Love Again' Burt Bacharach
> 'Moon River' Henry Mancini
> '(They Long To Be) Clost To You' The Carpenters

Although an incredibly popular performer – especially with the ladies – Liberace was panned by the critics for his sentimental style. He coined a phrase in response to this, saying that he cried all the way to the bank.

Krautrock & *Electro*

Krautrock, which emanated from West Germany during the late-1960s, fused the Velvet Underground's white noise experiments and Pink Floyd's psychedelic rock with the free form jazz aesthetic and funk-based rhythms.

Avoiding the dull virtuosity of progressive rock and the sanitised R&B pop of the late 1960s, Krautrock's grand vision of reinventing the rock guitar as well as exploring the untapped possibilities of the electronic sound has seen it influence dance and electronic music as well as experimental rock.

The most influential Krautrock bands were Neu, Can and Faust. From the mid-1960s through to the early 1970s Faust juxtaposed melodic songs like 'Jennifer' with screeching walls of noise, while Neu favoured a pulsating electronic sound as well as making blissful ambient passages. Michael Rother from Neu also explored a pure electronic sound on his *Harmonica* collaboration with Hans-Joachim Roedelius and Dieter Moebius from Cluster. However, Can – who formed in the mid-1960s – were the most important Krautrock band. Consisting of bassist Holger Czukay, guitarist Michael Karoli, keyboardist Irmin Schmidt, drummer Jaki Leibezeit and vocalist Damo Suzuki, the band's free-form approach saw them jam for hours before translating their improvizations into arrangements. On works like *Tago Mago*, *Ege Bamyasi* and *Future Days*, the band fuses spacious, atmospheric textures with sparse, live funk rhythms.

"If you want to make something new, you shouldn't think too far beyond one certain idea."
Holger Czukay

Occupying the middle ground between guitar rock and the clean, synthesized techno sound, Krautrock, especially Can, is a fascinating paradox. Its proponents used guitars for purposes they weren't intended for – to emulate synthesized sounds – as well as gelling rock's often forgotten sense of rhythm with precise repetition, an aesthetic common to electronic rather than live music. The wide range of artists and acts Can and their Krautrock contemporaries inspired straddles the rock and electronic worlds.

Pioneers of the exploratory sounds of post-psychedelia, Can's innovative sound would go on to influence the boom of technopop artists during the 1980s and 1990s.

Electronic *Heirs*

By the 1980s, the Krautrock legacy was still strong amongst rock music's experimental proponents. Sonic Youth's free-form guitar work alluded to the German sound; Julin Cope's frazzled acid rock made references to Krautrock's deranged sound; and, on a lighter note, the shoegazing indie style of Ride was shaped by Krautrock's wall of sound.

The 1980s act Spacemen 3 also embodied the Krautrock mentality. Their work was characterized by layers of feedback, pulsating hypno-rhythms and electronic textures, key components of the band's superb *Playing With Fire* album.

By the 1990s, Krautrock influences were most notable in the electronic environment. The angular, difficult work of Tortoise, To Rococo Rot and Mouse On Mars gave way to Andy Votel and the Twisted Nerve label's skewed, lo-fi approach, while indietronica acts like Lali Puna, Dntel, Tarwater, Peaches, Kreidler and Schneider TM fused guitar elements with melodic, quirky and even sleazy electronic elements.

However, Germany is where the most apparent modern day heirs to Krautrock can be found. Uwe Schmidt has succeeded in reinventing Krautrock's legacy under a number of guises. Together with Burnt Friedmann as Flanger, he explores its free form, jazz-based rhythm approach, and as Sieg Uber Die Sonne, Schmidt makes deep electronic music. Most famously, he has released a series of quirky, salsa-inspired cover versions of Kraftwerk under yet another incarnation, Señor Coconut.

Key Artists:
Can
Neu
Faust
Drexciya
Cybotron

For different reasons, the stripped-down electronic sound of the Scape label and its owner, Stefan "Pole" Betke is also an obvious Krautrock heir. Bearing similarities to the contemporary stripped-down, dub-influenced German techno sound, Betke's compositions lack the rhythmic focus of 1960s Krautrock, but, together with like-minded producers Matmos, the jazz-inspired Jan Jelinek – who also records for Scape – and Russian act Fizzarum, he has inherited the Krautrock mantle.

Having released their debut album, Taking Drugs To Make Music To Take Drugs To in 1986, Spacemen 3 were notorious for recording songs that lasted for upwards of 20 minutes at a time.

The Evolution of *Electro*

Despite the current hype and mainstream acceptance of the music, Electro has always enjoyed a strong cult following. This is due to the music's many different strands and its constant need for reinvention.

Although electro wasn't solely a product of the 1970s band Kraftwerk's pioneering synthesized sound, the German act's importance cannot be overestimated. By the early 1980s, Kraftwerk had influenced synth pop and new romantic acts like Depeche Mode, the Human League and Ultravox. US producer Juan Atkins took inspiration from Kraftwerk's rigid beat structures and futurist sense of dislocation to kick start Detroit's electro movement. In particular, his Cybotron and Model 500 projects as well as seminal acts like Underground Resistance and Drexciya were all influenced by Kraftwerk, but developed their own distinctive styles.

Not only was Atkins the first producer to coin the term "techno" for his sci-fi obsessed dance floor material, he also put out tracks like 'Clear' as Cybotron, setting Detroit's influential electro scene in motion. Electro's sci-fi themes were also furthered by militant techno/electro act Underground Resistance. The collective's exploration of deep techno and dance floor friendly electro funk was, and still is, riddled with outer-space references. Meanwhile, mysterious act Drexciya turned electro's space fixation inside out, documenting the mythology of the lost city of Atlantis and the concept of an "inner space" on textured resonating releases like 'Deep Sea Dweller' and 'Aquatic Invasion'. Like its techno sound, Detroit's electro innovations laid down a blueprint for others to follow.

Key Tracks:
'Autoban' Kraftwerk
'Hallogallo' Neu
'Spoon' Can

It would be too simplistic, however, to credit Kraftwerk and Detroit for bring solely responsible for the vast contemporary electro scene. Funk bands like Parliament, Trouble Funk and Cameo, as well as composer John Carpenter's eerie film soundtracks were vital. Of equal importance are the ebm (electronic body music) and Italo disco sounds.

Kraftwerk became a dominant and influential force in electronic music's development.

Leaders of the New *School*

While the Detroit sound was revered, few producers outside the Motor City were making this complicated, intricate music. It seemed electro would remain a highly specialized sound. However, in 1997, Dutch producer I-F released the classic 'Space Invaders Are Smoking Grass' track, a record that looked to Italo Disco as much as it did to the Detroit sound for inspiration. This dance floor sound found favour with Techno DJs who could play their tracks without dropping the tempo.

In 1998, German DJ/Producer DJ Hell set up the International Deejay Gigolos label. Although he released ebm-influenced work by David Caretta and Terence Fixmer as well as putting out material by some of Drexciya's offshoot projects, Hell also sought out a poppier, synth pop-flavoured variant of the Adult/I-F sound. Dubbed electroclash by New York club promoter Larry Tee, Hell's label brought glamour, style and accessibility to electro.

Key Albums:

Neu *Neu*
Playing With Fire Spaceman 3
Tago Mago Can

Despite mainstream interest, electro has never been in a healthier state, evident in the increased variety of styles. Apart from the ongoing development of electroclash, many producers have veered away from this glitzy style. They are taking the music back underground and are looking to older influences again.

Meanwhile, Detroit's booty bass sound keeps growing in popularity. A brutally raw, high-octane version of the expletive-filled Miami bass sound, it is the work of Motor City's DJ Assault and Godfather, who have forged links with UK producers like Debasser and Andrea Parker. Similarly, maverick producer Andrew Weatherall and his studio partner Keith Tenniswood's work as Two Lone Swordsmen contrasts starkly with the glamour-obsessed electroclash sound. It seems that not even the untimely demise of Drexciya's James Stinson in late 2002 can stop electro's forward march.

While still a teenager, DJ Hell began mixing different genres of music from punk and new wave, to hip hop and house, until he found his niche in trance and hardcore.

Eighties *Pop*

Although many would contend that 1980s pop was typified by an empty, aspirational overload of bad haircuts and cynical blandness, the decade produced many of pop's most individual artists. In addition, it was arguably defined by 1985's Live Aid – a global charity event unmatchable in its reach, and definitive in its marking of the period.

"I came here to play music, and I didn't really realise the full extent and magnitude of what it is all about. Now I'm here. It's the greatest event ever."
Ozzy Osbourne on Live Aid

The pop of the 1980s was directly shaped by three developments, which significantly changed the musical marketplace. Firstly, the extraordinary technological leap that saw the humble synthesizer progress to the sampler, the sequencer, programmable drums and the practical, affordable means to replicate the sound of an entire orchestra at the touch of a button. Secondly, the advent of MTV and the success of the promo video meant that, as 1980s super-producer Trevor Horn's Buggles sang in 1979, 'Video Killed The Radio Star'. And, last but not least, the lines between "black" and "white" music became irrevocably blurred as, encouraged by the astonishing success of Michael Jackson's *Thriller*, everyone chased the ultimate crossover dollar by mixing soul, rock, pop and disco into an increasingly homogeneous whole.

Pop's New Royalty

Former child star Michael Jackson became the self-proclaimed King Of Pop during the 1980s, with his Quincy Jones-produced albums *Off The Wall* (1979) and *Thriller* (1982). They defined the new commercial rules: sophisticated dance-pop combined with pop melody and occasional rock raucousness; lyrical themes that flitted between the self-referential and the more general pop languages of love, sex and dancing; and massively expensive and lavish video promotions, with the television premiere of the 15-minute movie made for the 'Thriller' single synchronized into a global event. His sister Janet also threw off her teen-poppet image with the Jimmy Jam/Terry Lewis-produced *Control* in 1986 – a tough, feminist soul-pop album that took her immediately out of Michael's shadow.

Michael Jackson, renowned in the 1980s for his distinctive voice and fancy footwork, meets and greets his new waxwork at London's Madame Tussauds.

Pop *Prodigies*

**Jam and Lewis's Minneapolis funk band the Time numbered a pocket-sized but potent performer/
singer/composer/multi-musician in their ranks by the name of Prince Rogers Nelson. His lascivious
blend of funk, soul, pop and classic rock went supernova in 1984 with the soundtrack to his *Purple
Rain* movie. His Hendrix-meets-Little-Richard-and-learns-James-Brown's-dance-moves image seduced
the world, and saw him go on to be the decade's most talented and prolific pop prodigy.**

Meanwhile, in New York, an ambitious ex-dancer was plotting her path to glory. The disco bounce
of Madonna's first hit, 'Holiday', progressed into cheeky, smart and unforgettable dance-pop in 1984's
'Like A Virgin'. Ms Ciccone then embarked on almost two decades of unparalleled invention and
reinvention, seamlessly staying one step ahead of each pop trend without breaking a sweat.

The soul-pop crossover continued apace in the shape of two contrasting divas. Tina Turner had been
a rock'n'soul star since the 1960s, but had disappeared into obscurity until enjoying a comeback
smash with the *Private Dancer* album in 1984, featuring songwriting credits from the likes of Dire
Straits' Mark Knopfler and production work from the likes of British synth-popsters Heaven 17 and the
ubiquitous Rupert Hine. Her blend of electro-AOR and ravaged soul vocals, coupled with revelations
of abuse at the hands of former partner Ike Turner, transformed her into a survivor heroine.

5 Top 1980s UK Artists:		*5 Top 1980s US Artists:*	
1	Michael Jackson	1	Prince
2	Prince	2	Phil Collins
3	Madonna	3	John Mellencamp
4	Tina Turner	4	Sade
5	Gary Numan	5	The Police

At the other end of the age scale, the 22-year-
old, session singer Whitney Houston released
a self-titled album in 1985, which, with its glossy
blend of carefree dance pop and overwrought
balladry, became the most successful debut
album of all time. Despite talent and beauty
in abundance, the next 15 years saw decreasing
sales and increasing public humiliation for the crossover diva, amid rumours of severe drug problems,
rampant egomania and mysterious goings-on in her high-profile marriage to Bobby Brown.

The successful soundtrack that accompanied Prince's 1984 Purple Rain *spurned such hits as 'When Doves Cry' and 'Let's Go Crazy', further
increasing Prince's reputation for powerful lyrics and danceable guitar grooves.*

The New British *Invasion*

Eighties British pop and its success in America stemmed initially from its wave of pretty-boy acts crossing glam with synth-pop. But the key figure in 1980s Britpop was a producer, rather than an artist.

Trevor Horn moved from being a member of Yes, as well as his own one-hit-wonder pop act the Buggles, to manning the desk for a slew of influential and successful Brit artists, including ABC, Spandau Ballet, Dollar, Frankie Goes To Hollywood, the Art Of Noise and the Pet Shop Boys. Despite differences between the acts, his sound was immediately recognizable, as Horn pursued the sonic possibilities of the new Fairlight sampler and created an enormous wall of sound – crashing drums, cascading strings, fanfare brass, crunching bass, multi-layered vocals and sound effects which were either sugary sweet or speaker-blowing. This provided a high-concept contrast to the likes of George Michael, who moved away from the fun-poking dance-pop of Wham!, the band he formed with his school friend Andrew Ridgeley, into an increasingly personal, singer-songwriter style of pop, ending the 1980s as a major British pop star.

5 Top 1980s UK Tracks:

1 'Do They Know Its Christmas?' Band Aid
2 'Relax' Frankie Goes To Hollywood
3 'I Just Called To Say I Love You' Stevie Wonder
4 'Two Tribes' Frankie Goes To Hollywood
5 'Don't You Want Me' The Human League

5 Top 1980s US Tracks:

1 'Flashdance ... What A Feeling' Irene Cara
2 'Bette Davis Eyes' Kim Carnes
3 'Physical' Olivia Newton John
4 'Every Breath You Take' The Police
5 'Endless Love' Diana Ross and Lionel Richie

Electro-dance continued to be the major Britpop impulse, however, with bands as diverse as Eurythmics, Yazoo and Erasure, and punks-turned-electro-popsters the Cure and New Order producing successful, machine-driven pop containing varying degrees of light and shade. By the end of the 1980s, northern synth-pop duo the Pet Shop Boys had, in their deadpan, subtly political and strikingly intelligent way, combined all of the above Brit popsters' moods and methods into one cohesive, danceable, adult and enduringly popular whole.

Annie Lennox's powerful alto voice combined with Dave Stewart's innovative production techniques made Eurythmics one of the best pop acts of the 1980s.

Eighties Pop *Singer/Songwriters*

In the 1980s, the crossover ideal – not just between black and white music, but between rock and pop, and adults and kids – ruled the airwaves. Even the previously personal and introspective singer/ songwriters were forced to adjust, and to dilute their piano-based romantic ballads with uptempo, full-band, dance-friendly songs.

The brassy soul-pop nostalgia of New Yorker Billy Joel's 1983 hits, such as 'Uptown Girl' and 'Tell Her About It', were perhaps the ultimate examples of such crossover music. Nevertheless, those that managed to pull this balance off most successfully were an extremely varied bunch in style and approach, reminding us that, even in pop's most conservative periods, those artists with the most singular vision are those who tend to truly define their times.

English Eccentrics

Kent's Kate Bush became a superstar at the age of just 20 with her hysterical pop adaptation of 'Wuthering Heights' in 1978, and proceeded to illuminate the 1980s with a succession of increasingly adventurous and challenging pop concepts. On the one hand, her expressions of intense, freewheeling sexuality and gift for pseudo-classical melody made her a mainstream pin-up and hit-maker. On the other, her spooky, theatrical takes on subjects as wide-ranging as nuclear war ('Breathing') and the plight of aboriginal people ('The Dreaming') – plus her reclusive nature and often bizarre visual sense – gave her cult appeal and critical acclaim. Towards the end of the 1980s, she worked with the former Genesis frontman Peter Gabriel, a pioneer of globally attuned pop intellectualism. Gabriel's work incorporated elements of everything from synth-pop to African tribal rhythms, was often vividly political (particularly on the anti-apartheid anthem 'Biko'), and achieved a perfect compromise with dance-rock and the video age in 1986's 'Sledgehammer'.

"The contemporary hit radio format – they don't like jazz, they don't like hip-hop. It is against their formula. But because it is my record they have to take it seriously." Sting

---

Kate Bush's 1985 release Hounds Of Love *was produced and recorded in her own home studio and spawned the single 'Running Up That Hill' which brought her to the attention of the US audience.*

Kate Bush

Hounds Of Love

No Band *Required*

The man who took over Gabriel's lead role in prog-rockers-turned-adult-popsters Genesis spearheaded a wave of singer/songwriters who easily transcended their roots in massively successful bands.

Former child actor and drummer Phil Collins fused musicianly adult pop, the huge funky sound of Earth, Wind and Fire's brass section, the pop nostalgia pastiche typified by his cover of the Supremes' 'You Can't Hurry Love' and maudlin lyrics inspired by his marital problems to become one of the decade's most reliable unit-shifters. Collins's definitive brand of well-crafted divorce pop also made him a byword for blandness, according to the critics. A former member of the Motown funk band the Commodores, Lionel Richie was also critically dismissed while he delighted mature pop fans. This cardiganed creator of mawkish pop balladry and light dance-pop defined a particular brand of pop-soul crossover, influenced as much by mainstream country as by R&B.

Two other Englishmen who split era-defining pop groups before going on to even greater success were Gordon "Sting" Sumner and George Michael. The former Georgios Kyriacos Panayiotou had already left his north London Greek-Cypriot community far behind with teen-pop titans Wham!, in tandem with childhood friend Andrew Ridgeley. But 1987's *Faith* immediately redefined the pop prodigy as a more adult proposition, before *Listen Without Prejudice Vol. 1* matched a more Lennon/Elton John-derived introspection to the title's pretensions in 1990. Sting managed an equally seamless transition from new wave-meets-reggae Police pin-up in 1984, to self-consciously serious jazz-pop fusioneer in 1985. His high-profile association with various political and ecological causes exemplified what was expected from the mature rocker after the impact of 1985's Live Aid global charity event.

Key Artists:

Kate Bush
Sting
George Michael
Elton John
Stevie Wonder

George Michael's 1987 Faith *album was a transatlantic smash, selling more than 10 million copies and topping the pop music charts.*

The Soul *Side*

As Lionel Richie exemplifies, the 1980s adult-pop crossover did cut both ways. Two extremely good-looking black artists working out of London blended the new singer/songwriter's high-concept craft with classic black music grooves and textures.

Former US serviceman Terence Trent D'Arby put together his timely melange of old-school soul and modern pop production after a stint as a funk singer. His 1987 debut album, the hit-laden *Introducing The Hardline According To Terence Trent D'Arby*, melded his Sam Cooke-meets-Otis Redding soul scream with catchy pop-funk and ballads, appearing to herald the arrival of a pop genius. Sadly, D'Arby's sex-symbol impact and critical acclaim led to a loss of perspective, and his deliberately "weird" follow-up, *Neither Fish Nor Flesh*, became one of the most notorious "career suicide" albums in pop history, consigning him to subsequent near-obscurity. Meanwhile, a Nigerian/Brit female with equivalent model looks made no such mistake. Sade (born Helen Folasade Adu in Nigeria) forged a smooth and effortless blend of mellow jazz and sleepily sensual pop romance, making a string of albums that not only sold, but had a profound influence on black music – largely through being the late-night seduction choice for many of the male artists who ruled the rap and R&B roost in the 1990s!

Old, New, Borrowed and Blue

Two of the best-loved singer/songwriters from the 1970s adapted easily to the next decade's commercial demands. While Elton John reinvented himself as a pop survivor with the single 'I'm Still Standing', the great Stevie Wonder left the gritty experiments of his peak years behind. He enjoyed his biggest hit singles with 'Ebony and Ivory' and that wedding-reception perennial, 'I Just Called To Say I Love You'. Finally, one talented New Yorker continued and modernized the traditional female singer/songwriter lineage established by Joni Mitchell and Carole King. Suzanne Vega's cool, clever and melancholy ruminations on everything from bohemian cafés to domestic abuse ensured that the intelligent solo pop circle remained unbroken throughout the 1980s and beyond.

Key Tracks:

'Faith' George Michael
'If You Love Somebody Set Them Free' Sting
'I Just Called To Say I Love You' Stevie Wonder
'I'm Still Standing' Elton John
'Running Up That Hill' Kate Bush

Suzanne Vega's serene a cappella vocals on her single 'Tom's Diner' morphed into an unlikely club hit once it was remixed by British DJs D.N.A. with electronic beats and sounds in 1993.

New Wave

For many veterans of the punk era, New Wave is not a genre at all. The term was coined by the music press to encompass acts who were influenced by punk, but less overtly rebellious and with more traditionally crafted pop skills. New Wave acts traded largely on a back-to-basics desire to revive the short, sharp thrill of the classic, mid-1960s beat-pop single.

Their ethos was reflected in new wave's dress codes: tight, dark mod suits with skinny ties, short (or at least, shorter) hair, occasional biker-chic leather and Day-Glo pop-art dresses. The punk die-hards may have sneered, but new wave's legacy is one of the richest in pop history – a last blast of starkly produced, arty but direct, high-energy youth anthems, before the crossover hegemony of the 1980s swept it aside.

The Blank Generation

Like punk, new wave's mid-1970s origins can be traced to CBGB's, a small, smelly bar that became a gig venue on New York's Lower East Side. While Richard Hell, Television, the Ramones and Patti Smith were forging punk's template, fellow CBGB's regulars Blondie and Talking Heads were creating a punk-related, pop-styled sound that would conquer the world. Former Andy Warhol acolyte Debbie Harry (Blondie's vocalist) became one of late-1970s/early 1980s pop's most adored icons, fusing classic girl-group pop with punk aggression and a disco groove. Her perfect look and cut-glass voice simultaneously reinvented and satirized the "blonde bombshell" image, while her (male) band's extraordinary run of pop anthems virtually defined female intelligence and sexuality in the late-1970s and early 1980s.

"It was a pop that was very aggressive and with a female front person, and that had never really been done in pop."
Debbie Harry on Blondie

Madonna cites her as a major influence. By stark contrast, Talking Heads were nerdy, nervy and deliberately asexual, purveying a unique brand of 1960s art-pop and white lo-fi funk. As the 1980s moved on, the Heads transformed themselves into a globally inspired big-band with the classic 'Once In A Lifetime' single, even managing to throw country-tinged Americana into the mix before the band's acrimonious split in 1991.

Elvis Costello, a spikey, intelligent standard-bearer of the UK's new wave, recorded and performed with the Attractions between 1977 and 1985, establishing himself as a prolific songwriter. Johnny Cash and Roy Orbison are among the artists who have performed his work.

Stiff Upper *Lips*

Britain's new wave grew out of an independent record label. From 1977 onwards, London's Stiff Records cleverly mixed its roots in London's "pub rock" live scene with punk's eccentricity to introduce a number of unique alternative pop icons, including Nick Lowe, Ian Dury, Madness and the Pogues. But their key discovery was Declan MacManus.

MacManus was an Irish-Liverpudlian from a musical family who changed his name to Elvis Costello. He blended angry-young-man aggression with extraordinarily witty, literate songs and a strong US influence. Brit and Stateside hero worship followed, as his Buddy Holly look – tight office-worker suit, cheap spectacles, crew cut, skinny tie – established the dominant male imagery of new wave, and his increasingly sophisticated lyrical ruminations on love, sex and politics saw him graduate toward pop's top table, working with the likes of Paul McCartney and Burt Bacharach.

Key Artists:
Blondie
Talking Heads
Elvis Costello
The Jam
The Police

A group of other, equally striking Brit new wavers grafted pop craft onto various kinds of punk stance. The Jam injected youthful energy and anti-establishment bile into mod-era guitar pop, with young suburbanite Paul Weller crafting a string of sharp, relevant Who/Beatles-influenced UK chart-toppers while becoming a spokesman for a generation. The Stranglers added a sullen kind of London misanthropy to the Doors organ-dominated rock and became alternative pop icons throughout the late-1970s and early 1980s. Manchester's Buzzcocks made an early switch from scratchy punk to glorious pop love songs sung over a wall of guitars and thus laid the groundwork for every pop-punk act through to Blink 182 and Ash. Irishmen the Boomtown Rats mingled punk scruffiness with Stonesy rhythm and blues, Bowie-esque glam and even Springsteen-ish rock anthemics, striking paydirt with the power ballad 'I Don't Like Mondays' which was inspired by a shooting in an American school. Finally, the Police pulled off the cleverest fusion, with Sting, Andy Summers and their American drummer, Stewart Copeland, channelling their jazz-level musicianship into a sparse, haunting blend of rock, pop and reggae. In their hands, new wave became a global commercial concern.

Founded in 1975, the Stranglers were known for their dark lyrics, raucous sound and penchant for dressing in black. They enjoyed a loyal following throughout Europe and the US as the punk movement emerged.

America Strikes *Back*

Although Akron, Ohio's Chrissie Hynde had served her rock apprenticeship as a musician in Paris and a journalist in London, her friendship with the Sex Pistols helped her form a UK band that perfectly blended the leather-chic end of punk with her love of classic 1960s pop romance.

The Pretenders were the ultimate transatlantic new wave band, seducing with Hynde's soulful, French-influenced vocals and songs that carried echoes of US radio rock as much as the Kinks (Hynde went on to marry and divorce the Kinks' frontman, Ray Davies). Meanwhile, the Cars and the Knack successfully married new wave pop's skinny-tie image and love of 1960s beat with familiar FM rock production, creating hits ('My Best Friend's Girl' and 'My Sharona' respectively) that succinctly summed up the times. Another Akron band, Devo, came up with a strange strand of new wave activity, moving from marvellously atonal covers of the Stones' 'Satisfaction' and the baffling concept of de-evolution, to smartly subversive dance-pop hits that ingeniously satirized the synthetic 1980s values they appeared to embody.

Key Tracks:
'Denis' Blondie
'Don't Stand So Close To Me' The Police
'Going Underground' The Jam
'Once In A Lifetime' Talking Heads
'(The Angels Wanna Wear My) Red Shoes' Elvis Costello

With scene veterans Blondie, Patti Smith and even the New York Dolls still around in the new millennium, there remained room for NYC's Strokes to make their mark with 2003's million-selling *Room On Fire*. A sub-standard follow-up damaged their reputation, but 2006's *First Impressions Of Earth* impressed. Others to continue the New York new wave tradition included the Yeah Yeah Yeahs and Interpol, who followed their 2002 debut with the stunning *Antics*. Sadly CBGB's, the venue where it all started three decades earlier, was scheduled to close in October 2006.

The Pretenders released their self-titled debut album in 1980, which produced such sexually aggressive hits as 'Brass In Pocket' and a cover of the Kinks' 'Stop Your Sobbing'.

New Romantics & *Futurism*

Born out of a reaction to both punk and 2-Tone's politics and anti-star stance, the British synth-pop wave of the early 1980s brought almost instant change to the UK pop scene. Moreover, the US success of the principal protagonists signalled the biggest "British invasion" since the Beatles and the Rolling Stones transformed American pop in the 1960s.

Mixing a heavily styled, fashion-conscious image, machine-dominated and danceable tunes and a return to narcissistic and aspirational lyrics with a little theatrical, existentialist misery, UK synth-pop essentially blended the three major phases of David Bowie's 1970s trailblazing – peacock glam, smooth, white funk and arty, electronic alienation. Roxy Music and Germany's Kraftwerk were the other major influences on the two complementary strands of the new romantics and futurism.

Pirates and Posers

When Londoner Stuart Goddard saw the Sex Pistols, he changed his name to Adam Ant and, after several punkish false starts, delivered a vibrant pop fusion that brought colour back to the cheeks of British pop. Adam And the Ants' *Kings Of The Wild Frontier* album heralded a new decade in 1980, mixing pirate and Native American costume, glam-rock guitars and pure pop fun with original, even surreal noise. Adam's matinée-idol looks, joyfully silly pantomime imagery and theatrical promo videos enabled what would become the new romantic scene to blossom, opening the door for a number of former punks who wanted to dress up and embrace pop stardom.

"Such a puritanism has grown up of late. I'd rather dress up like Liberace." Adam Ant

The most cultish and influential of these were Japan, a London quintet led by David Sylvian, who was often referred to as "The World's Most Beautiful Man". Originally a rather limp copy of US glam-punks the New York Dolls, Japan reinvented themselves in 1979 with the electro-disco of *Quiet Life*. They went on to produce ever more subtle, atmospheric, Eastern-influenced art pop until their split in 1982, just as the shy, intellectual Sylvian was on the verge of a superstardom he did not want.

Upon reaching number one in the charts with 'Do You Really Want to Hurt Me?', Boy George's Culture Club was transformed from a band that believed themselves to be anti-establishment to a major radio-friendly, new romantic pop force that appealed to a diverse audience.

Romantic *Icons*

The quintessential new romantic group emerged from the trendiest end of London's club scene in 1980. Spandau Ballet mixed basic synth-disco, hilariously pretentious lyrics and the operatic vocals of Tony Hadley, before diminishing returns saw them become a showcase for Gary Kemp's increasingly smooth adult-pop songcraft, typified by the huge transatlantic hits 'True' and 'Gold'.

Gary and his bass-playing brother, Martin, went on to star in the film *The Krays* before Martin, after narrowly avoiding death by brain tumour, found more success in the 1990s as a star of the UK soap opera *EastEnders*. Spandau's even more successful rivals were Duran Duran, who came out of the Birmingham club scene to purvey an aggressively rockish take on synthetic dance-pop that saw them become the embodiment of the big-in-America, model-dating, hedonistic pop group.

Regional variants on the synth-dance-and-cheekbones formula sprang from every corner of the UK: the cheeky, camp, northern soul-influenced Soft Cell from Leeds; the funky, orchestral and wordy Trevor Horn-produced ABC from Sheffield; the grandiose Ultravox, led by Scotland's Midge Ure; and new romantic supergroup Visage, formed by London fashion faces and club promoters Steve Strange and Rusty Egan, and including Ure in its largely studio-based line-up.

Key Artists:

Adam Ant
Japan
Spandau Ballet
Duran Duran
Culture Club

Although he came directly from the same London club scene as Spandau and Visage, "Boy" George O'Dowd was a different kind of New Romantic icon. His extraordinary career took in the formation of Culture Club, flamboyant cross-dressing, a unique brand of white pop-soul that smoothly incorporated reggae ('Do You Really Want To Hurt Me') and MOR country (the ubiquitous 'Karma Chameleon'), a public fall from grace as a result of heroin addiction, America's rejection of his (surely always obvious?) homosexuality and a triumphant solo return as a DJ, raconteur and writer of the *Taboo* stage musical.

With their self-titled 1981 release, Duran Duran became instant worldwide stars, renowned for their good looks as much as for their synthesized, neo-disco songs and innovative videos featured on MTV.

Synths and *Sci-Fi*

Like Adam Ant, Gary Webb was a London punk who rejected rebellion for glam reinvention. As Gary Numan, he produced an electronic kind of pop-rock that traded on images of a nightmarish, dystopian future while somehow seeming cosy, which was no mean feat given that they were delivered by a chubby-faced cockney wearing eyeliner.

Heavily influenced by Bowie and cult figure John Foxx (who had led proto-futurists Ultravox before Midge Ure remade them as teen pop), Numan signalled the popular embrace of futurism, which had nothing to do with the Italian art movement and everything to do with noises and images that played with the mystery of a future dominated by machines.

The two most successful products of this school were Sheffield's Human League and Basildon's Depeche Mode. The League began as a superb, artful mix of synthetic throb, sly sci-fi imagery and arty slide shows, before the band split in two in 1980. Martyn Ware and Ian Craig-Marsh formed the British Electric Foundation in 1980, which then evolved into Heaven 17 the following year. Meanwhile, Philip Oakey hired pop tunesmiths Jo Callis and Ian Burden and girl backing singers/dancers Joanne Catherall and Susanne Sulley to form the new Human League line-up. Between them they created the magnificent *Dare*, the definitive synth-pop album of the decade and a huge transatlantic seller, courtesy of the ABBA-tributing anthem 'Don't You Want Me'.

Key Tracks:
'Do You Really Want To Hurt Me' Culture Club
'Don't You Want Me' Human League
'Girls On Film' Duran Duran
'Goody Two Shoes' Adam Ant
'True' Spandau Ballet

Depeche Mode suffered similar personnel problems when Vince Clarke, the composer of their early, lovably cute synthetic ditties, left in 1981. While Clarke found long-term synth-pop success with various, new songwriter Martin Gore and frontman Dave Gahan transformed the Mode into the ultimate stadium-friendly, synth-rock crossover, mingling sin, sadness, misery and mystery with globe-straddling appeal.

Gary Numan's experimental synth sounds earned him a fan base that remained loyal to his innovative sounds that began with the groundbreaking hit 'Cars'.

2 - Tone

Only two record labels in pop history have lent their name to an entire musical genre. The first is Detroit's Tamla Motown. The other is England's 2-Tone, a late-1970s/early 1980s imprint that still stands as the UK's most politically significant pop phenomenon.

2-Tone was set up in 1979 by the Special A.K.A., a multiracial ska- and reggae-inspired band from Coventry in England's Midlands. Comprising Jerry Dammers, Terry Hall, Neville Staples, Lynval Golding, John Bradbury, Roddy Radiation and Sir Horace Gentleman, this dynamic, working-class seven-piece revived the British/Jamaican Trojan label reggae of their childhoods, with the added extras of punk energy and angry, acerbic lyrics. Their songs of youth alienation, racism and working-class life were mostly sung by Hall with a blank, sneering sarcasm.

Black and White Unite

After building strong word-of-mouth supporting punk bands around Britain, the band set up their own independent label. Again inspired by Motown and Trojan, 2-Tone aimed for a strong visual identity, encapsulated by the label itself – a cartoon of a well-dressed, racially ambiguous "rude boy" in pork-pie hat and mod suit (a rude boy is the term for a young ska/reggae fan), illustrated in sharp, chessboard black and white. The 2-Tone name applied equally to the band's attitude to racial politics, a crucial and courageous stance at a time when the overtly racist political party the National Front was, with some success, recruiting among white British urban youth.

"The basic thing is Anglo-Jamaican music. It's trying to integrate those two."
Jerry Dammers

Released in the UK in July 1979, the Special A.K.A.'s first single, 'Gangsters', promptly reached number six. This surprise hit led to a licensing deal with the major label Chrysalis, a name change to the catchier the Specials and an almost instantaneous skinhead/mod revival among Britain's punk-and disco-fatigued youth.

Elvis Costello produced the 1979 self-titled debut release of the Specials, which launched their reputation as the forerunners of the 2-Tone ska movement and influenced countless other acts with their vibrant sound and stage performances.

Tales of Everyday *Madness*

By the end of 1979, 2-Tone had released Top 10 singles by all the main players in the 2-Tone wave. North London septet Madness's 'The Prince' was, like 'Gangsters', a tribute to the Jamaican ska legend Prince Buster, but with the punk attack replaced by a cheeky, cheery, but occasionally wistful, cockney music-hall attitude.

Graham "Suggs" McPherson and company soon left 2-Tone for Stiff Records and unleashed a string of hit singles and pioneering videos that established them as one of British pop's best-loved pop institutions until their split in 1986. The band still reform regularly for well-attended live shows.

Coventry's Selecter, led by the charismatic female vocalist Pauline Black, made a big initial impact with their debut single, 'On My Radio' and first album *Too Much Pressure*. But although they possessed an even greater ska-punk raucousness than their friends the Specials, they quickly ran out of steam. Finally, the Birmingham six-piece the Beat (called the English Beat in the US) emerged with a Christmas 1979 cover of Smokey Robinson's 'Tears Of A Clown' before forming their own Go-Feet label, again with the assistance of Chrysalis. Their strident punk-reggae protest songs, influenced by both Jamaican dub and classic 1960s pop, brought them transatlantic success before their split in 1983. Dave Wakeling and Ranking Roger went on to form General Public, while Andy Cox and David Steele found even greater success with Fine Young Cannibals.

Key Artists:
The Specials
Madness
The Beat
UB40
The Selecter

Meanwhile, other, non-2-Tone-affiliated UK groups also contributed to the reggae-and-mod-influenced spirit of the times. Birmingham's UB40 went for direct, albeit multiracial, dub and roots reggae, creating a mournful but infectious protest music that established them as the most successful non-Jamaican reggae act of all time. Of course, among all this protest and passion, someone had to come up with a lighter take. Step forward Bad Manners and their corpulent, skinhead frontman Buster Bloodvessel, with novelty ska revival hits such as 'Lip Up Fatty' and 'The Can-Can'.

Inspired by the Specials and Madness, Bad Manners created a name for themselves with their outrageous stage performances and amusingly original ska covers of classic songs, such as 'Monster Mash'.

2-Tone

Too Much Too *Young*

No matter how significant the achievements of these acts, the Specials remain the definitive 2-Tone band. But even as they were enjoying commercial and critical adulation for albums such as *Specials* and *More Specials*, and a UK number one single with a live version of the teen pregnancy-warning 'Too Much Too Young', the band were splitting under the pressure of musical and personal differences, as well as constant violence at their live shows from fascist skinheads who seemed unable (or unwilling) to accept the band's anti-racist stance.

Immediately after their greatest achievement, the single 'Ghost Town' – which topped the UK singles chart in 1981 as the anti-government riots it spoke so eloquently of raged through British inner cities – Hall, Golding and Staples quit to make excellent tribal pop with their own Fun Boy Three, while Radiation formed the short-lived Tearjerkers.

Reverting to the Special A.K.A. moniker, the bandleader Jerry Dammers recruited the vocalists Stan Campbell and Rhoda Dakar (the latter from a moderately successful 2-Tone act called the Bodysnatchers) to make a series of brave but less commercial political-issue singles, culminating in the Afro-pop anti-apartheid anthem 'Nelson Mandela'. The resulting album, *In The Studio*, was an undeserved flop, and a disillusioned Dammers split the band and the label in 1984, becoming a club DJ and full-time anti-apartheid activist.

Key Tracks:
'Ghost Town' The Specials
'On My Radio' The Selecter
'Tears Of A Clown' The Beat
'The Prince' Madness
'Too Much Too Young' The Specials

Although a version of the Specials reformed in the 1990s without Dammers, Hall and Bradbury, largely to cash-in on 2-Tone's nostalgic popularity in the US, the legacy of 2-Tone resides, more appropriately, in American ska/pop/punk acts such as No Doubt, Save Ferris and the Mighty Mighty Bosstones, as well as multiracial British dance-pop adventurers such as Tricky, Massive Attack and the Streets – the latter was paying homage by including a snippet of the Specials' 'Ghost Town' in their live sets.

Although popular in the UK, Madness's wild, ska/pop sound experienced only moderate success in the US, stemming from their single 'Our House' and its heavily played video on MTV.

Gangsta

Rumbling out of Los Angeles with different beats, a different look and a very different attitude, gangsta rap was hip hop's belligerent street child. This new sound grew up at black discos and parties away from mainstream interference, and so, much as the original hip hop had, it quite literally pleased itself and harked back to street funk for musical inspiration.

It was the first time rap had achieved any identity other than on the East Coast, but now, as hip hop moved closer to heavy metal and mainstream rock, upping its tempo and musical intensity, it appeared to be edging away from its home crowd. There had been signs that a change was due, when Eric B & Rakim's minimalist *Paid In Full* was the biggest rap album of 1987, and the following year EPMD's acclaimed *Strictly Business* proved how hip hop could still be funky. In the wake of these underground successes, it was not too much of a surprise when, at the end of the 1980s, west coast rap built itself almost exclusively on P-Funk samples – George Clinton's Parliament/Funkadelic always had huge support in California – for a bouncing, open-top car, hot-fun-in-the-California-sun type of vibe, laid-back in all but the lyrics.

"We called the label Death Row 'cause a majority of our people was parolees or incarcerated – it's no joke. We got people really was on death row." Suge Knight

Street Level

When NWA (Niggaz With Attitude, as they were known back then) unleashed their *Straight Outta Compton* album on an unsuspecting world in 1988, it epitomized the state of their particular nation; both geographically and situationally. The album's narrative told of the neglected world that was south central Los Angeles, which some 20 years after the Watts riots had slipped into decay and was ruled by the violent carryings-on of the Bloods and Crips street gangs. Songs from that LP like 'Fuck Tha Police', 'Straight Outta Compton' and the track that gave the genre its name, 'Gangsta Gangsta' summed up a situation in a way that came to represent black rage's new tone of voice – foul-mouthed, hate-filled, vitriolic and nihilistic.

NWA was formed in 1986 by former drug-dealer Eazy-E (Eric Wright). Its line-up included luminaries Ice Cube (O'Shea Jackson) and Dr. Dre (Andre Young), who both went on to successful solo careers. Eazy-E died of AIDS in 1995.

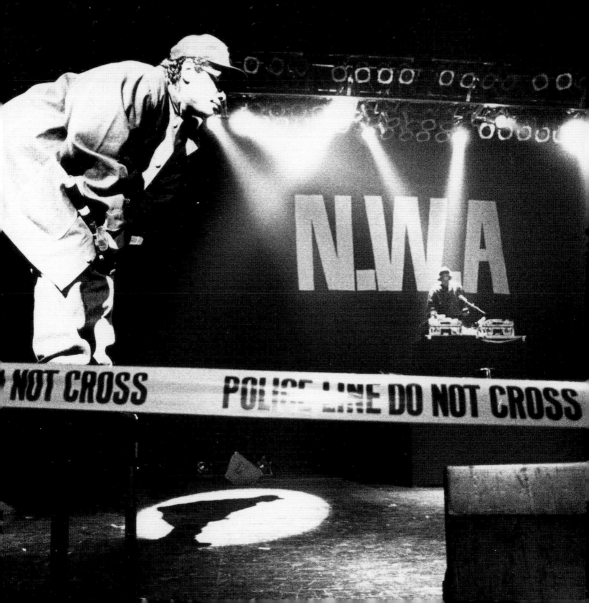

Mainstream *Disapproval*

In the city that, a few years later, would be notorious for the Rodney King beating, such an anti-authority attitude was understandable. The worrying factor was that in many ways this new attitude demonstrated a deep-rooted self-hatred, never more noticeable than in gangsta's apparent relationship with women.

At the time, the notions that women were nothing more than "bitches" and "hos", whose main role in life was to be scantily clad in videos, attracted more media flack than the preoccupations with violence. The fact that female rappers such as Foxy Brown and Lil' Kim endorsed that state of affairs – instead of using their success to prove the world otherwise – didn't help matters.

As Cool as Ice

But in spite of – or perhaps because of – initial mainstream disapproval, gangsta rap flourished, as NWA became the *alma mater* for the genre's two most significant figures, lyricist/rapper Ice Cube and producer Dr. Dre. Also out of Los Angeles was Ice-T, who may ultimately have fallen from grace, but earned respect as one of the genre's most powerful writers and performers for his *OG* album alone. Then there was the infamous Death Row Records, the label formed in 1991 by Suge Knight, a terrifying, physically huge figure who was rumoured to have connections with the Mafia. For him, gangsta was not just a musical style but a genuine way of life. However questionable Knight's methods were, Death Row attracted the cream of west coast talent, and before he was incarcerated in 1997, his company had released three of the genre's most memorable albums: *Snoop Dogg's Doggy Dogg Style*, Dr. Dre's *The Chronic* and Tupac Shakur's *All Eyez On Me*.

Key Artists:
Ice-T
NWA
Snoop Dogg
Notorious BIG
Tupac Shakur

Biggie Smalls, aka Notorious BIG, and Tupac Shakur were two of gangsta's biggest stars. Both were gunned down within six months of each other.

East Meets *West*

Naturally, New York was not going to be left out of the picture for too long. By the early 1990s, the Big Apple had its own thriving gangsta rap scene, but didn't achieve much wider acclaim until Notorious BIG released his *Ready To Die* album in 1994 which proved him to be one of the best gangsta rappers.

In his slipstream were the Junior MAFIA posse, MOP, Capone-N-Noriega, Mobb Deep and Jay-Z, all of whom were a match for most of what came out of LA, shifting the power base eastwards. Too often, though, the rivalry between the two coasts, which occasionally escalated from merely a war of words, became the industry's and the media's focus and the quality of some of the music got overshadowed.

Key Albums:

All Eyez On Me Tupac Shakur
Doggy Dogg Style Snoop Dogg
OG Ice-T
Ready To Die Notorious BIG
Straight Outta Compton NWA

But whereas gangsta rap may originally have been an expression of black rage or frustration, it was quickly co-opted as a kind of ghetto-style entertainment for thrill-seeking, socially rebelling whites. The audience changed and the artists began to play up to what was required of them. By the end of the 1990s, two of gangsta's biggest stars – Notorious BIG and Tupac – had been shot dead and the form had become a caricature of itself.

Ironically, the narrative power and vocabulary of the medium was taken up in spectacular fashion by Eminem to create a situation where the world's greatest rapper is white. But then the world's greatest golfer is black, so anything's possible.

The biggest waves in the new rap millennium were made by Eminem protégés 50 Cent and the Game. Both members of the group G Unit made top-selling solo records, while "50" managed to branch out into movies with his 2005 autobiographical feature *Get Rich Or Die Tryin'*. Fellow rappers Jay-Z and P Diddy also harboured wider ambitions, launching clothing lines. Meanwhile in 2005, producer turned artist Kanye West came up with his classic second album *Late Registration*, having put his neck on the line with political statements in the press knocking George Bush's administration and slating hip-hop's homophobia.

Detroit rapper Eminem has raised the credibility of white rap through his phenomenal worldwide success. His song 'Lose Yourself', from the semi-autobiographical film 8 Mile, won the singer an Academy Award.

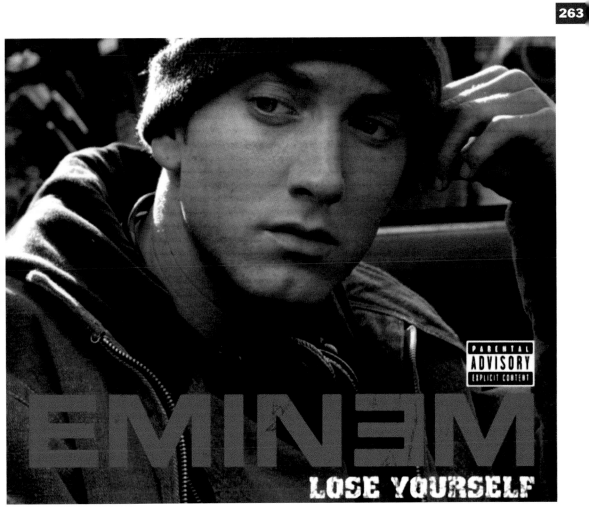

PARENTAL
ADVISORY
EXPLICIT CONTENT

EMINƎM

LOSE YOURSELF

Eighties Manufactured *Pop*

The term "manufactured pop" is, in many ways, a red herring. Despite the changes in our perception of pop talent brought about by The Beatles, much mainstream pop has been based on the "Tin Pan Alley" tradition, in which teams of producers, composers and music-business moguls find young, attractive performers (mainly singers) to front potential hits.

The term "manufactured pop" does not appear until the 1980s because of pop consumers' increasing knowledge of how pop is produced and presented. From the late 1980s onwards, the pop Svengalis became more open about the lack of creative and musical input on the part of their performers. In particular, two 1980s factory-pop providers were crucial in marking this change.

A S/A/W Point

Mike Stock, Matt Aitken and Pete Waterman (S/A/W) grew out of the north-western England soul, pop and disco tradition. They developed this into mainstream pop with their first major UK hit, 'You Spin Me Round (Like A Record)' by the Liverpool gay group Dead Or Alive in 1984. Using a true "hit factory" approach, S/A/W took the manufacture of pop one step further by stitching together songs out of computerized elements, taking a title out of a pre-written list, adding a numbered bassline, drum-pattern, melody line and so on, and then hiring a session singer to demo the song before the 'star' added their own vocals. S/A/W went on to dominate the charts in the late 1980s, writing and producing a string of unashamedly lightweight hits for Rick Astley, Bananarama, Mel & Kim, Sonia, Donna Summer and, most famously, Australian soap opera stars Kylie Minogue and Jason Donovan.

As important as the impossibly catchy music and clean-cut appeal of the stars was Waterman's bullish, amused approach to the antipathy shown towards S/A/W by music critics. His give-the-people-what-they-want attitude revealed a great deal of self-promotion at the expense of his artists, who – with the exception of Kylie Minogue – usually attempted to forge careers without him, only to fail. The manufacturer had stepped in front of the performer and the process became more apparent, reaching its logical conclusion with the *Pop Stars* and *Pop Idol* TV shows of the early twenty-first century.

Since splitting with S/A/W, Kylie Minogue has become one of the top pop stars in the world, with her hip, danceable grooves and supersexy looks, while Jason Donovan has gone on to a prosperous acting career.

Starr *Maker*

When writer/producer Maurice Starr of Boston put together the teen group New Edition, he could not have known how big an effect the quartet would have on future R&B after they "sacked" him in 1983.

Starr recovered from losing his protégés, however, and put together a new five-piece, the oldest members of which were 16. New Kids On The Block were, effectively, the white New Edition, becoming global teen idols in 1988 with their *Hangin' Tough* album, which cleverly mixed clean-cut, teen-girl-oriented romance with a timely, but unthreatening, bad-boy stance lifted from hip hop. Despite writing much of their own material, the group's contrivance made them even more of a joke figure than the S/A/W acts. Nevertheless, the New Kids' blend of stage-school dance routines, heartthrob looks and diluted street style forged the template for what we now know as the "boy band".

Songs of Innocents

S/A/W and Starr defined the future of manufactured pop in the late 1980s, but the decade had already brought plenty of more traditional teen-formula pop idols to short-lived prominence. Virginal US teen queens both, Tiffany and Debbie Gibson became America's darlings in the late 1980s, performing classic radio bubblegum for nice kids. Gibson became a symbol of toothy female conformity, too, inspiring satirical punk songs (Mojo Nixon and Skid Roper's wonderful 'Debbie Gibson Is Pregnant With My Two-Headed Love Child') and a hilarious Jimi Hendrix-meets-Debbie onstage skit by the controversial late comic Bill Hicks.

> *Key Artists:*
> New Kids On The Block
> Kylie Minogue
> Jason Donovan
> Tiffany
> Bros

Meanwhile, the UK gave us Bros, fronted by the terrifyingly blonde, London-based brothers Luke and Matt Goss. Bros reached their peak in 1988-89 with eight consecutive UK Top 10 hits, before falling out of favour and slipping into solo obscurity. Like New Edition, Londoners Five Star favoured the Jackson 5 approach, with the black British Pearson family group notching up transatlantic pop-soul hits in a short but prolific career. They peaked with their 1986 album, *Silk And Steel*, before the drug problems and public fallings out took their toll.

Mike Stock (left), Pete Waterman (right) and Matt Aitken of S/A/W helped to create more than 90 Top 40 hits, including 13 UK number ones, including Rick Astley's 'Never Gonna Give You Up' and Donna Summer's 'This Time I Know It's For Real'.

Nineties *Pop*

If you ask a young music consumer what kind of acts represent pop music, they will undoubtedly reel off a list of teen-orientated, manufactured bands. Pop has come to represent a narrowly focused genre, as far away from the initial, revolutionary rock-meets-pop appeal of Elvis Presley and the Beatles as can be.

Since the 1950s, pop has been a catch-all term for almost all popular music made in the wake of rock'n'roll. But each generation has seen the development of more musical sub-genres, with the music business's increasing success at identifying these sub-genres, and marketing narrowly and heavily towards their fans, effecting a gradual change in the way the public views pop.

"I'm an old-fashioned entertainer doing it in a nineties stylie."
Robbie Williams

Nevertheless, the 1990s still boasted some artists who, in different ways, transcended the limitations of genre-specific forms of music. The decade also saw various completely manufactured acts achieving a credibility, longevity and unit-shifting power in the pop marketplace. Britain's Spice Girls, Australia's Kylie Minogue and America's Britney Spears attained a kind of commercial and critical success that no one would have predicted when they emerged. Another UK teen band who pioneered this level of manufactured pop profile, Take That, produced one of the key 1990s pop stars, Robbie Williams, a former dancer who successfully mixed the sound and promotional devices of manufactured pop with a more individual vision.

Stoke-On-Trent's Williams was just 21 when he stage-managed one of the most public band splits in pop history. Within two years, he established himself as Britain's biggest pop star with a heavily produced blend of Britpop and mature balladry on the *Life Thru A Lens* album. Since then, he has effectively rewritten the rules of pop, dance and rock crossover, jumping easily from the pseudo-rap and gory, banned video of the single 'Rock DJ' to the Sinatra-tributing, big-band standards of the *Swing When You're Winning* album. He remains, at the time of writing, Britain's only truly transcendent pure pop star, overcoming musical limitations with his film-star good looks and boy-next-door cheek.

Increasingly featured in tabloid articles and notorious for his cheeky behaviour, Robbie Williams has continued to dominate the music world with his infectious mix of pop and rock and his good looks.

The Princesses of *Wails*

Many of the biggest pop sales phenomena continue to derive from virtuoso vocalists who blend chart-oriented pop with mature MOR torch song. Two female singers who broke through in the early 1990s challenged the position of Whitney Houston as the FM radio, adult-pop queen of the divas.

Discovered by soul mogul Tommy Mottola (they married in 1993 and divorced in 1997), the New Yorker Mariah Carey made an immediate impact with her Olympian, five-octave voice and self-titled, largely self-written 1990 debut album. This definitive black/white crossover diva went on to become the first artist to top the US charts in each year of the 1990s and broke the Beatles' record for weeks spent in the Hot 100. The melodrama of her vocally self-indulgent songs turned out to be based on reality. After signing an $80m record deal with Virgin at the end of the 1990s and enduring disappointing sales and a critically savaged flop movie in *Glitter*, she posted sprawling suicidal messages on her website and spent time in rehab. Virgin dropped her in 2002, but it was not all bad news: the record company gave her a $28m pay-off. She later returned to the charts on the Universal label.

Her Canadian rival Celine Dion also married her mentor, manager Rene Angelil, despite a 26-year age difference. The couple fell victim to a different kind of tragedy, though, as Angelil was diagnosed with throat cancer, prompting Dion's temporary retirement from music. Of course, the big-voiced chanteuse could afford the break, having achieved mega-lunged stardom with her brand of housewife-slaying MOR pop weepie. This was typified by her Grammy Award-winning songs for the movies *Beauty And The Beast* (with smooth soul man Peabo Bryson) and *Titanic* (the ubiquitous 'My Heart Will Go On', which, somewhat appropriately, became the Western world's most popular choice to be played at funerals). In 2003, Dion returned from her sabbatical with a new album and a three-year deal to perform in a top Las Vegas hotel-casino.

5 Top 1990s UK Artists:	5 Top 1990s US Artists:
1 Oasis	1 Madonna
2 Madonna	2 Mariah Carey
3 Simply Red	3 Whitney Houston
4 Alanis Morrissette	4 Celine Dion
5 The Spice Girls	5 Britney Spears

With her epic style and belting voice, Celine Dion has established herself as one of the world's mega stars and is currently a five-times Grammy Award winner.

Stars Old and *New*

Though most pop phenomena continued to rise and fall quickly, some 1980s icons remained relevant to the new decade. Madonna remains pop's biggest star, keeping one step ahead of dance-pop trends and changing image with each release. Manchester's Mick Hucknall led Simply Red's blue-eyed pop soul to great success. And electro-popsters the Pet Shop Boys maintained their loyal fans as they became more overt about their bittersweet celebrations of gay life.

New, unmanufactured pop voices also rose to prominence. The Irish family group the Corrs mixed mainstream dance with Irish folk; Scotland's Texas struck with a glossy take on FM rock and Manchester and London's M People moved from pop-house to heroic, adult-oriented anthems.

On the other side of the Atlantic California's No Doubt emerged from their local, 2-Tone-influenced scene with a smart blend of ska, pop and punk. All, of course, were led by women with strident singing voices and sex appeal, the likes of Sharleen Spiteri (Texas) and Gwen Stefani (No Doubt) entering the world of youth pop music with their adult, pin-up looks.

5 Top 1990s UK Tracks:	*5 Top 1990s US Tracks:*
1 'Candle In The Wind 97' Elton John	1 'One Sweet Day' Mariah Carey and Boyz II Men
2 'Unchained Melody' Robson Green and Jerome Flynn	2 'I Will Always Love You' Whitney Houston
3 'Love Is All Around' Wet Wet Wet	3 'End Of The Road' Boyz II Men
4 'Barbie Girl' Aqua	4 'Take A Bow' Madonna
5 'Believe' Cher	5 'Water Runs Dry' Boyz II Men

Adopting the monikers Sporty, Baby, Posh, Scary and Ginger, the Spice Girls became a worldwide phenomenon with their professions of "Girl Power", sugary pop vocalizations and cutting-edge fashions. Retrospectively, their massive appeal has stayed firmly rooted in nineties pop.

Nineties Pop *Singer/Songwriters*

After a decade that saw the art of the singer/songwriter being somewhat submerged by the demands of electronic over-production, disco crossover and relentless fashion horrors, the 1990s saw a rebirth of the solo artist with a genuinely individual style.

This proved to be of particular benefit to female artists who, while still having to conform to demands for feminine "sexiness", were at least able to broaden the scope of what that could mean, both in terms of looks and attitude. There were some new men on the block, but it was female artists, five women in particular, who achieved major success in the 1990s without having to make the compromises usually involved in aiming at a specific type of audience.

The Dubliner Sinéad O'Connor continues to pursue one of pop's most controversial careers. Emerging in the late 1980s with her angelic features hardened by a severe skinhead crop, her powerful, Celtic-influenced vocals became universally recognized in 1990 with her emotional cover of Prince's 'Nothing Compares 2 U'. The accompanying album, *I Do Not Want What I Haven't Got*, was a global smash, but the strength of her opinions may have stolen some of its musical thunder. O'Connor followed her outspoken criticisms of the history of the British in Ireland with attacks on the anti-abortion stance of the Catholic church and in 1992, she refused to play at an American show that began with the US national anthem. Despite her commercial fall from grace, O'Connor has had a profound influence on female solo artists throughout the 1990s and beyond.

"I see my body as an instrument rather than an ornament."
Alanis Morissette

The equally questioning, but far less controversial, North Carolina native Tori Amos became an overnight star with her 1992 debut album, *Little Earthquakes*. Although her rustic glamour, theatrical vocals and piano-led musical sophistication initially led to many comparisons with Kate Bush, Amos's new age, therapy-speak lyrics and kooky persona made her entirely unique, and the pure pop of her tunes led to an unlikely club hit with Armand Van Helden's hard-house reworking of 'Professional Widow' in 1996.

Controversial Irish singer Sinéad O'Connor has worked with such diverse artists as the Chieftains, Afro-Celt Sound System and The The.

The Strange and the *Strident*

Also finding a place in dance music, and also kooky, Iceland's Björk Gudmundsdottir split from the arty indie-goth band the Sugarcubes and released an astounding debut album (entitled *Debut*) in 1993.

Unlike the previous decade's dance-rock crossovers, Björk possessed a genuine love and understanding of cutting-edge dance music in the post-techno era. Her blendings of rumbling beats with ambient textures, flights of romantic fancy with abstract electronic noise, and Asian melodies and motifs with deep and restless basslines, is made all the more striking by her baby-faced features, flamboyant visual sense and skyscraping vocals.

Perhaps the bravest stance of all belongs to Kathryn Dawn Lang, an androgynous Canadian who began her career as a camp alternative cabaret performer tapping into an almost unnoticed enthusiasm for country music among Stateside lesbians. But kd lang (her name is always kept lower case) had talent above and beyond ironic country and a truly gorgeous voice. In 1992, the lush *Ingénue* album turned her into a unique star, with its erotically charged love songs, musical mix of country, soul and pop and a subtly gender-bending image. Along with the adult-rocker Melissa Etheridge, lang broke through the silence surrounding lesbianism in pop, building a loyal and large (and mainly female) following in supposedly conservative America.

Key Artists:
Alanis Morissette
Tori Amos
kd lang
Björk
Sinéad O'Connor

Borrowing something from all of the above heroines, another Canadian, Alanis Morissette, completed a journey from manufactured Canadian pop poppet to Voice Of Modern Woman with the release of her massively successful album, 1995's *Jagged Little Pill*. Taking Amos's therapy-speak to a logical conclusion and applying O'Connor's kind of howling anger to the subject of inadequate and abusive males, Morissette's muse became so influential that it is now rare to hear a female artist without a yodel in her voice and righteous indignation at the expense of men in her lyrics. Her nouveau-hippy, just-got-of-bed image and catchy soft-rock anthems have made her the ultimate symbol of pop feminism, with the likes of Sheryl Crow, Fiona Apple and Jewel all benefiting directly from her breakthrough.

kd lang's 1992 release Ingénue *marked her foray into adult alternative/pop and spawned the beautiful hit 'Constant Craving.'*

Male *Survivors*

While new female voices were defining the 1990s pop singer/songwriter art, veterans made the biggest impact among men. The likes of Sting and Elton John continued to enjoy success by doing exactly what they had always done, with the former Reg Dwight scoring his biggest-ever worldwide hit with his maudlin Princess Diana tribute, 'Candle In The Wind 97' and receiving a knighthood.

George Michael also continued to thrive, despite his notorious conviction for lewd behaviour in a Beverly Hills public toilet in 1998. Having previously moved away from the celebratory pure pop of *Faith* towards the self-consciously mature Elton John- and Lennon-influenced introspection of *Listen Without Prejudice Vol. 1* and *Older*, Michael responded to his humiliating outing by abandoning the heartfelt piano balladry and heading back towards light dance-pop and cover versions of standards.

There were no such personal confusions for ex-Jam leader Paul Weller, who became a harbinger of Britpop when the hit *Wildwood* album ended his solo wilderness years in 1993. Though his music is actually a gruff take on traditional late-1960s/early 1970s Britrock, the affection Weller continues to enjoy for his achievements with the Jam and the Style Council maintain his standing as a crossover between serious rock and chart pop.

The most striking new male singer/songwriter was the Nigerian/Brazilian Londoner Sealhenry Samuel, who, as Seal, used his vocals on dance artist Adamski's 1990 'Killer' hit (later covered by George Michael) as a stepping-stone to solo stardom. His slick blend of MOR pop and FM radio-friendly soul, typified by 1990's 'Crazy' and 1994's 'Kiss From A Rose', and unique physical presence (six-and-a-half foot, with childhood facial scarring) saw him enjoy global stardom throughout most of the decade.

Key Albums:

Debut Björk
I Do Not Want What I Haven't Got Sinéad O'Connor
Ingénue kd lang
Jagged Little Pill Alanis Morissette
Little Earthquakes Tori Amos

Before finding success in his own right as Elton John, Reg Dwight played in a band called Bluesology. They began by backing visiting US singers, becoming Long John Baldry's support band in 1966.

Contemporary $\mathcal{R}\&\mathcal{B}$

Although contemporary R&B prefers to align itself with its ruder and more street-credible cousins in hip hop, the roots of its mainstream practitioners lie firmly in manufactured pop. In a throwback to the Motown era, R&B has become a global phenomenon by combining producer-led factory formula with a high level of musical innovation and adventure.

This balance of pop smarts and muso credibility has produced many of the twenty-first century's most vital artists, entrepreneurs and recordings, while simultaneously conforming to many of pop's most facile stereotypes, particularly when it comes to gender issues and the worship of money.

Boys to Men

When Boston boy band New Edition sacked their mentor Maurice Starr in 1984, their subsequent move into a tougher, funkier blend of dance pop and balladry set the contemporary R&B train in motion. In 1986 Bobby Brown quit the group and by 1989 had become the new sound's first superstar with his *Don't Be Cruel* album, and the rest of the band had split. While Gill and Ralph Tresvant enjoyed successful solo careers, Michael Bivins, Ricky Bell and Ronnie Devoe formed Bell Biv Devoe. Bivins also discovered vocal group Boyz II Men, and the R&B era was brought into being by hugely successful male vocal groups with the above, Jodeci, R. Kelly and Public Announcement all treading a clever line between graphic teen girl seduction, hip hop attitude and increasing musical sophistication.

"It's her aura, her whole personality, her music as well, it definitely touches your heart."
Romeo of So Solid Crew on Ms Dynamite

The key producer/composer in this wave was Teddy Riley, who coined the term "New Jack Swing" in an infectious anthem for hip hop crew Wreckx-N-Effect. His sophisticated melanges of synthetic soul, pop, rap and P-Funk in productions made swingbeat a household term, turning US success into global recognition. With few exceptions, swing vocals were light, nasal and hugely indebted to Stevie Wonder, aiming squarely at a youthful black market that found hip hop just a little too hardcore.

Bobby Brown pioneered new jack swing during the 1980s. His hits continued into the 1990s, but by 1997 headlines about his bad-boy behaviour and marital problems with Whitney Houston had begun to take precedence over his music.

The Ladies in the *House*

But any universal black pop sound needs equal female input to thrive. Enter entirely male producers Denzil Foster and Thomas McElroy, who, at the end of the 1980s, decided to put together a girl group who could challenge swing's growing appeal with an altogether earthier take on the hip hop-inspired times. En Vogue were stylish, sassy and sang with gospel-derived maturity, providing the world with a new jack feminist Supremes on 1990 debut album *Born To Sing*.

Pundits played with the term "New Jill Swing", as less vocally ferocious but equally feisty and entertaining girl groups such as SWV and TLC began to emerge. All this changed when a young ghetto New Yorker, Mary J. Blige, teamed up with on-the-make producer Sean "Puffy" Combs. Combs labelled Blige's debut What's The 411? album "hip hop soul", and Blige's strident vocals and "ghetto fabulous" style sold millions and made swingbeat a redundant term, but set the troubled diva on the road to alcohol and drug problems, a traumatic private life, and enduring superstardom. She released her fifth album, *No More Drama*, in 2001 and the title of the album and quality of the tracks reflect the personal and musical development Blige has achieved during her ten years in the business.

Key Artists:

New Edition
Bobby Brown
En Vogue
Mary J. Blige
Destiny's Child

Combs, of course, went on to rename himself Puff Daddy and P. Diddy, mentor the likes of Biggie Smalls and Faith Evans, and become the embodiment of the obscenely rich, constantly bragging ghetto superstar, admired and reviled in equal measure.

Mary J. Blige shot to stardom with her first album in 1992.

The New *Bohemians*

To balance the extravagant, cash-flaunting excesses of the R&B mainstream, a set of artists emerged touting a less style-conscious, more bohemian and organic form of black music. The likes of Maxwell, Ben Harper, Macy Gray, Angie Stone, India Arie and former Fugee Lauryn Hill have all made key records in this vein. But the two crucial artists in what is often termed nu soul are both singular talents from America's southern states.

D'Angelo from Richmond, Virginia grabbed immediate acclaim with his 1995 debut album *Brown Sugar*, which blended hip hop beats and attitude, classic soul melodies and textures, jazzy technique, and vocals reminiscent of both Al Green and Marvin Gaye. All that, and with the looks and six-pack to match, the world is truly his.

The female version emerged in 1997 from Atlanta, Georgia. Erykah Badu's debut, *Baduizm*, was both sexual and spiritual, a sparse soundscape of low-tempo funk rhythms, jazzy songcraft and Ms. Badu's smoky, Billie Holiday-esque voice singing lyrics soaked in love, religion and politics. Again, the visual anti-image was strong, as accusatory as it was beautiful.

The new century sees vocal trio Destiny's Child firmly established as brand leaders in R&B's rise to global popularity, with Beyoncé Knowles & co. fusing sex, money, feminism, vocal virtuosity and pure pop fizz into a seamless and irresistible whole. Credible British R&B stars have finally arrived, with Craig David and Ms Dynamite bringing in influences from UK garage and Jamaican reggae respectively. The team of Missy Elliott and Tim "Timbaland" Mosley continue to mix R&B and rap so thrillingly that their influence makes it increasingly difficult to tell where hip hop begins and R&B ends. But, despite the impact of all the artists mentioned, R&B remains a producers' medium, its sound shaped and dominated by the likes of Teddy Riley, LA & Babyface, Rodney Jerkins, P. Diddy, Jermaine Dupri, Timbaland and the Neptunes, who all have a loyal following.

Key Albums:

Born To Sing En Vogue
Don't Be Cruel Bobby Brown
The Writing's On The Wall Destiny's Child
What's The 411 Mary J. Blige

The ambitious Sean Combs quickly made a name for himself in the music industry and formed his own record label, aptly named Bad Boy. He has courted controversy throughout his career; most famously through his feud with Death Row records.

Acid Jazz

Acid jazz is a lively, groove-oriented music style that combines elements from jazz, funk and hip hop, with an emphasis on jazz dance. The term "acid jazz" was first used during the late 1980s, both as the name of a record label and the title of a British jazz funk, "rare groove'" compilation series.

Interest had originally been sparked by a thriving London club scene, where hip DJs were playing rare 1970s jazz funk records. This encouraged British and American underground musicians such as the Brand New Heavies, Jamiroquai, Stereo MC's, Galliano and Groove Collective, who began to popularize the style by the 1990s. One of the first DJs to be identified with acid jazz was the London-based Gilles Peterson, who began broadcasting jazz funk sets from his garden shed at home and DJing at London clubs in the late 1980s. Peterson teamed up with Eddie Piller, who had

"Acid jazz was the most significant jazz form to emerge out of the British music scene."
Q magazine, UK.

previously released a debut album by a young, contemporary Hammond organ virtuoso, James Taylor, to form Acid Jazz Records. The label's first releases were a series of compilations titled *Totally Wired*, which alternated jazz funk obscurities from the 1970s with updated tracks from the new acid jazz movement. Peterson later formed his own acid jazz label, Talkin' Loud Records.

(Right) N'Dea Davenport, as a member of the Brand New Heavies, was an important figure in the development of acid jazz. After leaving the band in 1994, she embarked on a solo career. (Above) Stereo MC's, whose 1992 breakthrough album Connected won them two Brit Awards.

Mainstream Acid Jazz

Acid jazz entered into the mainstream in 1990, after the Brand New Heavies released their self-titled debut album on the Acid Jazz label. Formed in 1985 by drummer Jan Kincaid, guitarist Simon Bartholomew and bassist/keyboardist Andrew Levy they were originally an instrumental band inspired by James Brown and the Meters.

The band began recording their own material, added a singer and a brass section, and gained exposure via the club circuit. Their first album was a success and it was followed by a string of hit singles in 1991 in the UK and US. The 1994 album, *Brother Sister*, went platinum in Britain, and the band's success has since continued on both sides of the Atlantic with *Original Flava* (1994) and *Delicious* (1997).

After the emergence of the Heavies, Galliano and a few smaller UK acid jazz bands, a spate of compilations were launched en masse by record labels, leaving many consumers confused over exactly what the style was or who played it. The confusion increased when even more independent acid jazz communities began to spring up all over the US during the early 1990s. By then, the term could refer to anything from Jamiroquai's commercial soul funk to the James Taylor Quartet's rendering of the 'Starsky And Hutch Theme', or from the ethnic eclecticism of the Japanese producers United Future Organisation to the hip hop poetry of New York's Groove Collective.

Key Artists:

The Brand New Heavies
Jamiroquai
Galliano
Groove Collective
James Taylor Quartet

The creation of the UK singer/songwriter Jay Kay, Jamiroquai has perhaps popularized acid jazz more than any other band. The band has experienced chart success all over the world with an irresistible blend of house rhythms and 1970s-era soul/funk. As he did not originally have a band to back up his songs, Jay assembled a group of musicians and produced some demos, which impressed the Acid Jazz label enough to issue the debut single 'When You Gonna Learn?' in late 1992. A hit, it led to a long-term and lucrative recording contract with Sony, who released Emergency On Planet Earth (1992) and The Return Of The Space Cowboy (1994), both major hit albums in the UK. This success spread to America with Jamiroquai's third effort, *Travelling Without Moving* (1996), which contained the worldwide hit 'Virtual Insanity'.

Jay Kay and Jamiroquai have been largely responsible for bringing the acid jazz sound into the musical mainstream. The themes explored in the songs include the environment, government incompetence and space travel.

Nu Jazz

A number of more "serious" jazz artists, including the UK's Courtney Pine, the American veteran Pharaoh Sanders (both saxophonists) and the American Pat Metheny (guitarist), were also associated with acid jazz forms during the 1990s. Pine and Sanders both contributed to a British compilation series titled *Rebirth Of The Cool* (named after the classic *Miles Davis album Birth Of The Cool*), while the Pat Metheny Group used hip hop-style grooves to great effect on their *We Live Here* (1995) album.

Since the 1990s, acid jazz has moved more left-field, evolving into the nu jazz (nu-fusion or future-jazz) movement via the house music-led club dance floor. The cutting edge, springing from the underground, has been exploited commercially by France's St. Germain and even the 'establishment's Herbie Hancock (Future2Future, 2002). A serious jazz vibe is being combined with percussion-led, acousto-electric keyboards and programmed beats transfused with the hip hop/drum 'n' bass repetitions of house music, Afro-Brazilian beats and live jazz. Leading the nu jazz field are labels such as Germany's Compost (Jazzanova, Beanfield, Les Gammas, Kyoto Jazz Massive and Minus 8) and UK's 'West London collective' working with producer-DJ IG Culture and artists such as Kaidi Tatham, Modaji and Seiji. In nu jazz, vocalists are coming into their own again, high in both profile and mix – Vikter Duplaix, Robert Owens, Peven Everett and Ursula Rucker in the US, Victor Davies, Joseph Malik, Kate Phillips (Bembé Segué) and Marcus Begg in the UK and Europe.

Key Tracks:

'Dream On Dreamer' The Brand New Heavies
'Midnight At The Oasis' The Brand New Heavies
'Starsky And Hutch Theme' James Taylor Quartet
'Virtual Insanity' Jamiroquai
'When You Gonna Learn' Jamiroquai

Producers collaborating with live musicians are mixing (today's technological equivalent of scoring/arranging), remixing and sampling to brilliant effect, and new technology is opening up even more possibilities for jazz. Indeed, as Sun Ra predicted as long ago as 1972, "Space Is The Place", especially for the MP3 generation.

The James Taylor Quartet has kept acid jazz alive through continual gigging and recording. They have also been involved in writing film music, including the theme to Austin Powers: International Man Of Mystery.

Nineties Latin *Pop*

Latin pop has been around for as long as latin music itself. As far back as the 1920s, Mexico, Argentina and Spain were veritable fountains of popular music, which they exported to all Spanish-speaking nations. An international audience was found in the United States, along with the steady influx of Latino immigrants in the late twentieth century.

Prior to this, Latin music made its rounds through the decades via the boleros – traditional romantic songs – of composers such as Mexicans Agustín Lara ('Noche de Ronda', 'Granada') and Consuelo Velázquez ('Bésame Mucho'). Their songs were translated into English and popularized by various acts, ranging from Nat King Cole to Ray Charles. Latin music also managed to supersede language barriers thanks to various Latin dance crazes criss-crossing the globe, primarily the Cuban mambo. Its best-known representative was Pérez Prado, a big-band leader and composer whose catchy compositions and simplified arrangements propelled the music to international renown in the 1950s.

"I will never stop singing in Spanish ... that's who I am ... but this was always part of the plan."
Ricky Martin on making the transition with an English LP

The Pioneers

However, the rise of widely popular Latin acts remained relatively rare outside the Spanish-speaking world. Among the few exceptions are the Spanish balladeer Julio Iglesias, who crooned his way to fame in more than a dozen languages and Miami Sound Machine, the group created in the 1980s by the music mogul Emilio Estefan, then a fledgling bongo player. With Estefan's wife Gloria as the lead singer, Miami Sound Machine brought to the table a dynamic mix of Latin percussion and heavy brass, blended with disco beats and performed in English. The combination, which the Cuban-born Estefans often described as rice and beans (Cuban staples) with hamburger, turned songs such as 'Conga' into international hits and paved the way for what many now refer to as the "Latin music explosion" of the late 1990s.

The son of Julio, Enrique Iglesias' 2001 release Escape *spawned such hits as the title track and the ballad 'Hero', which was adopted as an unofficial tribute to those who perished in the World Trade Center attack.*

Ricky *Martin*

The Latin music explosion was spearheaded by Ricky Martin, a Puerto Rican singer whose hip-swivelling moves were reminiscent of Elvis Presley and whose generic, Western-world good looks made him internationally appealing.

Martin started out in show business with Menudo, a 1980s boy band who performed bubblegum Spanish-language pop. As a soloist, he became enormously popular throughout Latin America by singing Latin ballads, but gradually developed a parallel, upbeat style characterized by his use of Caribbean dance rhythms, percussion and brass.

That sound characterized 1998's 'La Copa De La Vida', or 'The Cup Of Life', a song conceived as the football World Cup anthem, which Martin recorded in several languages. Its worldwide success set the stage for Martin's self-titled English-language debut album in 1999, which featured 'Livin' La Vida Loca', a track that would become an international anthem in its English- and Spanish-language versions. 'Livin' ' was typical of Martin in its use of Latin rhythms, while its electric-guitar intro – reminiscent of 1960s California surf rock – gave it a far greater international feel. As well as propelling Martin to international superstardom, it opened the door for other Latin artists to embark on the crossover from Spanish to English.

Key Artists:

Ricky Martin
Marc Anthony
Luis Miguel
Enrique Iglesias
Jennifer Lopez

Ricky Martin's extrovert and flashy stage performances and music videos complemented his songs and helped propel him into superstardom.

The Latin *Explosion*

The late 1990s saw the international rise of Enrique Iglesias, the son of crooner Julio Iglesias, who, like his father, launched his career performing romantic ballads in Spanish. He ventured into English-language pop with 1999's *Enrique*, an album that featured romantic fare as well as more dance-oriented pop.

A more Latin direction was taken by Marc Anthony, a salsa singer born in New York to Puerto Rican parents. Anthony refused to sing salsa in English, something he once deemed a "sacrilege". But his 1999 English-language debut featured the single 'I Need To Know', whose rhythmic base was Latin and which featured Afro-Cuban percussion and hard-edged brass, culled from New York-style salsa.

Another New Yorker, the actress Jennifer López, launched her musical career after she played the leading role in *Selena*, a film based on the life of the Mexican-American singer who was tragically shot by a former employee in 1995. López's musical debut had more to do with urban and hip-hop beats than Latin music, but by virtue of her Hispanic name, she was thrown into the "Latin explosion" category. Equally importantly, her stature as a film star helped to raise awareness about the music performed by Selena. Called "Tejano", it is a hybrid of traditional Mexican cumbia, rancheras and polkas, with elements of American pop, blues and country.

Many other purveyors of Latin pop gained notoriety in the 1990s, among them the German singer Lou Bega, who revamped Pérez Prado's decades-old hit 'Mambo No. 5' with saucy English lyrics and renamed it 'Mambo No. 5 (A Little Bit Of...)'. Within the broad Spanish-language marketplace, the Mexican crooner Luis Miguel was, by and large, the king of the decade with his successive recordings of boleros dating back to the 1940s, which he modernized with string orchestra and drums, and re-introduced to a new generation of listeners. At the same time, rock movements in Argentina and Mexico yielded major acts such as Maná, Latin rock's biggest-selling band to date.

Key Tracks:

'Hero' Enrique Iglesias
'I Need To Know' Marc Anthony
'If You Had My Love' Jennifer Lopez
'Livin' La Vida Loca' Ricky Martin

Since arriving on the music scene in 1999, Jennifer López has become the media's darling. Her high-profile relationships and frequent merchandising of products, has eclipsed the importance of her music.

Big *Beat*

The 1990s electronica that came to be known as big beat is recognised by its rhythmic clout and propulsive force. With their fx and 303 acid lines set to "block rockin' beats", the Chemical Brothers were the architects of this fusion of hip hop and techno but Norman Cook, a.k.a Fatboy Slim, would later emulate their sound.

First at Naked Under Leather in Manchester, and then at the Heavenly Social in London, Tom Rowlands and Ed Simons (the Chemical Brothers) DJ'd across the board, Balearic-style. There was already a rich history of dance music to plunder by the early 1990s, from old-skool hip hop to breakbeat house, through indie dance or Northern soul, but Tom and Ed wanted to make their own mark. Their 'Chemical Beats' track is considered to be the first 1990s big-beat record, the "chemical generation" already being a much-used term for post-acid house, ecstasy-using clubbers. The Chemical Brothers would draw on old hardcore sounds, breaks and, crucially, guitars for their own tracks. Recorded in 1996 with Oasis guitarist Noel Gallagher, 'Setting Sun' topped the UK charts, and the album it came from, *Dig Your Own Hole*, sold a million and helped convert a swathe of alt-rock fans to electronica.

> *"I like to make the music more accessible to people, rather than being cooler-than-thou and moody or whatever."*
>
> Norman Cook, a.k.a Fatboy Slim

A former bassist in the Housemartins, Norman Cook had been dabbling in dance music since the mid-1980s, first fronting the band Beats International, then putting out house records under names such as Mighty Dub Katz and Pizzaman. Legend has it that Norman Cook (Fatboy Slim) took fellow Brighton pal Damian Harris to the amyl nitrate-fuelled Heavenly Social in London to give the Midfield General (Harris) a vision for his new label, Skint. They soon started a night in their seaside hometown, with Norman as resident – the Big Beat Boutique.

Considered by some as the definitive big beat album, You've Come A Long Way, Baby *(1998) was the second of Norman Cook's albums to be released under the name of Fatboy Slim. It lived up to all expectations.*

Party Time

While some dance music innovations inevitably became clichés, the big beat DJs kept ahead of the pack with their interest in technological developments. Crescendos, explosions, time-stretching, sirens, huge hip hop samples – no quick-fix trick was too much for the emerging sound.

This was blasphemy for some, a dumbing-down of refined electronic tweakery that turned dance music into pub rock, but its importance in converting rock doubters to dance music is inestimable.

Big beat also re-introduced a sense of fun to a dance scene that had become quite po-faced and studied. Trainspotting trip hop or chin-stroking, obscure European electronica was all very well, but hardly the heady "abandon and party" spirit of original acid house. Big beat's "Fuck art, let's party" ethos would soon lead to a number of other artists, DJs and labels banding together under this umbrella – although virtually everybody soon professed disdain for the terminology.

Key Artists:

Norman Cook (a.k.a. Fatboy Slim)
The Chemical Brothers
Bentley Rhythm Ace
Propellerheads
Les Rhythmes Digitales

Aside from Skint, Wall Of Sound with Wiseguys, Propellerheads, Les Rhythmes Digitales and Monkey Mafia were the other chief label exponents of big beat. Acts such as Eboman, the Lo-Fi Allstars, Bentley Rhythm Ace, Dub Pistols, FC Kahuna, the Crystal Method, Lunatic Calm and Deejay Punk-Roc all became associated with the sound but, when the inevitable backlash came, most of them successfully side-swerved into other genres such as house, breakbeat or electro.

Jacques Lu Cont is the man behind Les Rhythmes Digitales. Despite both the French names, he is English. A colourful character, he is known for his excellent live shows.

Trip *Hop*

Jungle and UK garage are often cited as the only real British contributions to electronic music, but the slow motion beats of trip hop are also steeped in the multi-cultural sounds of UK music.

Influenced by 1980s dub acts like On-U-Sound, Adrian Sherwood and African Headcharge and their own sound system backgrounds, Bristol based acts like Smith & Mighty and Massive Attack, as well as London outfits Pressure Drop and Renegade Soundwave, had been experimenting with the fusion of dub influences with hip hop and break beats since the mid-1980s.

Renegade Soundwave also released club-based, dub-influenced tracks like 'Biting My Nails', and Massive Attack even drafted in dub pioneer the Mad Professor to do a dub version of their *Protection* album, called *No Protection*. The dub ethic was also adopted by second wave Bristol producer Tricky, whose *Maxinquaye* album went to paranoid extremes – a mixture of dense, claustrophobic beats and ominous rapping.

"I don't want to be pigeon-holed. It's an attitude that describes what I do rather than a particular style".
James Lavelle, Mo'Wax

It was Portishead, however, who brought the fusion of heavy basslines and dead-paced beats, as well as dub's sense of mournful spaciousness, to the wider public's attention. Captured on the duo's debut album, *Dummy*, Portishead's melancholic outpourings ensured that the album became a brooders' favourite without sanitizing blueprints explored by their predecessors.

Tricky began collaborating with the teenage Martina Topley-Bird during the early 1990s, while a member of Massive Attack. She launched her solo career in 1999.

The Mo'Wax *Connection*

In the US, producer DJ Shadow started to release his own haunting compositions. Unlike its progenitors, his 1994 'In/flux' release dispensed with the notion of vocals, especially the violent, misogynist gangster rhymes, breaking with the traditions of US hip hop and opting for barren, otherworldly instrumentals.

London DJ James Lavelle, who had already put out instrumental hip hop tracks on his Mo'Wax label, signed Shadow. Lavelle's label also put out the *Headz* compilation, which became a landmark release. Pre-empting the glut of compilations keen to cash in on the trip hop sound, Mo'Wax was also the first imprint to document the music's development from a narrow set of influences to a wide range of flavours, with contributions as diverse as Warp stalwarts Autechre's menacing 'Lowride' and US West Coast act Tranquility Bass's uplifting 'We Came In Peace'. With Shadow's debut album, *Entroducing*, selling half a million copies, it looked like trip hop was set to follow an inclusive rather than an exclusive blueprint.

Trip hop's diverse approach was borne out by the individualistic approach other producers embraced. Washington DC act Thievery Corporation embraced dub and bossa flavours on their 1995 album *Sounds From The Thievery Hi-Fi*, Fila Brazilia looked to funk and jazz influences, Si Begg explored an unpredictable electronic sound, and Lamb's orchestral, vocal style, embodied on tracks like 'Gorecki', made clear that trip hop was flying in the face of purism and advocating a refreshing, eclectic agenda. Unsurprisingly, this eclectic modus operandi influenced trip hop's most prominent DJs, with pioneering DJ/production/multimedia outfit Coldcut laying down the gauntlet with their aptly named *70 Minutes Of Madness* mix CD. The mix was one of DJ culture's most important turning points.

Key Artists:

Massive Attack
Portishead
DJ Shadow
Renegade Soundwave
The Chemical Brothers

Madness proved that adherence to a specific tempo was no longer necessary and that with a degree of imagination and skill it was possible to pursue an eclectic musical agenda. This spirit was maintained by DJs like Jon Carter, Fatboy Slim, Midfield General and the Chemical Brothers who, conscious of dance floor demands, imbued their sets and their production work, with faster, more club-friendly breaks and beats.

The world of dance music would not be the same without the contributions of DJ Shadow and his seminal release, 'In/flux', which is widely regarded as a revolutionary and groundbreaking electro record.

The Beats Get *Bigger*

Pioneered at the Chemicals' Heavenly Social Club and originally captured on the duo's Cocteau Twins sampling 'Song To The Siren' debut release, a new breed of eclectic DJ and clubbing experience superseded the dead paced beats that characterized trip hop, and the music was rechristened big beat.

Artists like Dirty Beatniks, Wiseguys, Propellerheads, Death In Vegas, Freestylers, Cut La Roc and Dub Pistols and labels like Skint and Wall Of Sound followed in this new direction. Big beat's uncomplicated, good time party aesthetic turned Fatboy Slim and the Chemical Brothers into dance music's biggest pop stars, but it also took trip hop out of the media glare, allowing some of the music's most innovative artists the space to blossom.

As James Lavelle said on the release of his collaborative UNKLE album, Psycence Fiction, with DJ Shadow in 1998, "Big beat was such a blessing in disguise: finally trip hop can go and we can make a run for it!"

Despite Lavelle's detachment, trip hop's slow motion beats were revisited by Leftfield, who dedicated a sizeable chunk of their debut album, *Leftism*, to the dub-heavy rhythms and seismic dub basslines originally explored by Massive Attack and Smith & Mighty. Austrian act Kruder & Dorfmeister also brought trip hop back to the public's attention with the stoned grooves of their *K&D Sessions* album, which has become one of dance music's most popular releases.

Key Tracks:
'Glory Box' Portishead
'In/flux' DJ Shadow
'Kling To Me And I'll Klong To You' The Chemical Brothers
'Unfinished Sympathy' Massive Attack

True to electronic music's cyclical nature, trip hop had morphed into the new style of big beat before making a glorious comeback with these benchmark releases. Trip hop's legacy is still audible in the smoky grooves of chill out act Nightmares On Wax and in Zero 7's lush, down tempo compositions. It's unquestionable that trip hop left an indelible mark on electronic music.

Leftfield's 1995 album Leftism *includes vocals from Curve singer Toni Halliday, ex-Sex Pistol John Lydon and reggae vocalist Earl Sixteen.*

Britpop

By the early 1990s British pop and alternative fans were crying out for homegrown pop that combined old-fashioned rock charisma with lyrics and a definitively British sound, to counteract the manufactured teen acts, Euro-dance novelties and US imports. This arrived in the mid-1990s in the shape of Britpop: a wave of guitar bands with short, sharp pop songs.

The heavily 1960s-influenced basis of Britpop was heralded in 1990, with the release of the self-titled debut album by Liverpool group the La's (a Merseyside slang word for "lads"). Led by the singer/songwriter Lee Mavers, the La's purveyed a deceptively simple guitar pop in the vein of the Beatles, the Who and the Hollies, but somehow made entirely fresh by Mavers's poetic flights and choirboy-thug vocals, typified by their beautiful hit 'There She Goes'. Sadly, the eccentric Mavers, after complaining bitterly in the press about the production on the released album, split the band up and went into hiding in his native Liverpool. While their bassist, John Power, enjoyed some mid-1990s success with the similar but far less exciting Cast, Mavers remains missing in action, obsessively perfecting the ultimate pop sound that only he can hear. (The band re-formed for a tour in 2005).

"If you go back through 30 years of music we're the best bits all encompassed in one band. We're Oasis."
Noel Gallagher

Meanwhile, Bowie-worshipping Londoner Brett Anderson formed Suede in 1989. By 1992, the quartet had released their *Suede* album to huge critical acclaim, with the mix of Anderson's Bowie-esque tales of seedy sex and squalid glamour, coupled with guitarist Bernard Butler's virtuoso riffs and squalls, delighting a UK press and public desperate for new guitar heroes. Although Butler left for a solo career in 1994, Suede continued to please their loyal following with unreconstructed glam rock until their split. Anderson and Butler reunited in new band the Tears and released the 2005 album *Here Come The Tears*.

Britpop kings Blur have continued to create innovative music since their 1991 entrance into the music scene, with lead singer Damon Albarn's spin-off cartoon group Gorillaz also spawning a hit single in 2001.

The Britpop *Wars*

With Suede establishing a market for homegrown guitar pop, the three acts that define the Britpop era made their move. The superb London four-piece Blur summed up the mod-reviving, 1960s- and 1970s-quoting, anti-American mood on 1993's *Modern Life Is Rubbish* album and became a national phenomenon with 1994's *Parklife* – an irresistible blend of Kinks-ish English observational comedy, XTC- and Wire-influenced New Wave, and cockney singalong, with a sprinkling of glam and synth-disco. The album established Britpop as a UK commercial phenomenon overnight.

Hot on their heels were a Manchester band led by two confident and charismatic brothers. Noel and Liam Gallagher's Oasis were unashamed copyists, stealing riffs and melodies from Marc Bolan, the Sex Pistols and, most famously, the Beatles. But Liam's Lennon-meets-Johnny Rotten vocals and Noel's wall-of-sound guitar crunch made their first two albums, *Definitely Maybe* and *(What's The Story) Morning Glory*, almost universally popular in the UK, packed as they were with hard-rocking anthems and instantly classic power ballads.

Britpop reached its peak of homegrown national interest in August 1995, when Blur, arguably, contrived a popularity contest with intense rivals Oasis by releasing their long-awaited new single, 'Country House' on the same day as Oasis's 'Roll With It' in a race for the week's number one spot. Blur famously won the battle but lost the war, as *Morning Glory* outshone Blur's much-criticized follow-up to *Parklife*, *The Great Escape*, and the Gallaghers went on to become two of the most famous men on the planet.

Key Artists:

Blur
Oasis
Pulp
The La's
Suede

Since then, Blur's reinvention of themselves as an eclectic, art-punk proposition has ensured long-term success and respect, while Oasis have simply continued to make less exciting versions of the same records, albeit with healthy sales. Though Blur continued following the departure of their guitarist, Graham Coxon, in 2002, Damon Albarn created a chart-topping spin-off group in Gorillaz.

In May 2005 Oasis resurfaced after three years to produce their sixth album Don't Believe The Truth, *which entered the UK album chart at number one.*

Six-String *Wonders*

The third Britpop kings were Pulp, a Sheffield group led by the geeky and witty former art student Jarvis Cocker. Although Pulp had been in existence since 1978, it was not until 1995, with the era-defining, class-warfare hit single 'Common People', that Cocker became the Morrissey of the 1990s.

His own personal Britpop war was declared at the 1996 Brit Awards when, during a predictably self-aggrandizing cast-of-thousands guest performance from Michael Jackson, Cocker invaded the stage and started dancing before being bundled off by security. Cocker was arrested and Jackson's people accused him of assaulting the children onstage, before the threat of legal action forced them to withdraw the accusation. The accompanying tabloid furore turned Cocker into a symbol of plucky, rebellious England rejecting American celebrity excess.

The Britpop market remained open until the end of the 1990s. A host of traditional British guitar bands made their mark: the 1960s retro of Ocean Colour Scene, Kula Shaker and funky Madchester veterans the Charlatans; the spiky post-punk anthems of Oxford trio Supergrass and London's Elastica, whose frontwoman, Justine Frischmann, began her career with Suede and had a very public relationship (and break-up) with Blur leader Damon Albarn; the catchy mainstream pop of Wales's Catatonia and Liverpool's Lightning Seeds; and the moody rock atmospherics of Wigan's the Verve, led by lips-and-cheekbones idol Richard Ashcroft. Britpop fell dramatically from favour at the end of the century, but it remains the last time that a pointedly English variety of pop/rock made a genuine impact on a wide range of music lovers.

Key Tracks:

'Common People' Pulp
'Girls & Boys' Blur
'So Young' Suede
'There She Goes' The La's
'Wonderwall' Oasis

As the lead singer and lyricist of Pulp, Jarvis Cocker has become one of the most well-loved and admired musicians of the Britpop/ alternative scene.

Boy Bands

Groups of fresh-faced young men singing catchy tunes have been one of the mainstays of commercial pop since The Beatles. In the last two decades, manufactured boy bands such as New Kids On The Block and Take That have ruled the roost. Although their musical legacy bears no comparison to that of the Fab Fours, the devotion they inspired was just as fervent.

Marketing is everything for the modern boy band. Members are selected for characteristics that maximize their appeal to a fanbase largely made up of adolescent girls. Being youthful, squeaky clean and unthreateningly attractive are just as important as being able to sing in tune and dance in time. Few contemporary boy bands play instruments and most purvey lightweight pop, divided between uptempo numbers and slushy ballads. Due to the disposable nature of their music, and fickle young audiences with rapidly evolving tastes, boy bands rarely survive for more than five years, although artists such as Take That's Robbie Williams and *NSYNC's Justin Timberlake have been catapulted on to successful solo careers.

"In three years' time even though they'll be fans of another group, they'll never forget Take That."
Howard Donald of Take That on fans

Although the boy band evolved into its familiar form in the late-1980s, its history stretches back to the early 1960s and is entwined in the origins of, arguably, pop's greatest group. The Beatles wrote their own songs from the outset and their longevity, artistic scope and degree of control over their careers remain unmatched by any of today's boy bands. But in the clean-cut appeal of their mop-top days, and in the bubblegum melodies of songs such as 1963's 'I Want To Hold Your Hand', they foreshadowed their less-esteemed successors.

In the first half of the 1990s, Take That became a global phenomenon with their good looks and catchy pop hits. Their released a mixture of covers – such as 'Could It Be Magic' and 'Relight My Fire' – and original material, which included 'Pray', 'Babe' and 'Back For Good'.

The Fantastic *Five*

The boy-band concept took its next evolutionary leap in the late-1960s, when Joseph Jackson realized the commercial viability of putting his sons Jermaine, Jackie, Marlon, Tito and Michael on the stage.

One of the few post-Beatle boy bands whose music stands up well when revisited, the Jackson 5 combined pop, soul and disco to sublime effect. Their early sound was encapsulated by their breakthrough single, 'I Want You Back' (1970), a classic marriage of funky rhythms and sugary harmonies built around the sweet, expressive vocals of 12-year-old Michael.

The Jacksons' disciplinarian father, along with the legendary boss of their Motown record label, Berry Gordy, exerted tight control over their activities: they were not allowed to perform their own material until the mid-1970s. Every boy band since has been masterminded by similarly formidable figures, well-versed in the cut-throat whims of the music industry.

The 1970s saw several copycat groups appear, including the Osmonds, another sibling quintet with the focus on a talented younger brother – in this case, the cherub-faced Donny. Solo artists (including a liberated Michael Jackson) dominated the middle-ground of pop for much of the 1980s, but the boy band would be back with a vengeance by the end of the decade. With the increasing prevalence of synthesized backing tracks, acts abandoned live instrumentation in favour of choreographed dance routines and enlivened their music by diluting elements of hipper genres.

Key Artists:

The Beatles
The Jackson 5
New Kids On The Block
Take That
Backstreet Boys

The surge of boy bands in the late 1990s saw legions of worshipping and swooning teenage fans in hysterics over seeing their idols perform.

A Manufacturing *Boom*

The biggest of this new breed of boy band were New Kids On The Block, a quintet of Boston-based youngsters assembled by manager/songwriter Maurice Starr, who had considerable success earlier in the 1980s with New Edition.

With brothers Jon and Jordan Knight, Donnie Wahlberg, Danny Wood and Joey McIntyre, Starr combined some of the macho posturing of hip hop with the tight harmonies of R&B. Their best-known hit, 'Hangin' Tough', was a frothy mix of faux-street style and singalong choruses, and a global hit in 1988. It kicked off three years of chart domination for the Kids, who eventually split in 1994.

NKOTB's success paved the way for Take That, composed of Gary Barlow, Robbie Williams, Mark Owen, Jason Orange and Howard Donald. The five-piece bestrode the European charts in the first half of the 1990s, shifting more records than any British act since the Beatles. Mega-selling singles such as 1993's 'Could It Be Magic' incorporated the hi-energy rhythms of the club music that was sweeping Britain at the time, while the members' toned physiques, combined with a fondness for covering disco classics such as Tavares' 'It Only Takes A Minute', endeared them to the gay community as well as teenage girls.

Take That disbanded in 1996, but not before inspiring a slew of British and Irish boy bands. These included Westlife, who scored a British record with 10 consecutive number one singles. At around the same time, Backstreet Boys, yet another five-piece, emerged with an eponymous album that became the second-largest seller of the decade, shifting 28-million copies. Their style picked up where that of the New Kids left off, but borrowed even more heavily from black music than their predecessors. Monstrous hits such as 1999's 'Everybody (Backstreet's Back)' showcased their melodic synthesis of hip-hop, R&B, soul and pop, while Backstreet clones such as *NSYNC emerged throughout the late 1990s and early 2000s. Given the current popularity of R&B-infused acts, the public's appetite for boy bands shows no signs of being sated.

Key Tracks:

'Everybody (Backstreet's Back)' Backstreet Boys
'Hangin' Tough' New Kids On The Block
'I Want To Hold Your Hand' The Beatles
'I Want You Back' The Jackson 5
'Pray' Take That

The Backstreet Boys enjoyed phenomenal success during the mid-1990s, with their 1996 debut album landing in the Top 10 of nearly every European nation's music chart.

Noughties *Pop*

Although boy bands and girl bands held sway over Anglo-American pop for much of the 1990s, the end of the decade witnessed the return of the individual artist. While the likes of *NSYNC, Blue and Sugababes continued to fly the flag for groups, artists such as Britney Spears, Christina Aguilera and Pink emerged as arena-filling soloists.

The soaring popularity of R&B continued to leave its mark on the charts, with many pop acts making much use of tight harmonies, smooth melodies, streetwise beats and raunchy choreography. The period also saw huge hits for a succession of performers who had found fame as members of groups. Take That's Robbie Williams, *NSYNC's Justin Timberlake, Destiny's Child's Beyoncé Knowles, the Spice Girls' Geri Halliwell and Boyzone's Ronan Keating were now stars in their own right. But perhaps the most significant development in early twenty-first-century pop was the increasingly powerful role of television in making and breaking stars.

The Small Screen Comes to the Fore

Having been an important player in the music business since Elvis's scandalous appearance on *The Ed Sullivan Show* in 1956, television widened its influence in the 1980s with the introduction of MTV and the subsequent rise of the music video. In 2001, however, the partnership entered a new era with the launch of *Popstars*.

"People in the industry are musical snobs: it's all about being cool. That's always baffled me because pop music is popular music." Simon Fuller

Tapping into the British public's increasingly rabid obsession with both celebrity and reality TV, the show tracked thousands of young hopefuls as, through a merciless sequence of auditions, they were whittled down to a final line-up of five members. Myleene Klass, Kym Marsh, Suzanne Shaw, Danny Foster and Noel Sullivan adopted the name Hear'Say, and millions of viewers watched as they were groomed for stardom and recorded a debut single, 'Pure And Simple'. Crossing the identikit harmonies of Westlife with the bouncier grooves of S Club 7, it went straight to number one in the UK in 2001.

With a sex appeal that contradicts her squeaky clean image, Britney Spears has enjoyed phenomenal success both as a music artist and a major media fixture since her debut in 1999.

A Pop Idol is *Launched*

Critics accused *Popstars* of stifling creativity with unadventurous songs and formulaic marketing, as well as exploiting the power of television to line the pockets of its creators. Hear'Say certainly proved to be a short-lived sensation. Marsh left the band in 2002 and they split later in the same year, having plunged from being media darlings to hate figures in the space of 12 months.

But the format remained a hugely popular one with the public. In 2002, *Popstars* was followed by *Pop Idol*, a series that shifted the focus from groups to solo performers and allowed viewers to vote on who should win. Fourteen million people saw the vote go to Will Young, whose popularity looks set to far outlast that of Hear'Say. Blessed with a muscular, soulful voice, he breathed life into 'Evergreen', the uninspiring Westlife ballad with which he made his (inevitably chart-topping) debut in 2002. Young also resisted efforts to package him as an anodyne pop clone, becoming one of the first pop stars to be openly gay from the start of his career.

5 Top 2000s UK Artists:	5 Top 2000s US Artists:
1 Shania Twain	1 *NSYNC
2 Robbie Williams	2 Eminem
3 Dido	3 Jay Z
4 David Gray	4 Usher
5 Eminem	5 Nelly

The *Pop Idol* format was reproduced all over the world. *American Idol*, as it was known in the USA, launched a star in the huge-voiced Kelly Clarkson, whose debut single, 'A Moment Like This' (2002), sold a monstrous 236,000 copies in its first week of release. But it remains to be seen whether Clarkson, Young and Gareth Gates (Young's fellow Pop Idol alumnus), who all owe their fame to their familiarity with domestic audiences, will repeat the global success of three other former TV stars.

The phenomenal success of TV's Pop Idol in the UK resulted in runner-up Gareth Gates (left) also securing a record deal, along with the programme's winner, Will Young (right). Gates's success was such that his pop career initially eclipsed that of Young.

The Three *Mouseketeers*

Britney Spears, Christina Aguilera and Justin Timberlake began their careers in the early 1990s as Mouseketeers, youthful stars of Disney's *The Mickey Mouse Show*. A decade later, all three had swapped their over-sized ears for high-profile musical careers. The first to achieve supernova status was Spears, who debuted in 1999 with '...Baby One More Time', a huge-selling slice of commercial R&B laced with suggestive growls.

Spears' trump card was an ambiguous image that combined wide-eyed innocence with illicit sensuality. Although her publicity machine emphasized her wholesome upbringing and virginity, this contrasted with both the sado-masochistic undertones of the lyrics "hit me baby one more time" and the song's controversial video, in which Spears appeared dressed as a schoolgirl. Record buyers lapped it up and Spears became the most successful American teenager of all time. She was followed into the charts by a succession of solo American females, including Aguilera, who became infamous for her skimpy outfits, raunchy videos and libidinous vocals. This direct marketing strategy began to pay rich dividends with the considerable success of her *Stripped LP* (2002) and 'Dirrty' single (2003).

5 Top 2000s UK Tracks:		*5 Top 2000s US Tracks:*	
1	'Anything Is Possible' Will Young	1	'We Belong Together' Mariah Carey
2	'Unchained Melody' Gareth Gates	2	'In Da Club' 50 Cent
3	'It Wasn't Me' Shaggy featuring Rickrok	3	'Ignition' R. Kelly
4	'Pure And Simple' Hear'Say	4	'Yeah' Usher
5	'Do They Know It's Christmas?' Band Aid 20	5	'This Love' Maroon 5

Although Timberlake had been a mid-ranking star since the late 1990s through his involvement with *NSYNC, he was initially best known as Spears' boyfriend. He made his solo debut in 2002 with 'Like I Love You' and his star profile gradually eclipsed hers. Timberlake's blend of urban grooves and soulful pop hardly overflowed with originality. But he at least had the sense to work with respected producers and aim high by aping the sweet falsetto, high-pitched grunts and slick dance moves of Michael Jackson. By the beginning of 2003, on the back of his huge-selling *Justified* album, he looked poised to snatch the King of Pop's crown, though it took three years for a follow-up to emerge.

Christina Aguilera (pictured), Pink, Mya and Lil' Kim received a Grammy Award for their song, 'Lady Marmalade,' from the Moulin Rouge *soundtrack. The hit denoted a transition in Christina's music from sugary pop ballads to a harder, sexier, more urban sound.*

Noughties Pop *Singer/Songwriters*

While more and more of the mainstream is occupied by heavily manufactured and stylized rock, pop and R&B acts, the emergence of less-demonstrative artists – often from a self-financing, small-scale independent background – represents a quiet form of rebellion from the pop norm.

The success of mavericks such as Björk and Sinéad O'Connor in the 1990s continues to foster an independent spirit in the pop singer/songwriters of the new century. While the likes of Alanis Morissette, Sir Elton John, Paul Weller and Tori Amos remain relevant to a post-2000 audience, it is the new, low-key and rootsy pop singer/songwriters who are beginning to define the future of the genre.

Although very different in musical style, six key artists have all grown from humble beginnings in specific locales, striving long and hard under difficult circumstances before hitting paydirt. The most striking example is David Gray, a Manchester-born multi-instrumentalist who grew up in Wales but found initial success in Ireland. His first album, *A Century Ends*, was released in 1993, but it took another six years of Irish support slots – and his entirely self-financed 1998 album, *White Ladder* – for his Van Morrison-goes-pop songcraft to achieve a crossover impact, along with

"I'm as mystified now as when I started. I'm no closer to understanding the difference between the ingredients of a really great song and a mediocre one."
David Gray

friends in high places and a US release on Dave Matthews ATO label in 2000. Its 2002 follow-up, *A New Day At Midnight*, established him as a major adult pop star.

David Gray's emotional music speaks of infidelity, pain and love highlighted by his powerfully unique voice. His music has wowed thousands of fans, including Dave Matthews of the Dave Matthews Band, who offered Gray his American record deal.

Local Sounds from Local *People*

Macy Gray toiled for years on the Los Angeles jazz bar scene before establishing a highly individual blend of smoky and croaky vocals, eccentric performance, autobiographical lyrics and soul, rap, R&B, FM rock and pop stylings on her massive 1999 debut album, *On How Life Is.*

Alaska's Jewel Kilcher worked as a waitress and strummed and sang in dives in San Diego before becoming an "overnight success" with the folk-pop of 1995's *Pieces Of You*. Her blonde-sweetheart looks and intelligent songs have seen her build a transatlantic word-of-mouth following over subsequent years.

On the British side, Norwich's Beth Orton spent time as a Buddhist nun before she was discovered by the dance producer William Orbit in 1991. By the mid-1990s, she was collaborating with dance acts the Chemical Brothers and Red Snapper, and her quietly funky 1996 debut album *Trailer Park* made her the queen of post-clubbing chill-out for Brits. A gangly, shy six-footer, her appeal seems as as much due to her down-to-earth likeability as it is to her American roots-influenced songs.

The same could be said for Manchester's Damon Gough, aka Badly Drawn Boy, who remained a hometown obscurity until he set up his own Twisted Nerve label with producer Andy Votel. He began recording and quickly caught people's attention. His 2000 debut album, *The Hour Of Bewilderbeast*, saw him win Britain's Mercury Music Prize, while his legendarily shambolic live shows and penchant for scruffy woollen hats have not prevented his rapid ascent in the UK. In 2002, his soundtrack to Hugh Grant's *About A Boy* movie gained widespread popularity, aided by the singles 'Silent Sigh' and 'Something To Talk About'.

Key Artists:

David Gray
Macy Gray
Badly Drawn Boy
Alicia Keys
James Blunt

But perhaps the most striking advert for organic growth is Nova Scotia's Sarah McLachlan. Eight years, three albums of Celtic folk-pop and much mind-expanding travel passed between her first album, *Touch*, and her central role in organizing Lilith Fair, a 1997 tour designed to promote marginalized female artists. The same year saw her *Surfacing* album hit big in America and Europe, while Lilith Fair has quickly become an essential stepping-stone for women attempting to break the charts without shedding their clothes.

With a unique, growling voice and campy 1970s fashion style, Macy Gray has become renowned for her individual, funky sound and stage performances.

Barely Out of *Diapers*

The impact of the mature noughties artists was being mirrored and challenged by a wave of young female singer/songwriters. With the likes of Britney Spears establishing a new level of success and credibility for teen performers, the only thing better for a record company was finding equally young and visually appealing talent who could also write all their own material.

Cue a slew of American singer/songwriter prodigies. Harlem's Alicia Keys, whose extraordinarily articulate and soulful R&B debut album, *Songs In A Minor*, won the 21-year-old five Grammies. Canada's Nelly Furtado's career began with the rap duo Nelstar before success at 1999's Lilith Fair led to her hippy-chick mix of pop, Latin, folk, reggae and hip-hop on her 2000 album, *Whoa, Nelly!* The more traditional piano songcraft of Pennsylvania's Vanessa Carlton produced the global hit 'A Thousand Miles', as well as her precocious debut album, *Be Not Nobody*, in 2002.

The overnight singer/songwriter success of the decade so far occurred in 2005 with the rise to UK chart-topping status of former Army officer James Blunt, whose mournful *Back To Bedlam* proved the year's biggest seller. Katie Melua penned just two of her debut album's dozen offerings but could clearly join the clan in the future, while Scotland's KT Tunstall recalled Patti Smith with her edgy yet assured 2005 debut *Eye To the Telescope*. John Legend was pick of the stateside crop.

Key Tracks:

'Fallin'' Alicia Keys
'I Try' Macy Gray
'Something To Talk About' Badly Brawn Boy
'This Year's Love' David Gray
'You're Beautiful' James Blunt

Winner of Britain's prestigious Mercury Prize for Best Album in 2000, Damon Gough, or Badly Drawn Boy, has enjoyed increasing success outside the UK, quickly establishing himself as a thoughtful voice of his generation.

Noughties Latin *Pop*

Buoyed by its unprecedented international exposure in the 1990s, Latin pop greeted the new century with the first-ever Latin Grammy awards, which took place in the United States in September 2000.

Conceived as an internationally minded award, clearly distinct from – although related to – the Grammys, one of the objectives of the Latin Grammys was to "promote the vitality of the many regional forms of Latin music". What emerged in much of the pop showcased from different countries was music that mixed folk elements from specific regions with more universal elements, as well as more sophisticated orchestrations and arrangements.

Bringing traditional music to the forefront remains a clear trend in Latin pop of this decade, with the Spaniard Alejandro Sanz, whose pop is based on flamenco harmonies and improvizations, being one of the clear leaders in the field. With his insightful songs, Sanz became a star in Spain in the 1990s before achieving prominence in the Latin market with Corazón Partío, a mix of flamenco and pop that included virtuoso flamenco guitar solos and gospel-like backing vocals. Thanks to two award-winning albums, *El Alma Al Aire* and

"Writing in English was a major challenge. I didn't want other songwriters to write for me, I wanted to preserve the spirit of my songs in Spanish." Shakira

MTV Unplugged, and to collaborations with artists as varied as the Irish pop-folk band the Corrs and flamenco guitarist Vicente Amigo, Sanz expanded his reach – notably to the United States and Europe – in the early 2000s.

But even as an increasingly broad-minded audience has embraced rootsy Latin pop, the crossover trend from Spanish to English with a more international sound shows no sign of abating. Indeed, artists are now passing back and forth between languages with considerable ease.

Colombian Shakira has become the largest Latin crossover artist since Jennifer López with her hit singles, 'Whenever, Wherever' and 'Underneath Your Clothes'.

Christina Aguilera and *R&B*

The precursor for the decade was Christina Aguilera, a US teen act with a Latin surname, courtesy of an Ecuadorian father. After scoring a huge hit with her English-language debut in the late 1990s, Aguilera recorded a Spanish-language album, *Mi Reflejo*, in 2000, featuring translations from her English disc, original tracks and, in a move aimed to please traditional Latin audiences, a cover of a bolero standard, 'Contigo En La Distancia'.

Aside from this one track, there was nothing conspicuously Latin about Aguilera's sound. Instead, through songs such as 'Ven Conmigo', she introduced Latin pop laced with both an R&B vocal sensibility and hip-hop beats. The entire Aguilera package appealed to a younger Latin fan and in the ensuing years, R&B-tinged vocalizing has become a standard of Latin pop, particularly for a younger generation of acts, even as the more traditional renditions continued to hold court.

Key Artists:
Shakira
Christina Aguilera
Alejandro Sanz
Las Ketchup

Aguilera's success in both languages also signalled that Latin audiences were open to a kind of linguistic passing back and forth. Enrique Iglesias furthered his English-language career with a generic pop sound (*Escape*) that he carried over to his return to Latin pop in 2002. Marc Anthony also recorded in Spanish in 2001, but put forth a full salsa album, *Libre*, whose strong sales suggest that it was also purchased by his pop fans.

(Right) With Latin mania sweeping the world, it is not surprising that percussion instruments, such as the maracas, would become incorporated into mainstream music. (Above) Christina Aguilera's debut Spanish-language album Mi Reflejo *reached number one in the Latin album chart.*

The Latin *Crossover*

The most successful crossover of the current decade is that of the Colombian pop-rock star Shakira, whose English-language debut, *Laundry Service*, became one of the top-selling albums worldwide for 2001 and 2002. Like other crossover stars before her, Shakira came from a solid foundation in the Latin world and was, arguably, already the most successful female Latin act of her generation. But she also co-wrote her material, an important asset when singer/songwriters seemed to be back in vogue worldwide.

In a move that has become standard for crossover acts, Shakira's first single, 'Wherever, Whenever', was recorded in both English- and Spanish-language versions. The track featured Andean flute, perhaps the only concession to the singer's Latin side, and was otherwise a bouncy pop song with a slight edge, drawing more from British and American rockers than from Latin balladeers or folklorists. (She has been covering Aerosmith's 'Dude (Looks Like A Lady)' and AC/DC's 'Back In Black' in her concerts.) This is in keeping with past crossover success stories. While acts retain their personal "exotic" characteristics, the music becomes largely generic in an attempt to please all. Instead, the task of showcasing the elements that are commonly associated with Latin pop – the Afro-Cuban beats, Latin rhythms and percussion and instrumentation that can veer from the sound of guitar trios to the brash brass of salsa – has fallen largely on acts who record in Spanish.

But the multiple trends also indicate that Latin pop is more open to variations than ever before, from the traditional crooner, still embodied by the Mexican Luis Miguel as well as country mates Alejandro Fernández and Cristian Castro, to Las Ketchup. In June 2002, the latter trio of Spanish sisters released 'Aserejé', a novelty track that has been compared to its 1990s precursor, 'Macarena'. A nonsensical song stemming from the 1980s hit 'Rapper's Delight', 'Aserejé (The Ketchup Song)' became a number one hit in 21 countries, which demonstrated that Latin pop in Spanish can be universal.

Key Tracks:

'Aserejé (The Ketchup Song)' Las Ketchup
'Contigo En La Distancia' Christina Aguilera
'Ven Conmigo' Christina Aguilera
'Wherever, Whenever' Shakira

The infectious pop ditty, 'The Ketchup Song' by Spanish sisters Las Ketchup invaded the planet in 2002, earning the girls worldwide success.

UK *Garage*

The UK garage scene began in London in the 1990s when enterprising DJ's such as Norris "da Bass" Windross and Karl "Tuff Enuff" Brown set up after-hours parties in the capital's pubs for clubbers reluctant to end the revelry after spending the evening at one of London's new superclubs, such as the Ministry of Sound.

"We used to pitch it up a bit, give it a bit more energy cos people used to come from Ministry vibed up and we didn't want to chill them out," remembers Matt "Jam" Lamont, another of the London DJs. The records these DJs played were by Americans such as Todd Edwards, MK and Victor Simonelli. But London's poly-cultural creative musical heritage would, inevitably, lead DJs and producers such as Grant Nelson and RIP to put their own twist on the sound.

"London is a multicultural city.... It's like a melting pot of young people, and that's reflected in the music of UK garage."
MJ Cole, UK Garage DJ/ producer

It was another American, though, Armand Van Helden, who threw away the rule book, putting big basslines and junglist nuances into garage remixes of the Sneaker Pimps and Tori Amos, and thereby creating the space for disaffected drum'n'bass heads with drum programming experience to enter the scene. Records such as 'Closer Than Close', by Rosie Gaines, Double 99's 'RIP Groove' and 'Gunman', by 187 Lockdown, would break on illegal pirate radio stations before crossing over into the UK pop charts. The media dubbed the sound "speed garage", but the bubble burst after the initial 1997 hype as the scene to back up the hyperbole had not developed sufficiently.

Niomi McLean-Daley (a.k.a Ms Dynamite) was a former member of UK Garage act So Solid Crew, but with her solo career came a move towards British ragga and R&B. In 2002 she became the first female black solo artist to win the Mercury Music Prize.

So Solid Headline *Snatchers*

It was another American, Kelly G, with a remix of Tina Moore's 'Never Gonna Let You Go', who blueprinted the non-4/4 off-beat two-step sound of UKG. In 1999, songs such as Shanks & Bigfoot's 'Sweet Like Chocolate' and Craig David and Artful Dodger's 'Rewind' zoomed to the top of the UK charts. The national UK radio station, Radio 1, soon had its own UK garage show, hosted by the Dreem Teem.

Although varying musical styles would develop – from MJ Cole's smooth, soulful dubs to the breakbeat garage of Dee Kline or DJ Zinc, and from bassline-heavy bits by Wookie or DJ Narrows to the gangsta-rap stylings of So Solid Crew – it was the latter that inevitably stole the headlines. UK garage raves became peppered with gun-toting idiots, but with DJs such as EZ reintroducing the 4/4 sound and MCs such as the Mercury Prize-winning Ms Dynamite speaking out against violence, the music looks set to prosper once more.

Key Artists:

Armand Van Helden
Shanks & Bigfoot
Craig David
Artful Dodger
Ms Dynamite

(Above) Only 19 when he had his first UK number one in 2000, Craig David enjoyed a phenomenal rise to success. (Right) So Solid Crew, whose UK garage hits include 'Oh No' and '21 Seconds'.

New Jazz *Generation*

There are few who could have predicted the rise in popularity of today's jazz artists. A million miles from the image of traditional crooners in smoky bars, these young fresh faces have produced a string of top ten hits.

When sultry, 23-year-old singer/pianist Norah Jones swept the board at 2003's Grammy Awards, taking home five statuettes, she set in train the search for soundalikes – or, at least, similarly young, photogenic singers – to capture a slice of the "new jazz" market. Jones' surprise 18 million-selling debut album *Come Away With Me* swept the board in a manner reminiscent of Carole King's *Tapestry* some three decades earlier. Few realised that she was the daughter of world music great Ravi Shankar, but her dusky beauty as strategically featured on the cover was no hindrance to sales. Her 2004 follow-up, *Feels Like Home*, included canny covers of songs by Tom Waits, Townes Van Zandt and Duke Ellington, allowing listeners many ready-made reference points. She then upped her rock credibility by guesting on the Foo Fighters' *In Your Honour*, while Keith Richards dubbed her 'Billie Holiday reborn'.

My music is not about being groundbreaking ... it's about going back to basics and exploring the emotional side of music.
Katie Melua

Katie Melua, born in the former Soviet republic of Georgia but raised in Belfast and London, had a similar exotic lineage: her debut album *Call Off The Search* was released in November 2003 and knocked Jones off the top of the UK chart. Her Svengali was veteran Mike Batt, whose roles encompassed producer, songwriter (of exactly half the album), pianist and organist. Melua herself contributed two songs, the others being artful covers of numbers associated with John Mayall, Frank Sinatra, Nina Simone and Randy Newman. Melua's own 'Faraway Voice' paid tribute to Eva Cassidy, who died of cancer in 1996 – and it was BBC breakfast DJ Terry Wogan, Cassidy's champion, whose patronage of first single 'The Closest Thing To Crazy' gave Melua her break. Other female names to note included Renée Olstead, Jane Monheit, Diana Krall and Madeline Peroux.

Inspired by Eva Cassidy and Ella Fitzgerald, Katie Melua exploded onto the UK music scene with her unique mix of bluesy, folky and chilled sounds.

A Soul Diva Emerges

The arrival of 16-year-old prodigy Joss Stone on the scene in 2004 was cause for rejoicing – providing the listener didn't get too curious as to how the voice of an old-fashioned soul diva inhabited the body of a schoolgirl from Devon.

Stone's break came at age 12 when, as Joscelyn Stoker (her real name), she appeared on BBC TV's *Star For A Night*. A video found its way to a US record exec who paired her with Miami soul vet Betty Wright, and she was on her way. Albums *The Soul Sessions* (2004) and *Mind Body And Soul* (2005) sold by the (five) million, while a lengthy relationship with Beau Dozier, son of Motown tunesmith/producer Lamont, added credibility. She was the youngest performer at Live 8, singing on stage barefoot as is her custom.

Despite a multimillion-dollar contract promoting Gap, she refuses to exploit her looks by peeling off for cover pictures. She also avoids the showboating that can make Mariah Carey so tiresome, but will need to ring the changes to keep her many millions of fans on message. Given that she's started writing songs with Connor Reeves and Jonathan Shorten, her reliance on obscure pages from the classic soul songbook may yet diminish. Yet if her dramatic recasting of the White Stripes' 'Fell In Love With A Girl (Boy)' is anything to go by, she could sing a phone book and make it sound gospel.

Key Artists:
Norah Jones
Katie Melua
Joss Stone
Jamie Cullum

Joss Stone's debut album, The Soul Sessions, *established the teenager as possibly the most precociously gifted vocalist of her generation.*

Champion of *Cool*

The jazz-lite of Harry Connick Jr never made much of a dent in the British consciousness. But a home-grown champion of cool cropped up in 2003 in the shape of Jamie Cullum. Having financed one of two early albums on his credit card, the recent university graduate was understandably delighted when Universal Records offered him a contract that, with options, was worth more than £1 million.

He played the game with aplomb, serenading a lunch meeting at a major supermarket chain's HQ and touring local radio stations. The result was 2.5 million sales for *Twentysomething*, an album of all things to all men (and women). Overseen by George Benson and BB King producer Stewart Levine, it smoothly merged past and present by linking standards associated with Sinatra, Gene Kelly, Julie Andrews and Dinah Washington with contemporary material from Radiohead, Jimi Hendrix and Jeff Buckley – all delivered stylishly by the "David Beckham of jazz".

Having obediently toed the corporate line, the sticking point for Cullum came when he recorded a lamentable cover of 1960s pop classic 'Everlasting Love' to feature in the second Bridget Jones movie. "I never want to do anything like that ever again" he said, and recruited such hip names as Dan "the Automator" Nakamura, Guy Chambers and Ed Harcourt to add hipness to his mainstream appeal. The result was second major-label effort *Catching Tales* (2005). Cullum, a former punk, believes "you have more freedom in jazz than in punk, because in jazz you can play loudly and softly." Nevertheless, the new jazz generation aimed to seduce rather than shock.

Key Albums:

- *Call Off The Search* Katie Melua
- *Come Away With Me* Norah Jones
- *Mind Body And Soul* Joss Stone
- *Twentysomething* Jamie Cullum

Influenced by rock legends Kurt Cobain and Thom Yorke, Jamie Cullum has developed a sound that is an integration of jazz with rock and pop forms.

Rock *Introduction*

During the mid-1960s, America's military action in Vietnam was escalating out of control; students around the world were becoming more politically involved, civil rights and feminism were hot issues and the burgeoning youth movement was turning onto the effects of mind-bending drugs. Accordingly, certain strains of popular music melded attitude, experimentation and a social conscience, and the newly defined rock genre was the all-encompassing result.

By the second half of the decade, many record buyers regarded pop as a tame and dated form of escapism for oldies and prepubescent teens. Rock, by comparison, diverted some of its listeners through psychedelic, acid-drenched terrain, yet it also provided a heavy dose of realism, serving as an introspective outlet for a growing number of composer-performers, while expressing the concerns of those who were no longer prepared to look at the world through rose-tinted spectacles; Lennon-style granny glasses, perhaps, but ones whose lenses focussed on hard-hitting and sometimes controversial topics rather than the innocent themes of boy-loves-girl, boy-loses-girl.

Indeed, John Lennon and his fellow Beatles led the way among the handful of artists who made a successful transition from pop to rock. These included the Rolling Stones, the Yardbirds and the Who, who had already started out with a more aggressive rock sensibility.

"Pop music often tells you everything is OK, while rock music tells you that it's not OK, but you can change it." Bono

If one adds to them former folkies such as Bob Dylan and the Byrds, as well as emerging west coast acts like the Doors, Jefferson Airplane and the Grateful Dead, and it was clear that, echoing the musical revolution that had exploded on both sides of the Atlantic a decade earlier, rock was the new voice of youth.

The most incredible – and noisiest – drummer who ever lived, Keith Moon of the Who's talents were further fuelled by his diet of pills and alcohol and his larger-than-life "Moon the Loon" personality.

As the optimism of the Summer of Love gave way to late-1960s cynicism fueled by civil unrest, bloody anti-war riots and the hippy counterculture, so psychedelic and Eastern-tinged music were superseded by the vocal histrionics of Janis Joplin and Joe Cocker, as well as the blues-based hard rock of bands like Cream and the Jimi Hendrix Experience. Breaking with the pop tradition of producing catchy, radio- and jukebox-friendly three-minute songs, these acts indulged themselves and their followers with far lengthier numbers that were often distinguished by extended instrumental solos. In so doing, they paved the way for subsequent decades' purveyors of heavy metal, progressive, jam and arena rock.

Even though this was largely touted as music for the mind rather than for the body, it wasn't long before the record companies tried to match the popularity of so-called supergroups like Pink Floyd and Led Zeppelin. This was attempted with what many among the press and public perceived as the formulaic, watered-down product of "corporate" acts such as Boston, Kansas and Foreigner.

In a world where Alice Cooper and David Bowie were displaying a thespian-like theatricality, innovative psychedelia transmogrified into razzle-dazzle glam rock, people were pushing for bigger sounds onstage and in the studio and concerts were being produced on an increasingly grand scale. It was as if excess was being equated with success and it was also evident that, just 20 years after the likes of Elvis Presley, Little Richard and Jerry Lee Lewis had inspired teenagers, outraged parents and revolutionized Western culture, contemporary music had basically lost touch with its original *raison d'être*.

5 Top UK Rock Artists:	*5 Top US Rock Artists:*
1 Elvis Presley	1 Led Zeppelin
2 David Bowie	2 Eagles
3 Rod Stewart	3 Billy Joel
4 Status Quo	4 Pink Floyd
5 Paul McCartney/Wings	5 AC/DC

No longer all that exciting, liberating or even controversial, it promoted an instrumental virtuosity that was completely at odds with the easy-to-play, do-it-yourself appeal of early rock'n'roll. Then along came punk rock, and for a brief time, the entire scene was treated to the shakeup that it so badly needed.

Janis Joplin's incredible voice recalled the roaring blues vocals of Bessie Smith. Joplin was a big Bessie Smith fan and helped to buy her a gravestone in 1970, 33 years after she died in a car accident.

Between 1976 and 1978, the British punks in particular pumped up the aggression and devil-may-care attitude of their 1950s rock predecessors and quite literally spat in the face of authority, middle-class values and, just for the hell of it, one another. Drawing on often limited musical talents, outfits such as the Sex Pistols and the Clash channelled their anger and their energy into some blistering songs that once again helped to express the frustration and disenchantement of disaffected youth.

Punk was simply structured rock, and it had an invigorating effect on those who had grown tired of overblown, highly polished and, to their minds, soulless material. Nevertheless, almost as soon as the punk movement became an international phenomenon, it started to disintegrate, hijacked by kids from comfortable backgrounds who didn't have a clue about life on the streets, and undermined by some of the artists themselves, who embraced commercialism over independence when they signed with the major record labels.

Recalling how rock'n'roll had been usurped by parent-friendly pop at the start of the 1960s, the record companies attempted to broaden punk's appeal by associating numerous more mainstream acts with the genre, and the result was a watered-down hybrid that the media quickly dubbed "new wave". There were still traces of a surly attitude, and in the case of artists such as Elvis Costello there were clear musical skills, yet the spirit of punk had been laid to rest; for the next few years it would remain submerged while middle-of-the-road hard rockers and exotically-attired "new romantics" catered to the rapidly emerging MTV generation.

5 Top UK Rock Tracks:

1. 'Bohemian Rhapsody' Queen
2. 'Mull Of Kintyre' Wings
3. 'She Loves You' The Beatles
4. 'I Want To Hold Your Hand' The Beatles
5. 'Everything I Do (I Do It For You)' Bryan Adams

5 Top US Rock Tracks:

1. 'Hey Jude' The Beatles
2. 'Hound Dog' Elvis Presley
3. 'Another One Bites The Dust' Queen
4. 'Everything I Do (I Do It For You)' Bryan Adams
5. 'Love Me Tender' Elvis Presley

By the mid-1970s, rock had become sanitized and self-indulgent, as well as rather feminine. The punks stormed in and brought music back down to earth, with all the aggression and masculinity restored.

Once easy to categorize, rock music continued to fragment throughout the 1980s and 1990s, with heavy metal splitting off into subgenres ranging from thrash, speed and progressive to black, death and doom. At the same time, the alternative/indie tag served as a catch-all for a variety of styles, including that whose aesthetic – if not its unmelodic structure – was closest to that of vintage rock'n'roll, and which consequently had the most far-reaching impact on the latter-day rock scene.

Merging dissonant early 1970s heavy metal guitars with the hostile attitude, alienated lyrics and in-your-face music of punk, grunge first rose to prominence thanks to bands such as Soundgarden, Mudhoney and Green River, and then reached its apotheosis with the more melodic approach of Nirvana and Pearl Jam during the first half of the 1990s.

Still, history has a well-known habit of repeating itself, and in the case of the most successful rock music this is usually connected to financial considerations. For example, thanks to astute marketing and the cooperation of the media, Nirvana's name became synonymous with grunge, and when the band went the way of so many others by joining the mainstream, the genre did likewise, trading in its punk sensibilities for more widespread popularity.

At the beginning of the twenty-first century, rock music keeps subdividing and reinventing itself, continually absorbing new influences from other musical spheres. Yet partly due to this mutation process it also lacks freshness and vitality, and in the face of the cultural influence exerted by rap and hip hop, it no longer shapes opinions to the extent that it once did. Whether it can once again become the predominant force remains open to question.

5 Top UK Rock Albums:	*5 Top US Rock Albums:*
1 *Sgt Pepper's Lonely Hearts Club Band* The Beatles	1 *Eagles: Their Greatest Hits* Eagles
2 *(What's The Story) Morning Glory* Oasis	2 *The Wall* Pink Floyd
3 *Brothers In Arms* Dire Straits	3 *Untitled (IV)* Led Zeppelin
4 *Greatest Hits (Volume One)* Queen	4 *Back in Black* AC/DC
5 *Jagged Little Pill* Alanis Morisette	5 *The Beatles (The White Album)* The Beatles

Kurt Cobain, frontman of grunge pioneers Nirvana.

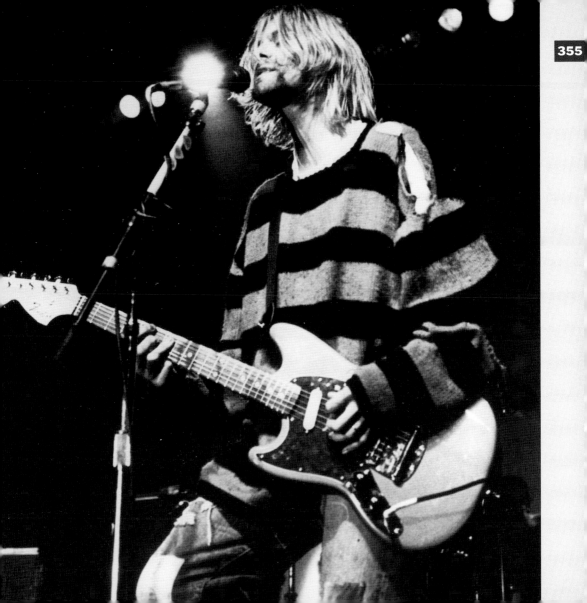

Blues *Rock*

Blues rock grew out of the British blues movement that started during the late-1950s, which was in turn developed in the 1960s. The Brits used more powerful amplification than their American counterparts, resulting in a harder, more imposing sound. Jimi Hendrix, Led Zeppelin and other artists developed this into a riff-oriented rock style.

Among the earliest blues rock bands were Cream, the Paul Butterfield Blues Band and Canned Heat. Cream were formed when Ginger Baker, drummer with the Graham Bond Organisation, decided to start his own band with guitarist Eric Clapton and bassist Jack Bruce. "Things were going badly with Graham," Baker told music journalist Chris Welch, "so I decided to get my own thing together. I was unaware that Eric had such a huge following. I just dug his playing, so I went to a Bluesbreakers gig in Oxford. In the interval Eric asked if I'd play a number with them, and it really took off! So I told him I was getting a band together and was wondering if he'd be interested. He said that he was and recommended Jack as the bass player."

"I had a Les Paul before Eric but I didn't have a Marshall. And when Eric got all of that together he was a delight to listen to. He really understood the blues." Jimmy Page

As all three band members were well known around the British blues circuit when they formed, each with a reputation for being a virtuoso on his respective instrument, Cream was, effectively, the first "supergroup". They were louder and more riff-oriented than previous blues-influenced bands, and their style incorporated extended solos – a regular feature for subsequent blues rockers. Despite only lasting for three years, Cream's first three albums, *Fresh Cream* (1966), *Disraeli Gears* (1967) and *Wheels Of Fire* (1967), are widely accepted as both blues rock classics and milestones in the birth of rock music. Influential American bands had also developed blues rock styles by the late 1960s: the Paul Butterfield Blues Band, with Mike Bloomfield and Elvin Bishop on guitars, and Canned Heat, a white blues band formed by singer Bob "The Bear" Hite and harmonica player Alan "Blind Owl" Wilson, were the most notable of these.

The brilliant Cream fused blues and rock.

A Dazzling *Showman*

Another key figure in the transition from blues to rock was the legendary Jimi Hendrix. Born Johnny Allen Hendrix in Seattle, USA, on 27 November 1942, he later changed his name to James (Jimi) Marshall Hendrix.

Influenced by legendary bluesmen such as Robert Johnson and B. B. King as a schoolboy, Hendrix taught himself to play guitar before working with musicians such as Little Richard in the early 1960s. His break came when Chas Chandler, the bassist with the Animals, heard him play in New York's Greenwich Village. Chas persuaded him to move over to London, where the Jimi Hendrix Experience was formed, with Jimi on guitar, Noel Redding on bass and Mitch Mitchell on drums.

Jimi was a dazzling showman, playing the guitar behind his head and with his teeth, but it was his extraordinary soloing and mastery of controlled feedback that set a new standard in electric blues lead guitar playing. As well as popularizing the use of feedback, he was a pioneering exponent of wah-wah. He widened the rock palette by his use of unusual intervals (e.g. the diminished fifths in the 'Purple Haze' intro) and chords (the so-called "Hendrix chord" of E7#9, also used in 'Purple Haze').

Key Artists:

Cream
The Paul Butterfield Blues Band
Canned Heat
Jimi Hendrix
Led Zeppelin

His best albums, *Are You Experienced?* (1967), *Axis: Bold As Love* (1968) and *Electric Ladyland* (1968), demonstrate that something seriously interesting was happening to the blues by the late-1960s. Although tragically he died in 1970, Jimi was to influence countless blues and rock players for many years to come.

Jimi Hendrix invented a new sonic vocabulary for the electric guitar, revolutionizing its use forever.

Broadening *Out*

By the end of the 1960s, blues rock began to diversify into heavy metal in the UK and southern blues rock in the US. Led Zeppelin was, perhaps, the first band to be described as heavy metal, but the group's blues roots are apparent in all of its recordings, including the hugely popular *Led Zeppelin II* (1969) and *Led Zeppelin IV* (1971) albums.

The band's guitarist, Jimmy Page, grew up listening to blues and rock'n'roll recordings, but one of his biggest influences was hearing Eric Clapton's Gibson Les Paul guitar through a cranked-up Marshall amp at a Bluesbreakers gig. "I had a Les Paul before Eric but I didn't have a Marshall," Page recalled. "And when Eric got all of that together he was a delight to listen to. He really understood the blues."

Meanwhile, in the States, the Allman Brothers Band was fusing electric blues with country and folk elements, to form what is now known as "southern rock". Albums such as *The Allman Brothers Band* (1969), *Idlewild South* (1970) and *Live At The Fillmore East* (1971) paved the way for a whole family of southern rock bands, including Lynyrd Skynyrd and Black Oak Arkansas. ZZ Top, a trio from Texas, also emerged out of the blues rock scene. Led by the bearded Billy Gibbons (guitar, vocals) and Dusty Hill (bass, vocals), the trio developed their own style of music, which became hugely popular in the 1970s and 1980s.

Key Tracks:
'On The Road Again' Canned Heat
'Stairway To Heaven' Led Zeppelin
'Sunshine Of Your Love' Cream
'The Burning Of The Midnight Lamp' Jimi Hendrix

Meanwhile, over in the UK, the group Free inspired generations of British blues rockers with major hits like 'All Right Now' (1970) and 'Wishing Well' (1973). Many other notable blues rock artists have since appeared on both sides of the Atlantic, including Bernard Allison, Bonnie Raitt, Walter Trout, Dave Hole and Ronnie Earl.

Led Zeppelin star Jimmy Page initially refused to join his first band, the Yardbirds, thinking he would make more money as a session musician.

British *Blues*

British blues was born when British musicians attempted to emulate Mississippi and Chicago bluesmen during the 1960s. Led by Eric Clapton and the Rolling Stones, these musicians copied the styles of Big Bill Broonzy, Muddy Waters, Howlin' Wolf and B. B. King, and, aided by powerful amplifiers, developed a sound of their own.

In the early 1950s, the first American blues musician to appear in England was Big Bill Broonzy. Although he was a popular, Chicago-style bluesman, his UK performances consisted of acoustic folk blues and protest songs. It was Muddy Waters' visit to the country in 1958 that really sparked off the beginning of the British blues movement. Muddy played with an electric, solid-body Fender guitar, backed by Chris Barber's English blues group featuring guitarist Alexis Korner and blues harpist Cyril Davies. They played at a volume that shocked folk purists, but delighted a growing younger audience.

"I spent most of my teens and early twenties studying the blues – the geography of it and the chronology of it, as well as how to play it."
Eric Clapton

Inspiration for a New Generation

After Muddy's tour, Korner and Davies pursued their musical ambitions even more passionately and formed Blues Incorporated, the first of the British blues bands. By 1962, the group had a regular slot at London's Marquee Club and a recording contract with Decca. Blues Incorporated inspired a younger generation of musicians, who then formed the three most influential British blues bands: John Mayall's Bluesbreakers featuring Eric Clapton, the Rolling Stones and the original Fleetwood Mac, with Peter Green. Clapton was a phenomenon with the Bluesbreakers – he turned his amp up to gig volume for recordings and obtained a more modern electric sound that influenced the likes of Jimi Hendrix and also Jimmy Page, who went on to form Led Zeppelin.

Alexis Korner was the main man behind the 1960s British blues scene.

Sex, Drugs and *Rock'n'Roll*

The Rolling Stones were perceived to be the definitive British blues band. They made a stream of hit records during the mid-1960s, including a chart-topping version of Willie Dixon's 'Little Red Rooster' (1964). They also covered songs by Muddy Waters and Howlin' Wolf, even insisting that Howlin' was a featured guest at a special US appearance. Their legendary "sex, drugs and rock'n'roll" lifestyle contrasted sharply with the Beatles' squeaky-clean image during the 1960s.

By 1966, British blues was in full flight: the legendary *John Mayall's Bluesbreakers With Eric Clapton* album was released that year. The inclusion of Eric Clapton on this album, fresh from the Yardbirds, helped British blues to reach a wider audience. Bands such as Fleetwood Mac, the Yardbirds (with Jeff Beck) and Ten Years After (with Alvin Lee) were forming, and the Animals started to develop their inimitable brand of blues pop.

Key Artists:
John Mayall's Bluesbreakers
The Rolling Stones
Blues Incorporated
Eric Clapton

By the end of the decade, the British blues movement was carried back across to the United States, where it was reabsorbed by larger audiences than the original Chicago and Mississippi bluesmen had enjoyed. The success of the British bands also encouraged early American blues rock bands such as the Allman Brothers and ZZ Top, who had already developed their own unique styles.

Although British blues is now seen by many as an early step in the conversion of blues into rock and heavy metal, it was a distinct style in its own right. Even today, musicians such as John Mayall, Eric Clapton and Aynsley Lister are waving the British blues flag.

The legendary John Mayall's Bluesbreakers With Eric Clapton *album was perhaps the most influential recording in the history of British rock guitar.*

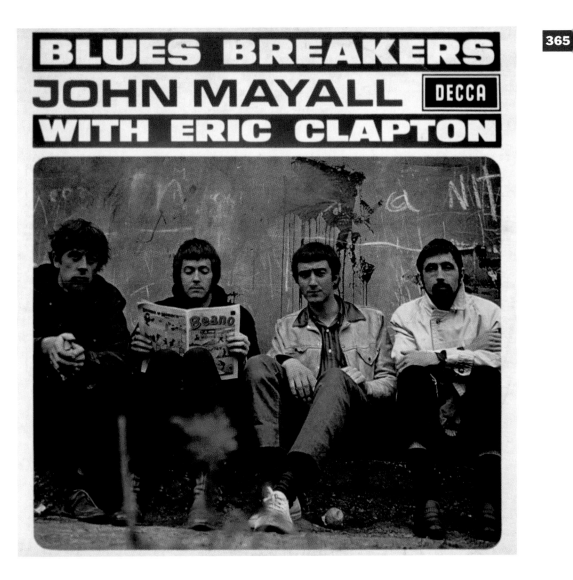

Country *Rock*

In terms of influences and origins, country and rock'n'roll draw so closely from the same antecedents that they are practically musical first cousins: branches from the same tree that share the same basic instrumentation of guitar, bass and drums.

Two of country music's greatest practitioners, Johnny Cash and Jerry Lee Lewis, launched their careers in the mid-1950s as part of the rock'n'roll/rockabilly explosion that took place at Sam Phillips' Sun Studios in Memphis. Even Elvis Presley was billed as a country singer and was a regular performer on Louisiana Hayride, a live country music radio extravaganza, broadcast from Shreveport.

An early harbinger of the modern country rock movement was Bob Dylan, who journeyed to Nashville in the mid- and late-1960s to record a trio of albums – *Blonde On Blonde*, *John Wesley Harding* and *Nashville Skyline*. For these projects, Dylan utilized "A Team" Music Row session musicians to underpin his dense and surreal lyrics with austere guitar- and steel guitar-driven country arrangements. Dylan's country rock explorations gave added impetus to a vital country rock movement that, by the late-1960s, was underway in southern California, spearheaded by pioneering bands like the Byrds, the Flying Burrito Brothers and Poco.

"So we tried the combination of putting country music, which was our roots, and rock'n'roll together to try to form something new." Jim Messina

The California Country Rock Explosion

These southern California bands grew out of a generation of young musicians who had been raised on rock'n'roll, but were just as influenced and enthralled by the bedrock country sounds of honky tonkers like Hank Williams, Merle Haggard and Buck Owens and the vintage bluegrass and western swing of artists like Bill Monroe and Bob Wills. In various ways, these California bands, like almost none before, melded the 1960s spirit of counter-cultural rebelliousness and the youthful hubris of rock'n'roll with the more down-home attitudes, arrangements and repertoires of country music.

Bob Dylan's 1969 album Nashville Skyline *saw the sometime-protest singer in a more mellow mood. Dylan's singing voice on the album is softer than his usual rasping tone and the songs are short and sweet, with simple lyrics.*

Californian Country *Rock*

A central figure in the California country rock scene was Gram Parsons, a Florida-born, Harvard University dropout and former teenage rock'n'roller. By the time Parsons joined the Byrds in late 1967, he was already resolutely pursuing a musical vision that sought a seamless fusion of acoustic rock- and blues-tinged country honky tonk into an elusive sound that he described as "cosmic American music".

Parsons found a country music-loving kindred spirit in California-born singer and multi-instrumentalist Chris Hillman, who was the Byrds' bass player at the time. Under Parsons' and Hillman's influence, the band immersed itself in a country idiom. Journeying to Nashville, the Byrds worked with Music Row session pickers on tracks that culminated in their 1968 album *Sweetheart Of The Rodeo*, a country rock landmark. Country music critic and historian Geoffrey Himes hailed the album as "perhaps the most influential alternative country album ever made...". Shortly after its release, Parsons and Hillman left the Byrds and formed the Flying Burrito Brothers, yet another cornerstone country rock ensemble. The Burrito Brothers' 1969 *Gilded Palace Of Sin*, like *Sweetheart Of The Rodeo*, masterfully blended country roots with rock'n'roll brio, and is still considered a country rock classic.

Key Artists:

Bob Dylan
Gram Parsons
Chris Hillman
The Byrds
The Flying Burrito Brothers

Parsons later struck out on his own and, in the early 1970s, recorded a pair of highly influential solo albums, *GP* and *Grievous Angel*, which featured his then-musical protégé Emmylou Harris. Chris Hillman, for his part, would resurface on the country scene in the late-1980s in the Desert Rose Band. Though the Desert Rose Band's records were heavily steeped in a traditional and bluegrass-flavoured harmony sound, intimations of the glorious 1970s southern California country rock era seemed to echo in every groove.

Poco, another influential California country rock ensemble included at various times both future members of the Eagles and former members of Buffalo Springfield. The band forged its own rousing country rock blending, in which Clapton- and Hendrix-style electric lead guitar runs were often thrillingly transposed on Rusty Young's electrified pedal steel guitar.

Gram Parsons was arguably the most influential figure on the countrry rock scene, inspiring everyone from the Rolling Stones to the Eagles. Parsons died tragically young from a drink and drugs overdose, aged 26.

Closing the Cultural *Gap*

It was the Eagles, including Poco alumni Randy Meisner and Timothy Schmit, with their smooth, soft rock/country-pop sound whose influence on modern country has been most widely felt and persistent. During the 1980s and 1990s there seemed to be at least a half-dozen different Nashville-based male harmony bands that were masterfully emulating the early Eagles' soft country rock groove.

In 1972, California-based country rock group the Nitty Gritty Dirt Band also played an important part in closing the cultural gap between country and rock audiences, when they came to Nashville and recorded the landmark LP *Will The Circle Be Unbroken*. This ambitious three-record set featured the Dirt Band in various traditional settings with country and bluegrass masters like Roy Acuff, Mother Maybelle Carter and Earl Scruggs.

Key Albums:

Blond On Blond Bob Dylan
Gilded Palace Of Sin The Flying Burrito Brothers
Nashville Skyline Bob Dylan
Sweetheart Of The Rodeo The Byrds

The 1970s saw the rise of a handful of Nashville-based country rockers like former Music Row session man Charlie Daniels. Hank Williams Jr., on the strength of landmark country boogie albums like *Hank Williams Jr. And Friends* and *Family Tradition*, won a huge national following of rowdy, youthful rock fans that were already tuned in to the music of formative southern rock bands like the Allman Brothers and Lynyrd Skynyrd. Williams, the son of honky tonk legend Hank Williams Sr., was actually more stylistically aligned with these formative 1970s southern rock ensembles than he was with his country contemporaries. While his records always contained elements of country, his live concerts, more often than not, were pure, eardrum-splitting hard rock.

In the 1980s, Texas singer-songwriters like Joe Ely and Steve Earle earned cult followings with muscular styles that incorporated the intensity of rock'n'roll with the twang and grittiness of Texas-style honky tonk. Also in the early 1980s a handful of Nashville bands like Jason & the Scorchers – once described as "non-compromising rock'n'rollers with hillbilly hearts" – pioneered a frenzied strain of punk country rock that foreshadowed the alt. country movement of the 1990s.

The Nitty Gritty Dirt Band started out jamming together in the 1960s, influenced by folk and rock'n'roll. As they delved more deeply into their musical heritage, they discovered bluegrass music, which began to appear in their own repertoire.

Folk *Rock*

**For many people in the 1960s, folk was equated with acoustic music or even unaccompanied music –
and electric guitars were the great taboo. The sense of propriety among the revivalists of the time
made them fiercely protective of the music, determined to preserve its purity in the face of attack
from the evil forces of pop. Many saw the electric guitar as the enemy.**

That is why Pete Seeger is said to have tried to pull the plug on Bob Dylan during his infamous
performance at the 1965 Newport Folk Festival with members of the electric Paul Butterfield Blues
Band. In England, the cry of "Judas" was heard when he repeated the formula. In essence, though,
the first rumblings of a new fusion of folk and rock came not from the hardcore folk fraternity, but
from rock bands seeking a fresh ideology. There had long been a course of great blues artists
interpreted by young white guys, and with spectacular results from the likes of Elvis, the Rolling Stones
and the Yardbirds, among others. As rock music diversified in the late-1960s, it was not unnatural for
young musicians to seek to develop what they saw as a rigid format for playing folk music.

*"To me it seemed a very natural and exciting
experiment for a rock band to explore its own
culture of folk music."* Ashley Hutchings

Dylan's move towards rock opened the doors.
Subsequently, when the Byrds began to have hits
with Dylan songs, and bands such as Jefferson
Airplane emerged with a strong folk blues flavour,
it was obvious that the times were indeed a-
changin'. In England, Fairport Convention modelled themselves on Jefferson Airplane, but it led them
to the realization that there was a rich treasury of indigenous music in their own backyard. It was the
bass player Ashley Hutchings who really led Fairport Convention's drive into traditional music, with the
landmark album *Liege & Lief*. The record was hailed as the first British folk rock album, attracting a new
audience to both the band and the traditional music they were experimenting with, although it did lead
to dissension in the ranks. The two obvious front members of the band, Sandy Denny and Richard
Thompson, were both keen to develop their own songwriting rather than pursue the traditional path.
Ultimately, this rift resulted in the departure of Denny and Thompson, as well as Ashley Hutchings.

*Fairport Convention, who have had a phemomenal number of changes in their line-up over the years, performed revved up versions of traditional
folk songs from the British Isles to great critical acclaim.*

A Blend of Ancient and *Modern*

Ashley Hutchings, former member of Fairport Convention, went on to become the seminal figure in English folk rock, forming Steeleye Span with two young stalwarts of the folk club scene, Maddy Prior and Tim Hart. When Martin Carthy, the most admired young revival singer on the scene, joined too, a lot of hardcore purists had to revise their attitudes towards the folk rock fusion.

Steeleye, named after a character in the traditional song 'Horkstow Grange', released a second album, *Please To See The King*, a bold, seminal blend of ancient and modern that genuinely captured the spirit of traditional songs in a modern format. It caught the imagination of the public, too, and despite changes of personnel along the way (neither Hutchings nor Carthy were to stay long), Steeleye became an enduringly successful outfit. They not only achieved the seemingly impossible feat of making folk music hot again, but sold out tours all over the world and even enjoyed some unlikely hit singles, notably with a song in Latin, 'Gaudete', and a feelgood version of the traditional standard 'All Around My Hat'. The singer Maddy Prior, like Martin Carthy, was later awarded the MBE.

While Steeleye was achieving pop success, Ashley Hutchings was experimenting ever more deeply with traditional song and dance through numerous incarnations of the Albion Band. He achieved his most spectacular results with his then-wife, Shirley Collins, singing on the classic *No Roses* album, which featured most of the leading British folk musicians of the day. Hutchings also masterminded *Morris On* and (with John Kirkpatrick) *The Compleat Dancing Master*, early 1970s albums stimulating a rebirth of dance tunes. At one point, the Albion Band even toured with a morris-dancing side in tow.

Key Artists:

The Byrds
Fairport Convention
Steeleye Span
Albion Country Band

One of the most successful and enduring British folk rock groups in the 1970s was Steeleye Span, whose lead singer Maddy Prior's impressive vocals helped promote the group's success.

A Lasting *Legacy*

The early success of folk rock had a profound effect on folk music. For one, it triggered the emergence of a host of Steeleye/Fairport/Albion imitators. Few of them brought anything new to the party, however, apart from Bob and Carole Pegg's Mr Fox (playing contemporary songs written in a traditional style), Five Hand Reel (with Dick Gaughan on lead vocal and electric guitar) and the Albion offshoot Home Service, gloriously fronted by two of the scene's most colourful characters and best songwriters, John Tams and Bill Caddick.

By the 1980s, the record industry and the media had lost interest, and hard economics prevented many folk rock outfits from surfacing. The one group to buck the trend has been the Oyster Band (later Oysterband), which emerged from the folk dance circuit to achieve credibility and success as folk rockers well versed in traditional music, but using it as a launch pad for their own highly charged, often political material.

But more than that, folk rock had a lasting legacy with a new generation familiar with the music. The long-term result is that its influence has spread far and wide, and continues to do so. In 1970, rock band Traffic played an elaborate arrangement of the trad song 'John Barleycorn', while other iconic artists – such as Robert Plant and Jimmy Page of Led Zeppelin, Mike Oldfield and Jethro Tull – have drawn on elements of the tradition.

Key Albums:

Liege & Lief Fairport Convention
No Roses Albion Country Band
Please To See The King Steeleye Span

More recently, the Northumbrian piper Kathryn Tickell has found herself playing on records by Sting, and nobody bats an eyelid when they hear bass, drums and electric guitar on a folk record. Or, more significantly, a traditional song or folk arrangement creeping into a rock record.

Jethro Tull's sound incorporated influences of classical, folk, ethnic and jazz music, as heard on their 1969 album Stand Up.

Hard *Rock*

Hard rock is a cross between rock'n'roll and blues, but played louder – everything on "11" or "one louder", as guitarist Nigel Tufnell in spoof rock band Spinal Tap would say. The electric guitar is the prominent instrument in hard rock, and most hard rock songs are based on a guitar "riff".

The classic example of a hard rock guitar riff is the "dur, dur, dur..." beginning of Deep Purple's 'Smoke On The Water' from *Machine Head* (1972) – gloriously simple and yet spectacularly effective and memorable. A "riff" is a short series of notes, often in a low register, repeated several times at the beginning of a song and then repeated several times later in the song.

"Every great rock song has a great riff, be it a single-note melody or a chordal-based sequence, and that's probably what makes it a great song."
Billy Corgan, Smashing Pumpkins

The first hard rock bands such as the Jimi Hendrix Experience, Cream and Led Zeppelin, emerged at the end of the 1960s. It is difficult to overestimate the contribution Jimi Hendrix made to rock music in general and hard rock in particular by revolutionizing the electric guitar, inventing a whole new sonic vocabulary including harnessing distortion and feedback for musical effect, as can be heard in 'Foxy Lady' from *Are You Experienced?* (1967). Cream, featuring Eric Clapton on guitar after he left John Mayall's Bluesbreakers, made onstage jamming for rock musicians a viable proposition, as can be heard in their rollercoaster ride through Robert Johnson's 'Crossroads' from *Wheels Of Fire* (1968), and many hard rock bands place an importance on instrumental prowess.

Formed by guitarist Jimmy Page, Led Zeppelin demonstrate that hard rock is a broader arena than its critics would have listeners believe. Their first album *Led Zeppelin* (1969) is heavily blues-based, *Led Zeppelin II* (1969) includes the bombastic 'Whole Lotta Love' which, along with Black Sabbath, was heavily influential on the heavy metal style. *Led Zeppelin III* (1970) shows a folky, acoustic side, and *Led Zeppelin IV* (1971) includes the famous 'Stairway To Heaven', one of the band's most ambitious and popular songs.

Originally planning to call themselves the New Yardbirds, Led Zeppelin's name came from either Keith Moon or John Entwistle, who commented that the band's new, raw sound would go down like a "lead zeppelin".

Swagger

Many listeners may regard hard rock and heavy metal as interchangeable, and while there is an overlap there are also significant distinctions. Hard rock is generally blues-based and sometimes played with a swing feel or at least a certain blues-derived "swagger", whereas heavy metal, as inspired by the Zeppelin's 'Whole Lotta Love' and Black Sabbath, is far less blues-based and is more brutal.

British band Queen took hard rock to a new level of sophistication with the semi-operatic 'Bohemian Rhapsody' from *A Night At The Opera* (1975), which includes a long multi-tracked vocal section which the band were understandably unable to recreate live, followed by a pummelling riff section – contrast between delicate interludes and fortissimo ("as loud as possible") riffing is popular in hard rock bands. It certainly cannot be termed as subtle ...

Interest in hard rock declined in the mid-70s as the scene became rather stale and punk rock and new wave captured listeners' attention, but was rejuvenated by American band Van Halen and their debut album Van Halen I (1978). Guitarist Eddie Van Halen, who played with an enthusiasm, aggression, energy and showbiz panache lacking in many hard rock bands, is credited with re-inventing the electric guitar vocabulary. Eddie Van Halen started on drums, with his guitarist brother Alex, until they switched instruments. Their band, with David Lee Roth on vocals and Michael Anthony on bass, was spotted by Gene Simmons of Kiss.

Key Artists:

Deep Purple
Jimi Hendrix Experience
Cream
Led Zeppelin
Queen

Queen
A Night At The Opera

(Right) Eddie Van Halen of US rock band Van Halen. (Above) Queen's outstanding fourth studio album A Night At The Opera *(1975) has recently been certified triple platinum in the US.*

Sex and Drugs and *Rock'n'Roll*

Just as much of the music is bombastic and larger than life, many hard rock musicians enjoy a lifestyle of excess – until it kills them that is. Ironically, AC/DC came back stronger than ever after the death of their singer Bon Scott, with Back In Black (1980).

Aerosmith seemed destined for the "where are they now?" file after the ravages of drugs sidetracked their career – singer Steve Tyler survived being pronounced dead – but a collaboration with rappers Run-DMC on 'Walk This Way' in 1986 introduced them to a new generation, followed up by the highly successful *Pump* (1989).

And speaking of mad, bad and dangerous to know, Guns 'n' Roses' *Appetite For Destruction* (1987) drew on 1970s rock but played with a punk attitude, making them an exciting proposition to younger listeners who had missed hard rock the first time around.

Key Tracks:

'Bohemian Rhapsody' Queen
'Crossroads' Cream
'Foxy Lady' Jimi Hendrix Experience
'Smoke On The Water' Deep Purple
'Stairway To Heaven' Led Zeppelin

Partly because many hard rock musicians take their music and craft seriously, many hard rock bands and musicians have enjoyed long careers; at the turn of the millennium, Deep Purple, Eric Clapton from Cream, Jimmy Page and Robert Plant from Led Zeppelin, Aerosmith and AC/DC were still enjoying productive careers. This "old guard" of hard rock has been joined by newer bands such as Metallica and Pearl Jam, who made the crossover from thrash metal and grunge respectively.

Steve Tyler of Aerosmith in a classic image of the 1970s rock star en route to the next gig. Aerosmith's film and soundtrack work has helped to keep them in the charts since their late-1980s comeback.

Psychedelic *Rock*

Several musical movements are associated either directly or indirectly with a specific recreational drug or drugs; psychedelic rock went a step further, and was practically born out of LSD or acid, as well as other hallucinogens including peyote, mescaline and even marijuana.

Much psychedelic rock attempts to recreate the mind expanding and awareness-enlarging sensations of an acid trip – the counter-culture of the 1960s put great emphasis on expanding one's mind through mind-altering drugs. So, musicians made use of the burgeoning new studio technology available and used effects such as the fuzzbox on guitars and exotic instruments such as the sitar, and broke away from traditional song structures of intro, verse, chorus, verse, chorus, middle eight, verse, final chorus. They also looked further afield for inspiration and forms of expression, to jazz or Indian music, for example. The Beatles' George Harrison became interested in the sitar that was used for an Indian restaurant scene in the Beatles film *Help!*, which led to the band becoming interested in Eastern culture.

"The psychedelic ethic ... runs through the musical mainstream in a still current. Musical ideas are passed from group to group like a joint."
Richard Goldstein

The Yardbirds made a tentative exploration of this area with their 'Heart Full Of Soul' single in 1965. In an effort to expand their sound and blend east and west in a kind of cross-cultural melting pot, the band drafted in a sitar player to play the song's instrumental hook. Unfortunately, the hapless sitar player was so used to playing complex eastern rhythms that he couldn't get the hang of the basic rock beat, so guitarist Jeff Beck imitated the sound of the sitar with a fuzzbox.

This anecdote neatly illustrates the problem with some psychedelic rock – mixing disparate musical elements may sound fine on paper, but in practice it might not work. Consequently, when it works psychedelic rock can represent rock music at its most ambitious and breathtaking, but when it doesn't work it can appear incompetent, over-ambitious and foolhardy.

Artwork played an important role in psychedelic rock, with record sleeves and concert posters becoming increasingly colourful and ornate. This example is a poster for the 1967 Monterey Pop Festival.

Drug-Induced *Sounds*

One of the first psychedelic records, the Byrds' 'Eight Miles High' (1966), saw the band's guitarist Roger McGuinn attempting to emulate jazz saxophonist John Coltrane and also displaying an Indian influence in his rambling improvisation. The lyrics were assumed to be drug-inspired – an accusation often aimed at the psychedelic bands – although the Byrds denied this.

John Lennon attempted to recreate the mood of an LSD trip on the Beatles' 'Tomorrow Never Knows' from *Revolver* (1966), with multiple tape loops, a processed lead vocal, backwards guitar solo and lyrics inspired by LSD guru Timothy Leary and *The Tibetan Book of the Dead*; George Harrison contributed a sitar part. The Rolling Stones' 'Paint It Black' single (1966) used a sitar to great effect and their fleeting psychedelic incarnation culminated in *Their Satanic Majesties Request* (1967).

The Summer of Love

1967, the so-called "Summer of Love", was an important year for psychedelic rock in America and Britain. In the US, the Doors released their self-titled debut album; singer Jim Morrison's highly poetic lyrics, keyboard player Ray Manzarek's hypnotic organ and the flamenco-trained guitarist Robbie Kreiger's improvizations proved an intoxicating mix. Fellow Americans Jefferson Airplane's *Surrealistic Pillow* featured 'White Rabbit' with its *Alice In Wonderland*-like lyrics and flamenco-influenced, moody introduction. Led by Arthur Lee, Love produced a classic in 1967's *Forever Changes*, whose highlights included the classic 'Alone Again Or'; the album was not commercially successful, but it is regularly acclaimed by critics.

Key Artists:
The Yardbirds
The Byrds
The Beatles
The Rolling Stones
The Doors

Love's Forever Changes is a psychedelic masterpiece, with inspired arrangements and delicious, dark undertones.

The Psychedelic *Sound*

On the other side of the Atlantic, Pink Floyd's debut album, *The Piper At The Gates Of Dawn* revealed an English sense of whimsy on 'Bike', spacey, sci-fi rock on 'Astronomy Domine' and a taste for avant-garde experimentation on 'Interstellar Overdrive'. The Move captured the psychedelia of London's underground scene with 'I Can Hear the Grass Grow', conveying the experience of a marijuana high.

The Beatles embraced the psychedelic spirit of the times on *Sgt Pepper's Lonely Hearts Club Band*, as exemplified in 'Lucy In The Sky With Diamonds' – John Lennon denied that the song was about LSD, but the dreamy and surreal lyrics clearly reflect the LSD experience, whether intentional or not. For 'A Day In The Life' on the same album, a full symphony orchestra was asked to start from each musician's lowest note, then play up to their highest note in a non-synchronized manner in an attempt to simulate the effect of a drug rush. One of the longest lasting psychedelic bands was the Grateful Dead. Improvization was a big part of the Dead's musical make-up, as can be heard on the *Live/Dead* album (1969) which features 'Dark Star', a song never performed the same way twice.

Overall, psychedelic rock was a relatively short-lived phenomenon with bands either splitting up or moving onto new musical territory such as the Byrds, who moved onto country rock, and Pink Floyd who succeeded in making progressive rock commercially successful.

Psychedelic rock was largely a 1960s phenomenon, although in Britain Jason Pearce led a valiant one-man crusade for its revival in the late-1980s and 1990s, first with the ramshackle Spaceman 3, whose chaotic and overwhelming blend of neopsychedelia can be heard on *Playing With Fire* (1989), then as the leader of Spiritualized with the altogether more accomplished and critically acclaimed *Ladies And Gentlemen We Are Floating In Space* (1997). Psychedelic rock's most notable revival, however, occurred with the rise in popularity in the 1990s of trance, a style of dance music of which it is considered to be a forerunner.

Key Tracks:

'Eight Miles High' The Byrds
'Heart Full Of Soul' The Yardbirds
'Light My Fire' The Doors
'Lucy In The Sky With Diamonds' The Beatles
'Paint It Black' The Rolling Stones

George Harrison's forays into Indian music added another exotic flavour to psychedelic music. He is shown here with Ravi Shankar, who taught him the rudiments of sitar playing.

Southern *Rock*

Taking its lead from the loud blues rock of late-1960s bands such as Cream and the Grateful Dead, southern rock materialized with the release of the Allman Brothers Band's eponymous 1969 debut album, which embellished a fusion of rock'n'roll, blues, country and jazz with a distinct good ol' boy edge from directly below the Mason-Dixon Line.

Natives of Macon, Georgia, the Allmans always resisted the southern rock label. The band underwent many personnel changes over the years, the first of these being due to the motorcyle death of guitarist Duane Allman in October 1971, and that of bass player Berry Oakley just over a year later. Before Duane's fatal accident, through the *Idlewild South* and *Live at the Fillmore East* albums, he and fellow lead guitarist Dickey Betts traded solos with keyboardist/vocalist Gregg Allman in a balanced line-up that enhanced its blues rock performances with sophisticated jazz structures and classical techniques. Following Duane's death midway through the recording of the *Eat A Peach* album, Betts assumed all of the lead guitar duties and, while also emerging as a singer and songwriter, he led the band in a more laid-back, country-oriented direction, evident on 1973's, *Brothers And Sisters*.

Hereafter, a combination of internal disputes and drink and drug-related problems would contribute to the Allman Brothers' diminishing accomplishments throughout the remainder of the decade. Nevertheless, the band had changed the musical map of America, and in so doing it had also paved the way for numerous other southern rock acts to enjoy mainstream success.

"Rock'n'roll was born in the South, so southern rock is like saying rock rock."
Gregg Allman

Ironically however, the band who brought the southern rock sound closest to the mainstream were a Californian outfit, Creedence Clearwater Revival. Their stomping, bayou-influenced rock is encapsulated in hits such as 'Proud Mary' and the ubiquitous 'Bad Moon Rising', which has since become a standard in every amateur band's repertoire.

One of the defining bands of the southern rock sound, the Allman Brothers.

The Success of *Skynyrd*

The definitive southern rock outfit, Jacksonville, Florida natives Lynyrd Skynyrd boasted a heavy blues rock sound, the songwriting talents of lead singer Ronnie Van Zant, and the three-pronged guitar formation of Allen Collins, Gary Rossington and Ed King that featured prominently on the band's first hit song, 'Freebird', a tribute to the late, lamented Duane Allman.

In 1974, following a support slot on the Who's *Quadrophenia* tour, Skynyrd achieved a multi-platinum breakthrough with its sophomore album, *Second Helping*, which spawned the hit single 'Sweet Home Alabama' and helped to cement the group's credentials both in the studio and on the road.

Van Zant was flowering as a composer and lyricist, yet tragedy struck in October 1977 when, just three days after the release of the band's *Street Survivors* album, he was killed in a plane crash en route to Baton Rouge, Louisiana. The accident also claimed backing vocalist Cassie Gaines and her brother Steve, who had joined Skynyrd as a guitarist following Ed King's departure.

Key Artists:

The Allman Brothers Band
Creedence Clearwater Revival
Lynyrd Skynyrd

Like the Allman Brothers Band, Lynyrd Skynyrd broke up and subsequently reformed with a revamped line-up. Despite the emergence of outfits such as the Georgia Satellites, the Black Crowes, Widespread Panic and the Dave Matthews Band during the 1980s and 1990s, the halcyon days of southern rock were over having, never recovered from the decimation of its two leading lights.

Southern rock band Lynyrd Skynyrd fused the overdriven power of blues-rock with a rebellious southern image.

Prog Rock

"To boldly go where no band has gone before ..." could have been the motto of the progressive rock bands, taking rock music to places it had never been in terms of harmony and structure. They tend to favour long songs with lengthy instrumentals, guitar and keyboards being the foremost instruments, with an emphasis on instrumental dexterity and virtuosity.

Many prog rock songs have different sections or parts, like a classical symphony. For example, Yes's 'Starship Trooper' from *The Yes Album* (1971) has three different sections – Life Seeker, Disillusion and Würm. Essentially, prog rock is music of the mind rather than music of the body.

Inspired by the psychedelic scene of the late-1960s, bands such as the Nice, the Moody Blues and Procol Harum started writing a strain of music influenced by classical and symphonic sounds and musical structures, producing a form of symphonic rock which laid the foundation for progressive rock. This can be heard in Procul Harum's debut single and best-known song, 'A Whiter Shade of Pale' (1967) in which the chord progression was influenced by J. S. Bach.

"Historically musicians have felt real hurt if the audience expressed displeasure. We didn't do that. We told the audience to get f****d."
Frank Zappa

The late-1960s saw the beginnings of two of the longest lasting progressive rock bands, King Crimson and Yes, who took instrumental virtuosity and songwriting structures to new levels. King Crimson's stunning debut *In The Court Of The Crimson King* (1969), which includes their trademark song '21st Century Schizoid Man', not only has the instrumental prowess associated with prog rock, but also rocks harder than the other prog rockers. After distinctly psychedelic beginnings, Yes forged their unique identity on *Close To The Edge* (1972), with album side length "suites" enabling all five band members to flex their musical muscles.

King Crimson, whose sound was described by one critic as "organized anarchy". Constant personnel changes within the band have left Robert Fripp (second from left) as the only original member.

Theatrical and *Grandiose*

Some prog rockers put on theatrical stage shows, and Genesis' then-lead singer Peter Gabriel would wear bizarre costumes as a visual extension of the music. Genesis made the transition to mainstream rock/pop band in the 1980s, but in the early 1970s they were a prog rock band, as can be heard on *Foxtrot* (1972).

Three already established musicians, Emerson, Lake and Palmer formed the first prog rock "supergroup" (formed by members who had already made a name for themselves in other groups) and their reworking of Mussorgsky's *Pictures at an Exhibition* (1972) took the combination of classical and rock to its logical extreme with a band reworking a piece of classical music.

Key Artists:

Procol Harum
The Moody Blues
Yes
King Crimson
Pink Floyd

Pink Floyd started their career as a psychedelic band, then after songwriter Syd Barrett left they moved more towards progressive rock, although Barrett's replacement David Gilmour brought a distinct blues influence. Pink Floyd managed to make prog rock more accessible with their best-selling album *Dark Side of the Moon* (1973), curbing the excesses of the genre.

To their critics, the prog rockers were overblown and self-indulgent, as epitomized by Yes's notorious triple concept album *Tales Of Topographic Oceans* (1974), or quite simply BOFs ("boring old farts"); they were also perceived as being elitist since it required considerable musical proficiency to play prog rock. And for every action there's a reaction; running alongside prog rock, pub rock took music back to its roots, offering a more earthy alternative, then punk rock spat in prog rock's face and attempted to destroy it altogether.

Pink Floyd made some of the most accessible prog rock music. Their grandiose The Wall *(1979) provided them with their first number one single, a lavish tour and a spin-off film.*

Like Punk Never *Happened*

While punk gained all the headlines and sidelined the prog rockers in the mid-1970s, it seems you couldn't keep a prog rocker down, and many of the progressive rock groups survived to enjoy far longer careers than the punks. Despite almost ever-changing line-ups, both King Crimson and Yes have continued to record and tour, King Crimson's *THRAK* (1995) showing that they are still a creative force with something to say.

Almost meriting a musical category of his own, Frank Zappa started his musical career in the mid-1960s with *Freak Out* (1966) and continued writing and recording until his death in 1993. As with prog rock, Zappa's music drew from a multitude of musical styles, often demanding the highest instrumental standards from an ever-changing band of musicians, but unlike the prog rockers his lyrics were often humorous or highly sarcastic.

Key Tracks:

'A Whiter Shade Of Pale' Procol Harum
'Nights In White Satin' The Moody Blues
'Starship Trooper' Yes
'21st Century Schizoid Man' King Crimson

In the 1980s, UK band Marillion bravely flew the prog rock flag, defiantly swimming against the tide, with their *Misplaced Childhood* (1985) concept album even spawning a couple of hit singles. In the 1990s, US band Dream Theatre introduced prog rock to a new, younger generation, played with impeccable musicianship by highly-schooled instrumentalists.

Yes's Rick Wakeman's trademark sound came from the Mellotron and MiniMoog.

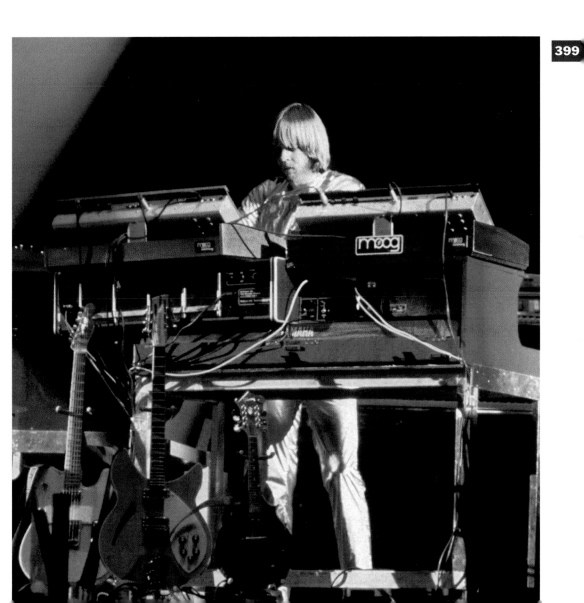

Jam *Bands*

When the Grateful Dead started attracting a large fan following on the San Francisco Bay Area concert scene during the late-1960s, courtesy of free-form jams that showcased the band's fusion of folk, rock, country and blues, it signalled that rock'n'roll was latching onto a tradition of improvization that had long been prevalent in other forms of Western music.

This had been a key feature of the classical music of the Baroque era in Europe, where composers such as Mozart were renowned improvizors on the keyboard. However, by the early-nineteenth century, at the height of the Romantic movement, the complex musical language of the composers was set down, providing little room for the musicians to improvize.

"It's like you're surfing: the wave is stronger than you. If you relax and have no fear, and you're with the flow of the wave, you can ride it. But if you try to fight it, you'll wipe out." Trey Anastasio, Phish

At the start of the twentieth century, this was still the norm in Europe, whereas in America an air of greater collaboration prevailed among the pioneering jazz musicians who virtually created music as they performed it. And it was this approach, passed down the generations by greats like Louis Armstrong, Duke Ellington, Charlie Parker, Ornette Coleman, Miles Davis and John Coltrane, which was subsequently adopted by, among others, the Grateful Dead, Frank Zappa & the Mothers of Invention and the Allman Brothers Band. They also echoed the jazz musicians' penchant for fusing diverse musical styles onstage and on albums such as the Dead's *Anthem Of The Sun* and the Allmans' *Idlewild South* and *Eat A Peach*.

Jamming was introduced to the rock scene by acts such as Frank Zappa.

Musical *Eclecticism*

During the 1990s, a new generation of jam bands emerged. Taking their lead from the Dead and the Allmans, while fusing anything from rock, soul and jazz to bluegrass and worldbeat, groups such as the Spin Doctors, Blues Traveler, Widespread Panic and Phish began carving out their own niche.

Building their following by way of constant touring, what they and their predecessors have usually shared is a solid bond with their audience – even encouraging them to tape concerts – as well as an understandable ability to fully transfer their live appeal to record. Nevertheless, this isn't to say that some of them haven't enjoyed chart triumphs.

Key Artists:

The Allman Brothers Band
Blues Traveler
The Grateful Dead
Phish
The Spin Doctors

New York's Spin Doctors saw sales of their 1991 album *Pocket Full of Kryptonite* rocket after radio and MTV helped turn 'Little Miss Can't Be Wrong' into a hit on the singles charts, and much the same was experienced by another band out of the Big Apple, Blues Traveler. *When Four*, Traveler's aptly-titled fourth album, was released in September 1994, it eventually achieved quintuple-platinum sales in the wake of the single 'Run Around' becoming one of 1995's biggest hits.

Conversely, the outfit that has led the way on the jam band scene while coming closest to assuming the Grateful Dead's mantle, is one from Vermont that has never been able to translate its concert following into record sales via studio albums such as *Junta* and *A Picture of Nectar*. Melding folk, bluegrass, country, jazz and rock'n'roll Phish has set new standards of originality in terms of free-form rock improvization, while becoming an institution on the American college circuit. And therein lies the appeal of the jam scene, which has far more to do with live performance than with recorded encapsulations.

The New York-based blues-rock quartet formed in 1988 by singer/harmonica player John Popper, Blues Traveler was part of a revival of the extended jamming style of the 1960s and 1970s.

Glam Rock & *Glitter*

A largely British movement, glam rock and glitter were highly popular in the early 1970s – so popular that one artist, Marc Bolan, was given his own TV series. Inspired by early rock'n'roll and bubblegum pop, glam rock was fun, catchy and melodic, played with crunchy, distorted guitars, with the musicians dressing up in outrageous and androgynous costumes.

While Britain has a long history of pantomime dames and drag queens, America was slightly wary of glam rock's blurring of gender identity, which partly explains why it never took off as strongly in the US. Similarities can be found between the British glam rockers and American hard rockers Kiss, especially in the dressing-up and make-up department. Kiss started their career with flamboyant costumes and theatrical face-painting in the mid-1970s. For the glam rockers, almost as much effort and creativity went into the appearance as the music, and while contemporary artists such as Elton John and Paul McCartney & Wings may not have been influenced by the music, they were certainly inspired by the fashion.

"Bowie has sold his talent for fame, fortune and a white fur rug; a once creative artist is now slipping on Woolworth's glitter; shameless, Bowie has become a showbiz star." Simon Frith

Starting out as folk rockers, T Rex, largely Marc Bolan's group, set the glam rock ball rolling with *Electric Warrior* (1971) and *The Slider* (1972) – fun, trashy rock'n'roll with catchy hooks and often inane lyrics, with T Rex refusing to take themselves too seriously. Although glam rock and glitter are essentially the same thing, the "glitter" bands are generally the more glitzy, trashy and throwaway bands, as inspired by T Rex – Slade, Sweet, Suzi Quatro and Gary Glitter.

After flirting briefly with a skinhead image, Slade's *Slayed?* (1972) established them as bona fide glam rockers, complete with foot-stomping beats and rousing, anthemic choruses. For better or worse, Slade still get airplay in Britain every year by unimaginative DJs who insist on playing 'Merry Christmas Everybody' come Christmas time, their saving grace being singer Noddy Holder who possessed one of the classic British rock voices.

With Noddy Holder's powerful vocals and guitarist Dave Hill's equally arresting dress sense, Slade were one of the most successful British chart bands of the 1970s, scoring seventeen consecutive Top Twenty hits.

Grannie's Old *Clothes*

Sweet adopted the glam dressing up, but, with the possible exception of the singer, ended up looking like bricklayers dressed up in their granny's old clothes – not a pretty sight, it must be said. Fortunately, they sounded better than they looked and were a significant influence on the New Wave Of British Heavy Metal band Def Leppard.

Despite all the experimentation with sexual identity, glam rock was very much a male-dominated genre, with one notable exception – Suzi Quatro. Singer and bass player Quatro is seen by some admirers as a proto-riot grrrl, although her music has none of the sexual politics and feminism championed by the riot grrrl movement. Famously leather-clad and diminutive, Quatro's self-titled 1973 album includes the hit single 'Can The Can'.

Real name Paul Gadd, Gary Glitter's *Glitter* (1972) consolidated his position as one of the leaders of the era, although musically he was even more of more of a singles artist than the other glitter acts, and is thus best represented on *Rock'n'Roll: Gary Glitter's Greatest Hits* (1998). Glitter was backed by – who else? – the Glitter Band, who went on to have their own successful career. After suffering bankruptcy in the 1980s and 1990s, Gary Glitter revived his live act, although his musical career was brought to an abrupt halt after he was convicted for paedophile offences in the late-1990s.

Key Artists:

T Rex
Slade
Sweet
Gary Glitter
David Bowie

Multi instrumentalist Roy Wood, one of the more eccentric and prolific British performers on the glam/glitter rock scene in the early 1970s, led the band Wizzard while also enjoying a solo career. Wood, former founder of the Move and Electric Light Orchestra, drew inspiration from a host of musical genres such as 1950s rock'n'roll, classical music and psychedelia. Wizzard had a hit with 'I Wish It Could Be Christmas Every Day' in 1973, which hasn't quite had the same longevity as Slade's Christmas hit, although it is not far behind.

Suzi Quatro was discovered in her native Detroit by British record producer Mickie Most, who was working there with Jeff Beck. Suzi's cool, leather-clad image later landed her a role in the TV sitcom Happy Days.

Art School

Alongside the glitter bands, David Bowie and Roxy Music took a more arty perspective on glam rock. Bowie revelled in the theatrical aspect of glam rock and reinvented himself with a new persona, Ziggy Stardust, as heard on the album *The Rise And Fall Of Ziggy Stardust* (1972), with his backing band the Spiders From Mars.

He also revived the career of hard rockers Mott the Hoople by giving them a glam rock makeover on *All The Young Dudes* (1972), producing the album and writing the well-known title track. Having lived through and weathered numerous rock movements, at the turn of the millennium rock chameleon David Bowie remained a creative force.

Roxy Music successfully combined their art-rock leanings with a glam rock setting, and showed that avant-garde and highly experimental ideas can work in a three-minute pop song context, as on *For Your Pleasure* (1973). This album was the last to be made with Brian Eno, who represented the experimental side of the band, and thus subsequent albums had a more conventional feel to them. Roxy Music singer Bryan Ferry released solo albums while still in the band, then pursued a more sophisticated and adult-pop sound after the demise of Roxy Music in 1983. (They have since re-formed).

Key Tracks:

'Ballroom Blitz' Sweet
'Can The Can' Suzi Quatro
'Cum On Feel The Noize' Slade
'I'm The Leader Of The Gang (I Am)' Gary Glitter
'Jeepster' T Rex

Although not primarily thought of as a glam rock act, Queen's self-titled debut album (1973) has one platform-shod foot firmly in the glam rock school. Bombastic and camp, Queen also showed themselves to be far more versatile and multi-dimensional than any of the other glam acts. Although very much an early 1970s phenomenon, a glam rock influence can be seen in several 1990s British bands such as Gay Dad, Suede and Kenickie. Ex-Felt member Lawrence Hayward formed Denim in 1990 as a tribute to glam rock, their debut album *Back In Denim* (1992) including a song entitled 'The Osmonds' after the US pop-singing family who flirted with glam rock, and contributions from two ex-members of the Glitter Band.

For many, Queen were the epitome of glam rock, combining high camp with wailing guitars and over-the-top arrangements. The band's mini-opera 'Bohemian Rhapsody' is a unique piece that manages to transcend its pretensions.

Fusion & Jazz *Rock*

"Fusion" can be applied to any music that blends two or more different styles, though it is normally used to describe the electronic jazz rock movement that emerged in the late 1960s. Some of the musicians expanded the boundaries of both jazz and rock, while others focused on producing sophisticated, but shallow, "background" music.

Although fusion records have never sold in huge quantities, the style has remained popular within the musical community during the past 30 years. The term "musician's musician" is often used to describe the top exponents.

It is widely accepted that Miles Davis's *Bitches Brew* (1969) album was the first influential jazz rock recording. It combined modal jazz with rock guitar and drum sounds, and introduced jazz to a wider rock audience. While not the first jazz artist to use electric guitar, piano and bass, Davis was the highest-profile leader to adapt the popular approaches of Jimi Hendrix, Sly Stone, James Brown and Stevie Wonder to his own ends. The album featured an extraordinary selection of musicians, including Joe Zawinul and Chick Corea (keyboards), Wayne Shorter (saxophone), John McLaughlin (electric guitar) and Lenny White (drums). These players went on to form three of the most celebrated and influential fusion bands in the early 1970s: Weather Report (Zawinul and Shorter), Return To Forever (Corea and White) and the Mahavishnu Orchestra (McLaughlin).

"Bitches Brew has a kind of searching quality because Miles was onto the process of discovering this new music and developing it." Dave Holland (bass player on Bitches Brew)

The groundbreaking Bitches Brew *marked an irrevocable change in the development of jazz. The dark but fiery combination of Miles Davis' trumpet and Wayne Shorter's saxophone on the album blew away all who heard it.*

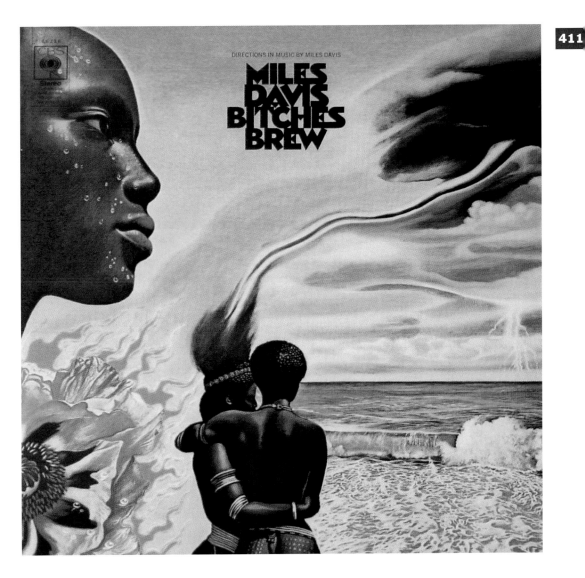

Weather Report and *Mahavishnu*

Weather Report was one of the most successful fusion bands, with albums reaching the Top 50 charts on both sides of the Atlantic. Their earliest recordings were patchy, but *Black Market* (1976) featured strong compositions and introduced the legendary Jaco Pastorius on fretless bass guitar.

The combination of strikingly original tunes, Shorter's searing sax lines, Zawinul's colourful synth passages (played on Arp and Oberheim instruments) and Pastorius's jaw-dropping bass work (ranging from "singing" melodic passages to unusual harmonics and ultra-fast riffs) proved to be an even bigger success with their next album, *Heavy Weather* (1977). Further recordings, such as *Mr. Gone* (1978), *Night Passage* (1980) and *Weather Report* (1982), confirmed the band's status as a top-flight jazz act, although Pastorius left in 1982 and the band eventually split in 1986. Sadly, Pastorius died in 1987 after he was beaten up outside a nightclub in Fort Lauderdale, Florida.

The Mahavishnu Orchestra was more rock-oriented than Weather Report. Formed by John McLaughlin during the early 1970s and influenced by Eastern mysticism, the original band featured McLaughlin on electric guitar, along with Jan Hammer (keyboards), Jerry Goodman (violin), Rick Laird (bass) and Billy Cobham (drums). Their explosive creativity broke new boundaries in jazz, both in terms of virtuosity and complexity, and their albums *The Inner Mounting Flame* (1971) and *Birds Of Fire* (1972) are widely regarded as fusion classics. Hammer, Goodman and Cobham left to work on their own projects a year later, and McLaughlin reformed the band with various other line-ups for the next two decades. He also formed Shakti, an exploratory 'Eastern' acoustic fusion band, with renowned Indian classical musicians such as L. Shankar (violin) and Zakir Hussain (tablas) during the mid-1970s, as well as a much-celebrated acoustic guitar trio with flamenco virtuoso Paco de Lucía and fusion ace Al Di Meola. The trio's live recording, *Friday Night In San Francisco* (1980), features some breathtakingly fleet guitar work that has to be heard to be believed.

Key Artists:

Weather Report
Mahavishnu Orchestra
Return To Forever
Tony Williams' Lifetime
Al Di Meola

Jaco Pastorius, who redefined the role of the electric bass in jazz, played with Pat Metheny and Weather Report, among others.

Other Influential *Bands*

The other primary 1970s fusion band to directly emerge out of the *Bitches Brew* scene was Chick Corea's Return To Forever. Their first line-up was a Latin-style band led by Chick on keyboards, but by 1975 the group had developed into an all-out fusion outfit featuring Al Di Meola (guitar), Stanley Clarke (bass) and Lenny White (drums).

Their *Romantic Warrior* (1976) recording was a landmark jazz-rock album, featuring six complex, intricately crafted instrumentals that were to inspire rock and jazz musicians for years to come. It also acted as a launching pad for Di Meola's solo career; he went on to record *Land Of The Midnight Sun* (1976), *Elegant Gypsy* (1976), *Casino* (1977) and *Splendido Hotel* (1979), which resulted in *Guitar Player* magazine readers voting him Best Jazz Player for five consecutive years.

There were a number of other seminal fusion recordings made during the 1970s: Believe It (1975) by Tony Williams introduced Allan Holdsworth's unique but influential legato lead-guitar style; Frank Zappa's Roxy & Elsewhere (1974) fused jazz and rock with a warped, but much-loved sense of humour; and the Pat Metheny Group with its self-titled album (1978) forged a new, earthy jazz style that eventually earned the group huge audiences critical acclaim and Grammy awards. Across the Atlantic, Brand X's Unorthodox Behaviour (1976) and Soft Machine's *Third* (1970) proved that British bands were also capable of producing world-class fusion, while the French and Belgians also showed their fusion mettle with violinist Jean-Luc Ponty's *Enigmatic Ocean* (1977) and Marc Moulin's *Placebo* (1973).

Key Albums:

Believe It Tony Williams
Heavy Weather Weather Report
Romantic Warrior Return To Forever
Roxy & Elsewhere Frank Zappa
The Inner Mounting Flame Mahavishnu Orchestra

By contrast, the 1980s were relatively quiet for fusion, although Corea, Holdsworth and the American guitarist John Scofield made some significant recordings during this period. In more recent years, Tribal Tech has kept the fusion flag flying. Their recent recordings, *Thick* and *Rocket Science*, show that jazz rock is still alive and kicking.

An incredibly talented and versatile pianist, Chick Corea made forays into fusion jazz that were only a part, albeit an important one, of his musical output. He also peformed Latin and free jazz and music from the classical repertoire.

Pub Rock

A British phenomenon, pub rock was a reaction to the self-indulgence of the progressive rockers and the vain preening of the glam rockers. The pub rock bands drew from a variety of roots-music styles, such as blues, folk and country, with the folk influence dating back to the UK folk-rockers of the late-1960s such as Fairport Convention.

The beginning of pub rock is largely credited to a little-known American band, Eggs over Easy, gigging at the Tally-Ho pub in London with a mixture of original songs and cover material which inspired other bands and, just as importantly, encouraged other pubs to book live bands on what was soon to become a vibrant gig circuit.

Opening Time

Brinsley Schwarz's mixture of folk, prog rock and hippie affectations on their self-titled debut album in 1970 sounds even worse on record than on paper, and along with a disastrous showcase gig in the US it effectively ended all interest there. Returning to the UK, the band honed their sound culminating with *Nervous On The Road* (1972), a pub rock masterpiece that helped pave the way for fellow pub rockers Bees Make Honey, Ace, Chilli Willi and the Red Hot Peppers and Ducks Deluxe.

"You don't have to be a musician to play rock'n'roll. You've just got to love it and want to play it."
Lee Brilleaux, Dr. Feelgood

Emerging towards the end of the pub rock era, Dr. Feelgood's lively and aggressive R&B sound made them an exciting live band who managed to capture that energy on their debut album *Down By The Jetty* (1975). Eddie & the Hot Rods were similarly energetic and had a hit single with 'Do Anything You Wanna Do' in 1977.

Dr. Feelgood's original line up included the menacing vocals of Lee Brilleaux (far right) and the Mick Green-styled guitar prowess of Wilko Johnson (far left).

Last Orders at the *Tally-Ho*

The music press and many listeners turned their attention to punk in the latter half of the 1970s and the pub rock bands were unable to compete. Most faded into obscurity or disbanded, the notable exception being Dr. Feelgood. Band members left and were replaced until the only remaining original member was singer Lee Brilleaux. Brilleaux died from cancer in 1994 but the band has carried on.

Pub rock had a significant influence on punk rock. The Clash's frontman, the late Joe Strummer, began his musical career with pub rockers the 101'ers. Ex-Brinsley Schwarz songwriter Nick Lowe became the in-house producer with the Stiff record label, one of the foremost punk labels, working with the Damned, the Pretenders and Elvis Costello, before going on to enjoy a successful solo career.

Key Artists:

Eggs Over Easy
Brinsley Schwarz
Bees Make Honey
Ace
Chilli Willie & the Red Hot Chilli Peppers

Singer/songwriters Elvis Costello and the late Ian Dury straddle the divide between pub rock and punk rock, albeit a more restrained and literate side of punk rock, and their pub rock roots can be heard on their respective debut albums *My Aim Is True* (1977) and *New Boots And Panties!!* (1977). Fellow singer/songwriter Graham Parker's debut album Howlin' Wind gained critical acclaim but unlike Costello and Dury he was sidelined by punk rock.

Ian Dury's debut album New Boots And Panties!! showcased his sharp, witty lyrics and funky pub rock sound, and contained character songs such as 'Billericay Dickie' and 'Clevor Trever'.

Proto-*Punk*

Proto-punk bands, like all "proto" genres, are by definition only identified retrospectively and generally share subversive and anti-establishment attitudes. Although punk rock was primarily a British phenomenon, there were several notable American punk bands and its musical roots lie more with these American bands than with British bands.

The energy of pub rockers like Dr. Feelgood and Eddie & the Hot Rods may be heard in the punk bands but they lacked the anger, nihilism, and artistic and political overtones.

Although the Velvet Underground's debut album *The Velvet Underground & Nico* (1967) didn't sell huge amounts on its release, its impact on non-mainstream forms of rock music was significant, with its disregard for conventional song structures and lyrics that dealt head-on with sex and drugs. The roots of punk rock, goth rock and glam rock can all be traced back to this album.

"We're musical primitives."
John Cale, Velvet Underground

Anti-Establishment

The MC5 gathered a loyal following on the strength of their exciting and anarchic live performances, so much so that they elected to record a live show for their debut album, *Kick Out The Jams* (1969). Beginning with singer Rob Tyner's rabble rousing cry of "Kick out the jams, motherfuckers", the early use of the "mf" word – nearly thirty years before it became commonplace on rap records – led to some shops refusing to stock the record. Elektra Records had to release an alternative version with "brothers and sisters" replacing "motherfuckers". With their radical anti-establishment politics, the MC5 became the figurehead for the White Panther Party whose manifesto included "an assault on the culture by any means necessary, including dope and fucking in the streets."

Distinctive artwork adorns The Velvet Underground and Nico *album of 1967, emphasizing Pop Art roots and Andy Warhol connections.*

Self-Destruction

You won't find an anti-establishment manifesto with Iggy and the Stooges, but they certainly helped themselves to the sex and drugs. A band with one finger permanently on the self-destruct button, singer Iggy Pop would cut himself onstage or smear himself with peanut butter or raw meat – then launch himself into the audience. *Raw Power* (1973) reveals a wild, wired and weird band, with raw and spontaneous music and lyrics, thanks to the habit of improvizing in the studio.

And speaking of self-destruction, the New York Dolls' second album *Too Much Too Soon* (1974) became a self-fulfilling prophesy and the band split shortly afterwards, despite hapless manager Malcolm McLaren's attempts to promote the band to a wider audience. McLaren would put his experience to use afterwards as the infamous Svengali of the Sex Pistols.

Having established herself as a poet, Patti Smith released her debut album *Horses* (1975) to critical acclaim, and revealed a poet's sensibilities with her imaginative use of language in loosely constructed song forms.

Smith described her music as, "three chord rock merged with the power of the word". Her debut single 'Piss Factory' (1974) describes the boredom of working in a factory, something the punks could relate to.

Key Artists:

The Velvet Underground
The MC5
Iggy & the Stooges
New York Dolls
Patti Smith

Britain was not without its proto-punk bands. The Troggs had a hit single in the UK in 1966 with 'Wild Thing', based on a three chord riff and the archetypical example of their "caveman rock". The Kinks also had a knack for primitive, aggressive guitar riff based songs such as 'You Really Got Me' and 'All Day And All Of The Night', the latter being covered by punk band the Stranglers.

Iggy Pop's legendary onstage performances were always controversial and caused one UK television show, So It Goes, to be withdrawn permanently after a bout of particularly colourful language.

British *Punk*

Punk exploded on to the stagnant British music scene in the mid-1970s with short, fast songs, played with maximum energy and often fuelled by angry lyrics. A musical and social phenomenon, punk was a reaction to the indulgence of glam rock bands, and the perceived elitism of the often highly musically proficient musicians who played in the prog rock bands.

It was also a reaction to the perceived artificialness of the "corporate rock" manufactured groups such as Boston, Kansas and Foreigner, and the perceived slickness of the equally artificial disco scene. Socially, punk appealed to the disenfranchised British youth who felt at best bored and at worst alienated by what British society had to offer them – unemployment or dead-end jobs.

Looking back from the perspective of a more permissive and (slightly!) more tolerant society, it is difficult to believe the profoundly shocking effect punk had on the nation's morals.

"This is a chord. This is another. This is a third. Now form a band."
Sideburns fanzine

Arguably the last musical movement to have such a huge social impact, British TV shows would earnestly debate the "evils" of punk rock. Goaded into swearing on live daytime television, Sex Pistols guitarist Steve Jones recalled this turning point: "It was hilarious, it was one of the best feelings, the next day, when you saw the paper. You thought, 'Fucking hell, this is great!' From that day on, it was different. Before then, it was the music: the next day, it was the media."

Johnny Rotten got the gig as vocalist for the Sex Pistols after he was spotted with green hair, wearing an "I Hate Pink Floyd" T-shirt.

No *Future*

At the height of their fame – or infamy – the Sex Pistols with Johnny Rotten (aka John Lydon) as their lead singer, had a number one single 'God Save the Queen' during the Queen's Silver Jubilee year of 1977, which was banned by the BBC on the grounds of its allegedly offensive lyrics. The opening of 'God Save The Queen' bears the hallmarks of classic rock'n'roll, albeit with a louder, faster and more aggressive character. Its anti-establishment lyrics and "no future" outro sum up the Sex Pistols' outlook perfectly: bleak and nihilistic. Fittingly, they imploded shortly after releasing their debut album, *Never Mind The Bollocks, Here's The Sex Pistols* (1977).

The Clash, fronted by the late Joe Strummer, were equally exciting but offered a more positive agenda, particularly with their anti-racism messages. The Clash were able to develop their sound from the impressive frenetic self-titled debut in 1977, culminating in *London Calling* (1979), which reveals influences as diverse as rockabilly, reggae, ska and hard rock.

Several other bands offered significant variations on the stereotypical manic punk three chord thrash. The Jam had an altogether smarter image than the punks, and *In The City* (1977) reveals 1960s mod leanings. After the Jam split up, singer Paul Weller went on to enjoy a successful solo career, although his solo offerings do not reflect his punk and mod roots with the Jam and he remains unwilling to play songs from that era. The Stranglers, significantly older than the other punk bands, offered a psychedelic tinge, as can be heard on the groovy organ solo on the title track of *No More Heroes* (1977). Other notable punk debuts included the Damned's *Damned, Damned, Damned* (1977) and the Buzzcocks' *Spiral Scratch EP* (1977). The Damned had a distinctly less political agenda than, for example, the Clash, and came across as drunken pranksters out for a laugh, although 'New Rose' and 'Neat Neat Neat' from their debut are classics of the punk genre – short, energetic and highly memorable. Inspired by the Sex Pistols, the Buzzcocks mixed punk and pop with occasionally humorous lyrics.

Key Artists:

The Sex Pistols
The Clash
The Jam
The Stranglers
The Damned

The Damned were the first UK punk band to release a nationally distributed single, 'New Rose', in 1976. They were also the first to play in America the following year at CBGB's, receiving mixed reviews.

New *Wave*

Elvis Costello started his career on the pub rock circuit, then successfully jumped ship to get lumped in with the punk generation, although lyrically and musically he was considerably more sophisticated, as demonstrated on *My Aim Is True* (1977). Consequently the media labelled him "new wave", a loosely-defined genre for artists less hard-edged than the punk rockers.

DIY

Punk's lasting musical legacy was its DIY (do-it-yourself) ethic, encouraging youngsters from all walks of life to form bands. In this respect, punk mirrored the skiffle craze that had swept the UK twenty years earlier, offering aspiring musicians a road to stardom regardless of their musical ability and standard of equipment. Punk also encouraged people to set up their own independent or indie record labels, so-called because they didn't rely on what punk rockers regarded as the BOFs ("boring old farts") and accountants in the traditional record companies.

Key Tracks:

'God Save The Queen' The Sex Pistols
'Going Underground' The Jam
'Golden Brown' The Stranglers
'London Calling' The Clash
'New Rose' The Damned

The Sex Pistols effectively destroyed their credibility by reforming for a tour in the 1990s, a shameless venture which they readily admitted was driven by financial reasons, the justification being that they didn't make any money the first time around. The Clash's mainman Joe Strummer died in 2002 before the Clash could reform for a proposed Rock'n'Roll Hall Of Fame gig when they were inducted the following year.

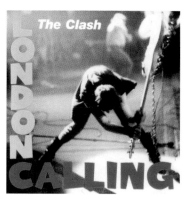

(Right) For many, the Clash were the ultimate punk rock band. It was supporting the Sex Pistols with his previous band that turned singer Joe Strummer on to punk. (Above) The Clash's London Calling (1979) album marked the band's critical and commercial breakthrough.

American *Punk*

Like the majority of their British counterparts, the original American punks had been making music for years before they began to receive acknowledgement in late 1975. In common with the Brits once again, the biggest problem was that nobody had a clue what to call it.

Drawing their wild, high-energy style from such Detroit-based rock acts of the late-1960s and early 1970s as MC5 and the Stooges, and boasting an androgynous, long-haired look that made the Rolling Stones look like choirboys, glammed-up east coast quintet the New York Dolls were America's first real punk rock band. Debauched and dangerous, loud and lewd, the Dolls had formed as far back as 1971, but it didn't take long for them to fulfill the cliché of living fast and dying young. Original drummer Billy Murcia succumbed to a mixture of alcohol and drugs during a British tour in late-1972, and was succeeded by Jerry Nolan.

"Punk was about creating new, important, energetic music that would hopefully threaten the stupidity of the 1970s. You can argue about whether Offspring sold out by signing to Sony until you're blue in the face, it won't feed the homeless person outside your front door."
Jello Biafra, Dead Kennedys

In 1973 and 1974, a pair of albums for Mercury Records – the Todd Rundgren-produced *New York Dolls* and *Too Much Too Soon* – barely dented the US chart despite receptive reviews, and the band were dropped, meeting future Sex Pistols manager Malcolm McLaren shortly afterwards. Still perfecting his manipulatory skills, McLaren attempted to revive their career by dressing the Dolls in red leather and demanding they pose in front of the USSR flag. Accusations of communism followed, and one by one the members began to depart. By 1977, with McLaren riding high as the Pistols manager, it was all over. Jerry Nolan and guitarist Johnny Thunders teamed up with Richard Hell to form the Heartbreakers, though former Television bassist Hell – who had turned down McLaren's offer to front the Sex Pistols – departed soon afterwards to form the Voidoids. After many notoriously drug addicted years, Thunders himself was found dead in 1991, with Nolan succumbing to a heart attack soon afterwards.

The New York Dolls were the missing link between glam rock and punk. Their gigs mixed cross-dressing with swearing and hard rock music.

An Undercurrent of *Subterfuge*

In early 1976, a new magazine called *Punk* gave the movement focus. The personnel and inner circles of the post-Dolls bands included more than their fair share of arty bohemian types – painters, filmmakers, writers, poets and artists; like the waitresses and house-decorators, all refreshingly free of the baggage of "serious" musicians.

Television, Suicide and Patti Smith were among the acts to play New York dives like Max's Kansas City and the Country, Bluegrass & Blues Club (CBGB's for short). The sounds of these bands, and others like the Ramones, Talking Heads and Blondie, were radically different, yet united by an exciting undercurrent of subterfuge. In the words of Smith, "I was wondering what I could do as a writer or poet to inspire people to reclaim rock'n'roll as a revolutionary, grass-roots base for the people."

Key Artists:

Richard Hell
Black Flag
The Dead Kennedys
Ramones
Talking Heads

A New Wave of Punk

The first of the new wave acts to be signed were the Ramones, a band that relied more upon goofy, dark humour than anarchy. Given their near-legendary musical minimalism, it was highly remarkable that the Ramones made music for some twenty years after *Ramones*, their May 1976 debut.

(Right) The Ramones specialized in a very basic sound. Their songs incorporated simple chords and lyrics and no solos. (Above) The Ramones *(1976) album established the band as three-chord garage rockers with a sense of humour.*

A New *Generation*

Cleveland chipped in with the Dead Boys, and over on the west coast, Black Flag, X, the Germs and the Dead Kennedys were spearheading a more aggressive, politically aggrieved strike at the nation's underbelly.

Of the four, Black Flag were more inclined to incorporate humour into their edgy blend of rage and sarcasm – an asset that frontman Henry Rollins retained when the band fragmented in 1986. The Dead Kennedys, meanwhile, were deadly serious ... and then some. 'California Über Alles', their debut single, lambasted San Francisco's then governor, Jerry Brown. In 1979, frontman Jello Biafra contested the city's mayorship, finishing fourth. Despite being banned, the group's 'Too Drunk To Fuck' single broached the British chart, but worse followed when a poster for 1985's *Frankenchrist* album resulted in an obscenity prosecution. The Kennedys fragmented after a two-year court battle with Biafra left hopping mad at the group's reformation without him, the re-issue of their catalogue and the pressing of the live album, *Mutiny On The Bay*.

If the DKs are guilty of undermining the original principles of punk rock, they're far from alone. The Offspring's reported $10 million (£6.7 m) switch to Sony Records subsidiary Columbia from Epitaph – a credible indie label owned by Bad Religion's Brett Gurewitz – created a backlash, though the Californians underlined both underground credentials and popularity by permitting an MP3 of their song 'Pretty Fly (For A White Guy)' to be downloaded an incredible 22 million times in just ten weeks.

Key Tracks:

'Psycho Killer' Talking Heads
'Six Pack' Black Flag
'Suzie Is A Headbanger' Ramones
'Too Drunk To Fuck' The Dead Kennedys

Consequently, survivors like Sick Of It All have had their noses rubbed in the success of airwave-friendly, younger acts like Sum 41, Blink 182 and Finch, not to mention Green Day who, though more pop today, started out with a punk attitude. As SOIA singer Lou Koller observes, punk is now freely "available at the mall".

Punks at New York's CBGB's club in 1978.

Arena Rock

The rise of arena rock began in North America during the mid-1970s with a surge in the popularity of bands like Journey, Foreigner, Boston and Styx. Embraced by a network of FM radio stations, these bands and others like them became so profitable to their record companies that they almost represented a licence to print money.

The formula was deliciously simple: slick, commercial material, underpinned by memorable hard rock riffs and a glossy production. Radio-friendly ballads also encouraged a wider audience, although these were used in moderation.

A Stylistic Journey

The arena rock sound resembled an aural marshmallow; with an apparently tough outer casing, but sticky and sweet on the inside. In fact, many of its original bands had gravitated towards the genre from other styles of music. Formed in 1973 by the ex-Santana guitarist Neal Schon, and joined later that year by keyboard player Gregg Rolie, Journey had made three poor-selling jazz rock albums before the simplified strains of *Infinity* enabled them to top a million sales in 1978.

"You have to be able to survive change and keep your integrity."
Tommy Shaw, Styx

Two years earlier, in 1976, a New York-based English guitarist/songwriter called Mick Jones had almost turned his back on the music business after the dissolution of the Leslie West Band, but fuelled by the success of the singles 'Cold As Ice' and 'Feels Like The First Time', Jones achieved out-of-the-box success with Foreigner's five-million-selling, self-titled debut.

The anthems on Journey's Escape *(1981) brought Steve Perry's powerful, sweeping vocals to the album and singles charts.*

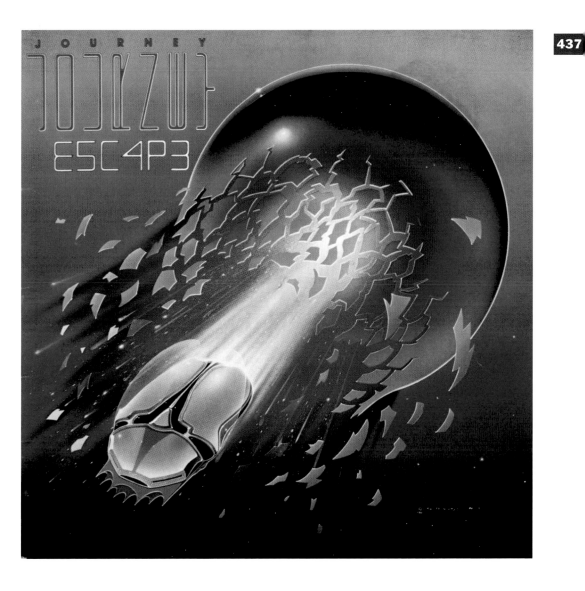

MTV and Mass *Appeal*

The rags to riches story of Boston was more unlikely still. Essentially a vehicle for guitarist/songwriter/ producer Tom Scholz, the band's 1976 *Boston* album – a glorified collection of basement demos – shot to the top of the US chart and became the best-selling pop debut effort in history until dislodged by Whitney Houston in 1986. By 1995, Boston had sold over 15 million copies in America alone, though the perfectionist streak of the reclusive Scholz has created just four more albums in the ensuing quarter of a century.

In the 1980s, Aerosmith, Heart and Whitesnake – all acts with different roots – moved in to stake their claims in the arena rock market. With their leaner, more blues-based heritage, Aerosmith had already tasted considerable success during the 1970s and brought their sound into a new decade with the help of songwriters Desmond Child and Holly Knight and producer Bruce Fairbairn.

Heart, too, already had a proven track record for folk-based acoustic melancholy, but the Heart album gave them their most popular release in 1985. Likewise, former blues-rockers Whitesnake, lead by former Deep Purple vocalist David Coverdale, cunningly engineered a re-birth to capitalize upon the MTV boom in 1987.

Rush, too, began to court mass appeal. Their prog roots were homogenized via such synth-friendly albums as *Power Windows* (1985) and *Hold Your Fire* (1987), although the Canadian trio were to become increasingly reclusive.

Key Artists:
Aerosmith
Styx
Journey
Foreigner
Boston

The grunge-rock revolution would render arena rock deeply unfashionable during the next decade. However, many of its big hitters live on, and continue to play live. Bands like Journey, Styx and REO Speedwagon continue to undertake major tours.

Foreigner's original line-up was a mixture of Londoners and New Yorkers. This was the basis of the band's name and went some way towards earning them mass appeal.

Melodic *Rock*

During the 1970s, tuneful hard rock loomed over the US charts like a fluffy, pink colossus. The arrival of baby-faced guitarist Tommy Shaw led Chicago rockers Styx to become the first American group to achieve four consecutive triple-platinum albums, and when Journey appointed singer Steve Perry it made them one of the biggest bands in the world.

Foreigner have now sold an incredible 60 million albums – 35 million of those in the US alone – as a consequence of such airwave standards as the 1980s hits 'Waiting For A Girl Like You', 'I Want To Know What Love Is' and 'Hot Blooded'.

"How did I feel during the grunge years? Unemployed."
Kip Winger, Winger

In the 1980s, British band Def Leppard utilized state-of the-art technology, clever marketing and widespread touring to tap into the pop market with their Pyromania and Hysteria albums, a blueprint later used more ruthlessly still by Bon Jovi.

The latter pair of bands were among the few to survive the grunge rock revolution, though Leppard surprised many by daring to flirt with the style themselves on their 1996 album *Slang*. Having overhauled themselves for a new generation of MTV viewers, ex-Deep Purple frontman David Coverdale and his former blues band Whitesnake also received long-overdue US attention as the 1980s drew to a close.

After landing a recording contract in 1983, New Jersey band Bon Jovi's extensive touring, phenomenal record sales and good-looking frontman quickly transformed them into one of the world's top rock acts.

Ebbing *Enthusiasm*

Post-grunge, the only real metamorphosis that melodic rock has undergone is a downsizing of its audience. All save a tiny minority of acts have long since abandoned the pretence of creatively advancing their music. Like no other genre, except perhaps progressive rock, fans of AOR (album-oriented rock) demand rehashes of the same old ideas.

At grass-roots level, Vaughan, Von Groove, Ten, Harem Scarem, Mecca and Westworld all represent a glut of highly entertaining though inward-looking artists. Even new albums from top-tier bands often elicit scant enthusiasm, and Journey and Van Halen both ended long-term deals with Sony and Warner Brothers in 2002. However, a decent living can be made on the lucrative summer touring circuit, and perhaps for that reason alone many of melodic rock's main players continue to exist. Although Journey sold just 200,000 copies of *Arrival*, their 1998 debut with ex-Tall Stories singer Steve Augeri replacing Steve Perry, they and others like them seem determined to continue.

Invaluable exposure on TV's *South Park*, *Austin Powers: Goldmember* and the Adam Sandler movie *Big Daddy* has rewarded Styx – these days without keyboard player Dennis De Young, the voice of 'Come Sail Away', 'The Best Of Times' and 'The Grand Illusion' – with an unlikely renewed credibility that peaked when Brian Wilson of the Beach Boys, Tenacious D and Billy Bob Thornton all made guest appearances on the group's fourteenth album, *Cyclorama* (2003).

Key Artists:

Bon Jovi
Journey
Styx
Foreigner
Def Leppard

Guitarist Mick Jones and vocalist Lou Gramm, the latter recovered from a life-threatening brain tumor, celebrated Foreigner's 25th anniversary in 2002 with fifty US dates and embarked upon their first album together since *Mr Moonlight* in 1994. Boston came back with a new album, *Corporate America*, in 2002. Unfortunately, it's now unlikely that Van Halen will work again with ex-singers David Lee Roth or Sammy Hagar, although Hagar and bassist Michael Anthony are both in Planet US, a project including Journey's Neal Schon and Deen Castronovo.

Although never a great hit with critics or "serious" rock fans, Styx enjoyed great popularity during their heyday, packing clubs throughout America and releasing three triple-platinum albums.

Goth *Rock*

Much derided by music (and fashion) journalists, goth rock is slow, introspective, gloomy and doom-ridden, with elements from hard rock and psychedelia, often with swathes of cold keyboards and angular guitar parts.

The dress code was rigid: black clothes, big black hair and face made up to look deathly white. Critics often found the music pretentious and overblown and the goth fashion cartoonish and reminiscent of the Addams Family, but that didn't stop hordes of angst-ridden adolescents finding something they could relate to.

"We were anti-rock'n'roll and that might be pretentious but there's pretence in every aspect of art. It's all an act." Peter Murphy, Bauhaus

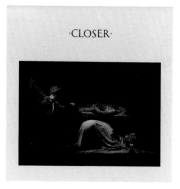

·CLOSER·

The roots of goth rock can be heard in Joy Division who provide the missing link between punk and goth rock. Formed in true punk style after an inspiring gig by the Sex Pistols by guitarist Bernard Sumner and bassist Peter Hook – but before they had had any musical experience – Joy Division replaced the energy of punk with melancholy, atmosphere and introspection, as heard on *Unknown Pleasures* (1979) and *Closer* (1980). On the verge of their first American tour in 1980, the troubled singer Ian Curtis hanged himself. The remaining members regrouped and formed New Order, taking the music in a more dance-oriented direction.

(Right) The dark, gloomy music of Joy Division, along with the untimely death of singer Ian Curtis, made the band a perfect role model for fledgling goths. (Above) Joy Division's Closer *(1980) album had a more sombre sound than their first album, with more use of synthesizers and studio effects.*

Horror and *Death*

The goth rock flag was handed over to Bauhaus, whose epic single 'Bela Lugosi's Dead' marked the beginning of full-on goth. Their debut album, *In The Flat Field* (1980), similarly provided a template for Goth – self-obsessed and despairing lyrics over moody and atmospheric music.

Starting as a post-punk band, by the time of their fifth album, *Pornography* (1982), the Cure had miserablism down to a fine art, firmly establishing their goth credentials and achieving a UK Top 10 album despite its rather relentless monotony. Of all the prominent goth bands, the Cure went on to enjoy the longest and most commercially successful career, with Robert Smith managing to combine their goth roots with a more varied, accessible and poppy sound – but without ditching the black clothes and the big black hair.

As goth established itself as a commercial proposition, Bauhaus had a hit single with a cover of David Bowie's 'Ziggy Stardust' in 1982 and their most successful album to date, *The Sky's Gone Out* (1982), reaching number four in the charts.

Zeppelin-esque

The Sisters Of Mercy's *Floodland* (1987) benefited from Meat Loaf producer Jim Steinman's widescreen production, which helped give the music the scale and depth it required to have full effect. In 1988, the Mission (a Sisters of Mercy splinter group) released their *Little Children* album. The record benefited from the production and playing of ex-Led Zeppelin bassist John Paul Jones, who not surprisingly gave the album a Zeppelin-esque tinge.

Key Artists:

Joy Division
Bauhaus
The Cure
Sisters of Mercy
The Mission

By the end of the 1980s goth had largely run its course, although its musical influence can be heard in doom metal and industrial metal, and its visual influence can be seen in artists like Marilyn Manson.

Actor Bela Lugosi, the subject of Bauhaus's landmark single 'Bela Lugosi's Dead', played Dracula during the 1930s. The song covered two of goth's top subjects – horror and death – in the title.

Doom *Metal*

Inspired largely by heavy metal founders Black Sabbath, the doom metal bands based their sound on the slower and more "sludgy" elements of Sabbath's sound, as can be heard on 'Planet Caravan' from *Paranoid* (1970) and 'Sweet Leaf' from *Master Of Reality* (1971), rather than the faster and more brutal elements of their music.

As the name suggests, doom metal is sad, melancholic and brooding, and like heavy metal the prominent instrument is distorted guitar, but unlike speed metal, doom metal is not particularly aggressive. Vocally, bands may use straightforward "clean" and traditional vocals or the more extreme "grunting".

The movement began to take shape in the mid-1980s with bands such as St Vitus, Trouble and Candlemass from Sweden. Doom metal contrasts strongly with, and was partly a reaction to, the speed metal bands of the early 1980s, such as Metallica and Slayer, who played as fast as possible – many of the doom metal bands make a virtue out of playing slowly.

"The Heaviest Band in the World"

Once described as "the heaviest band in the world", Candlemass' *Epicus Doomicus Metallicus* (1986) is a classic of the genre, and is thought to have christened the genre, although others believe the name comes from the Black Sabbath song 'Hand Of Doom' from *Paranoid*. Cathedral's *In Memorium* (1992) also sets the standard and illustrates neatly the musicians' motivation.

"To me, Doom Metal is a home for the troubled soul."

Hammy, Peaceville Records

Singer Lee Dorrian had previously been with the highly influential Napalm Death, whose style had been characterized by speed and brutality. With Cathedral though, he slowed the music right down, with detuned guitars for extra heaviness and his own unique 'singing' style.

The Black Sabbath-inspired Cathedral, with Lee Dorrian's grunting, gargling vocals perfectly punctuated by Gaz Jennings' power guitar riffs, created a new "doom-groove" sound.

The Doom *Effect*

In the 1990s, My Dying Bride, Paradise Lost and Anathema, three British bands on the Peaceville record label, mixed their Black Sabbath-derived doom metal influences with elements of goth rock.

Paradise Lost's *Gothic* (1991) acknowledges the goth influence in their music and, as befits the band's name, My Dying Bride create a mood of doomed romanticism as can be heard on *Turn Loose The Swans* (1993).

Stoner Metal, Drone Doom and Sludge Metal

Just as heavy metal inspired doom metal, doom metal in turn inspired the 1970s-obsessed stoner metal, and also overlaps with this 1990s style. As the name suggests, stoner rock has an added preoccupation with recreational drug use.

> *Key Artists:*
> St Vitus
> Trouble
> Candlemass
> Cathedral

In a seemingly limitless spiral of possibilities, another offshoot from doom metal is the so-called "drone doom" as practised by Earth. Retaining the heaviness, slowness and brooding of doom, Earth exploit drones in their music, that is, notes or riffs ringing on or being repeated against change in other instruments. On the other side of the Atlantic, yet another branch of doom metal crawled from New Orleans – the so-called "sludge metal" bands like Crowbar and Eyehategod who also drew inspiration from the Seattle grunge bands such as Soundgarden.

(Right) To the chagrin of many of their original fans, Paradise Lost have continued to grow creatively throughout their career, moving from their metal roots to electronic and pop music. (Above) Paradise Lost's fourth album Icon (1993) combines doom metal oppression with melodic heavy metal.

Heavy *Metal*

The term "heavy metal" came from the controversial US Beat Movement novel, *Naked Lunch*, in which the author, William Burroughs, talked about "heavy metal thunder". This phrase was used in Steppenwolf's 1968 single 'Born To Be Wild', and helped christen an emerging sub-genre of hard rock.

The origins of heavy metal are heard in the hard rock bands of the late-1960s and early 1970s such as the Jimi Hendrix Experience, Led Zeppelin and Cream, and in the strident guitar playing of Dave Davies in the Kinks and Pete Townshend in the Who in the mid-1960s.

The difference between hard rock and heavy metal is rather subtle – and for many listeners the terms are interchangeable. However, heavy metal is generally more brutal, louder and without the blues influence heard in hard rock, and often the lyrics have satanic, black magic or fantasy overtones. It's a male dominated style of music, and popular with angst-ridden adolescents. There's also a strict dress code – denim, leather, and perhaps most important of all, long hair. Needless to say, music critics hate heavy metal.

"It wasn't supposed to be a pretty thing."
Robert Plant, Led Zeppelin

The defining albums are Led Zeppelin's *Led Zeppelin II* (1969), particularly the bombastic 'Whole Lotta Love', and Black Sabbath's *Paranoid* (1971). While Zeppelin moved onto new musical pastures, Sabbath continued to plough the same furrow. Guitarist Tony Iommi came up with some of the style's most memorable guitar riffs such as 'Paranoid' and 'Iron Man', while singer Ozzy Osbourne added his trademark nasal whine.

Other prominent exponents include Judas Priest with singer Rob Halford's trademark semi-operatic vocals as heard on British Steel (1980), and Motörhead (*Ace Of Spades* (1980) is a prime example of their fare) who claimed to be so heavy that if they moved in next door to you then your lawn would die!

Before an MTV docu-soap relaunched his career, Ozzy Osbourne of Black Sabbath was known for many years as "the bloke who bit the head off a bat".

NWOBHM

Dead lawns notwithstanding, a younger generation of British musicians was inspired by the hard rock and heavy metal bands of the 1970s, spawning the New Wave Of British Heavy Metal, or NWOBHM for short. The NWOBHM included Iron Maiden, Def Leppard, Saxon, Samson, Venom, Diamond Head and many others.

Of all the NWOBHM bands, the most successful were Iron Maiden and Def Leppard. Maiden's trademark galloping rhythm and lyrics about fantasy or the Devil has changed little over the years. *The Number Of The Beast* (1982) marked a commercial breakthrough with little compromise in their sound. Def Leppard consistently strove to develop their sound and produced the best-selling *Hysteria* (1987), an expertly produced and painstakingly composed piece of pop metal.

The NWOBHM had a profound impact on drummer Lars Ulrich, who later formed Metallica, the most successful of the big four so-called thrash metal bands, the others being Slayer, Megadeth and Anthrax. As Metallica's sound developed they smoothed off their brutal edges and became a heavy metal band, with *Metallica* (1991) becoming one of the best-selling metal albums of all time.

Key Artists:
Led Zeppelin
Black Sabbath
Judas Priest
Iron Maiden
Def Leppard

Happy Families

Meanwhile, Ozzy Osbourne left and rejoined Black Sabbath, along the way releasing *Blizzard Of Ozz* (1980) under his own name, featuring the formidable guitar talents of the late Randy Rhoads. Bizarrely, instead of being revered as the Godfather of Heavy Metal, Osbourne is now better known as the hapless head of his dysfunctional, but loving, family thanks to the MTV real-life hit documentary TV series *The Osbournes*.

Eddie, Iron Maiden's album cover character and mascot, has saved the band members from being constantly recognized on the streets, even at the height of their popularity.

Speed & Thrash *Metal*

Speed and thrash metal sprang to prominence in America during the early 1980s, with fans around the globe forming their own groups. Equally indebted to the do-it-yourself ethos of the New Wave Of British Heavy Metal and the underground spirit of hardcore punk, the style's original progenitors were frighteningly young, but had spent years sharpening their musicianship.

Speed metal's culture of mindless exuberance was perhaps best summed up by Metallica's 'Whiplash', a galloping exercise in precision riffing that appeared on their 1983 debut album, *Kill 'Em All*. If other self-penned numbers like 'Jump In The Fire' suggested that Metallica had been influenced by the UK's Diamond Head, the covering of the Stourbridge quartet's 'Am I Evil?' on an early B-side was definitive proof.

"Lars [Ulrich, drummer] was always nervous onstage, so he'd play faster and faster. We just figured, 'Hell, we'll play faster, too.' "
James Hetfield, Metallica

More than any of their rivals, Metallica exhibited a willingness to grow, and although initially sworn against the music industry's corporate gamesmanship, the San Franciscans had signed to a major label by their fourth album, 1988's *...And Justice For All*. Sooner or later, the rest of the movement's so-called "big four" – Anthrax, Megadeth and Slayer – had done likewise. For other pacesetters like Exodus and Testament, approval from the mainstream came too late, sometimes even resulting in boardroom interference.

Regardless of the labels that released them, some of the best speed/thrash albums attained only cult status, among them *Bonded By Blood* by Exodus (1985), Testament's *The Legacy* (1987), *Darkness Descends* by Dark Angel (1986), *Terrible Certainty* by Kreator (1988) and Death Angel's *Act III* (1990). Swiss band Celtic Frost added their own fascinating idiosyncracies when creating *Into The Pandemonium* in 1987.

Metallica combined the band's rough sounds and hard riffs with the more commercial flavour brought by mainstream producer Bob Rock.

Extreme *Metal*

To many, Slayer made the definitive thrash metal album in the form of 1986's controversial, Rick Rubin-produced *Reign In Blood*. Less than half an hour in duration, the savagery of 'Necrophobic', 'Raining Blood' and 'Angel Of Death' – the latter written by guitarist Jeff Hanneman about war criminal Joseph Mengele – elevated speed metal to death metal and a new plateau of extremity.

By the early 1990s, Metallica's fabled *Metallica* (also known as *The Black Album*) had effectively put them out of reach of the chasing pack, topping the US chart and selling seven million copies. The combination of the ballads 'The Unforgiven' and 'Nothing Else Matters' and the crunching stadium rock of 'Enter Sandman' made Metallica more accessible than any had believed possible, and they had also moved the goalposts for hard rock bands in general.

Three years afterwards, Pantera's *Far Beyond Driven* entered the *Billboard* chart at number one, and later that decade, Megadeth – formed by Dave Mustaine, the sacked Metallica guitarist – released a string of platinum and multi-platinum albums before disbanding in 2002.

Key Artists:

Metallica
Slayer
Anthrax
Megadeath

With Metallica and Megadeth long since moving on, Anthrax and especially Slayer profited through remaining faithful to speed metal's roots. More recently, Swedish quartet the Haunted added a brutal, contemporary twist, with colourful Floridians Iced Earth demonstrating what a little extra ingenuity can achieve.

(Right) Manowar entered the Guiness Book Of Records *during their 1984 "Spectacle Of Might" tour as the world's loudest rock'n'roll band.*

(Above) Their Fighting The World *(1987) album was released three years after their previous album, but was well worth the wait.*

Death Metal & *Grindcore*

Death metal and grindcore both had roots in the decaying thrash metal scene of the mid-1980s. As that decade concluded, musicians on both sides of the Atlantic were looking for new and horrific ways to shock. The styles ended up gravitating towards one another, but began life as very different entities.

Musically death metal and grindcore have much in common with thrash metal and black metal, but with a biting satirical element to the lyrics that adds intensity.

"We're out to wind up as many people as possible" Jeff Walker, Carcass

Death metal bands like Morbid Angel and Death set their violence, suffering and pain-obsessed lyrics to a more intricate framework than the more punk rock-influenced early grindcore acts. As well as the sharing of guitarist Bill Steer, the debut albums from Napalm Death and Carcass (1987's legendary *Scum* and the following year's *Reek Of Putrefaction*) had much in common. Both were showcases for breathtakingly fast and often jarringly short material as well as biting social comment. However, both quickly realized the limited possibilities of what they were doing and began more rounded careers.

Carcass eventually found themselves stranded in no man's land with the more mainstream *Swansong* album in 1996, fragmenting soon afterwards. Fiercely defensive of their underground status, Napalm Death have rarely sounded more ferocious or incisive than on their last two albums, *Enemy Of The Music Business* and *Order Of The Leech*.

Napalm Death's sound was so extreme that at first some critics though it was a joke.

A Gruesome *Glut*

Just as Napalm and Carcass lit the touchpaper in the UK, Chuck Schuldiner's band Death were doing likewise with their own 1987 debut, *Scream Bloody Gore*. Fellow Floridians Morbid Angel weren't lagging far behind guitarist/singer Schuldiner, and by the early 1990s the North American death metal scene included thousands of bands. Each seemed personified by a gruesome name and indecipherable logo.

Among the first to make an impression were Slayer, Cannibal Corpse, Obituary, Deicide, Immolation, Autopsy, Malevolent Creation, Gwar and Suffocation. Brazil also had Sepultura, with Scandinavia throwing forth Dismember, Entombed, At The Gates, Carnage and Hypocrisy.

As quickly as death metal became big business, its quality control mechanism flew out of the window. Major labels began signing such generic second-wavers as Cancer, and before too long records were being judged upon who had produced them, and where.

Melodic Death Metal

After a period of stagnation, In Flames, Dark Tranquillity, Soilwork and Sentenced have all revitalized death metal. The juxtaposition of tuneful segments and traditional intensity has resulted in a melodic death metal that is known as the Gothenburg sound. Meanwhile, former Carnage/Carcass guitarist Mike Amott and his fellow Scandinavians Arch Enemy have dared to appoint an unknown female, Germany's Angela Gossow, as their lead vocalist and are reaping the increased rewards of their best release to date, 2001's *Wages Of Sin*. South Carolina's Nile have also given death metal a cinematic, symphonic twist with their highly recommended 2002 album, *In Their Darkened Shrines*.

Key Artists:
Morbid Angel
Death
Napalm Death
Carcass

"Sepultura" is the Portuguese word for "grave". While translating Motörhead's, 'Dance On Your Grave' into his native tongue, singer and guitarist Max Cavalera thought it would make a good name for a band.

Madchester

Occasionally, a town or city is so integral to a style of music that the music takes its name from the place. In the early 1960s, Liverpool gave rise to the Mersey sound and Merseybeat; in the late-1980s and early 1990s, England's Manchester spawned so-called Madchester.

As much a clubbing scene and youth sub-culture as a style of music, Madchester was also known as "Baggy" due to the baggy clothes worn by the kids. The foremost band of the Madchester scene was the Happy Mondays with their drugged-out, almost psychedelic take on dance music. Embracing funky rhythms and hip hop beats topped off with stream of consciousness lyrics, often with a menacing undercurrent, the Mondays' *Bummed* (1988) shows their unique style beginning to gel.

"Manchester's got everything except a beach."
Ian Brown, singer, Stone Roses

Manchester had already produced arguably the most important British guitar band of the 1980s, the Smiths, and then went on to produce another significant British guitar band – the Stone Roses. Both were heavily influenced by 1960s guitar pop, and although the Stone Roses self-titled debut album from 1989 has little in the way of dance influence, a more dance-orientated remix of 'Fool's Gold' helped establish the Stone Roses as the main Madchester band alongside the Happy Mondays.

The Happy Mondays came into their own with their second album, *Pills, Thrills And Bellyaches* (1990). An intoxicating and heady mix of trippy beats and surreal lyrics sung in a thuggish and occasionally threatening tone by vocalist Shaun Ryder, the album represents the pinnacle of the Madchester scene. It also revealed the Mondays' shameless appropriation – 'Step On' is basically John Kongos' 'He's Gonna Step On You Again' and the melody of 'Kinky Afro' is "borrowed" from LaBelle's 'Lady Marmalade'.

The Happy Mondays perhaps best summed up the spirit of Madchester, combining vocalist Shaun Ryder's deadpan drawl, Bez's frenzied onstage antics and a dancey, "urban folk" sound.

The Madchester *Sound*

The Stone Roses and the Happy Mondays were by no means the only players in the scene. Eclectic leftfielders James and their *Gold Mother* (1990) album produced the hit single 'Sit Down', a mini-anthem for the Madchester generation, although their sound was too diverse to make them a pure Madchester band, with their distinctly folky influences and even stadium-rock leanings.

The Hammond organ played a big part in the sound of both the Inspiral Carpets and the Charlatans. Clint Boon's organ work makes an integral contribution to Inspiral Carpets' *Life* (1990), although the band's inconsistency meant their lasting claim to fame in music history was that Oasis songwriter and creative force Noel Gallagher started his musical career as a roadie for the band, learning the ropes of the music business.

The Charlatans' *Some Friendly* (1991) reveals them to be a more traditional rock band than the Stone Roses and the Happy Mondays with their Rolling Stones-ish swagger and "wakka wakka" organ, as blueprinted by Deep Purple on their 'Hush' single way back in 1968.

Key Artists:

The Happy Mondays
The Stone Roses
James
The Charlatans
Inspiral Carpets

On the fringes of the scene, the Farm's struggled for an identity before aligning themselves with a Madchester-inspired sound. Perceived as rather goofy and a bit of a novelty act, their album *Spartacus* (1991) nevertheless produced two hit singles, 'Groovy Train' and 'All Together Now', the latter of which lifted the melody from classical composer Johann Pachelbel's 'Canon'.

The Hacienda was opened in 1982 by a group of people – including Manchester band New Order – who felt that the city did not offer a nightclub suited to their needs. The innovative, space-age venue soon gained legendary status as the home of the madchester scene.

Drugs and *Clubs*

Just as psychedelic rock was heavily influenced and associated with LSD, the Madchester scene was heavily influenced by and associated with the drug Ecstasy. "Es", as they are known, induce a feeling of blissed-out "loviness" and an understanding of one's fellow clubber.

In fact, clubbing played a big part in the scene, and Madchester often utilized the acid-house dance rhythms heard by the musicians while out clubbing. As with many labels, the precise origins of the "Madchester" term are open to speculation, although it is thought that the Happy Mondays *Rave On Manchester EP* (1989) gave the scene its name. However, it also ties in the Manchester expression "mad fer it" meaning "up for it", and the "mad" part is appropriate since the the the drug taking associated with the scene gave rise to some, well, pretty mad behaviour.

Key Tracks:
'One Love' The Stone Roses
'Sit Down' James
'Step On' The Happy Mondays
'The Only One I Know' The Charlatans
'This Is How It Feels' Inspiral Carpets

The Stone Roses became embroiled in a long-running court case with their former record company, then a bout of laziness resulted in a five-year delay before the release of their modestly-titled second album, *The Second Coming* (1994). The loss of momentum led to the end of the band, with singer Ian Brown pursuing a solo career and guitarist John Squire leading the ill-fated trad rock band the Seahorses. The Happy Mondays disintegrated, largely due to Ryder's drug abuse, although he got himself sufficently together to form Black Grape who continued where the Happy Mondays had left off.

The Stone Roses found widespread success with their psychedelia-influenced jangly guitar pop, but legal battles with their record companies led to an early retirement from the limelight.

Alternative/Indie Rock

Rather a "catch-all" category that includes many musically diverse bands from the 1980s and 1990s, "alternative" is generally an American term referring to any remotely leftfield and non-mainstream band, whereas "indie rock" originally refers generally to the UK bands recording for smaller, independent labels, again usually meaning non-mainstream bands.

Alternative encompasses many sub-styles. To complicate matters, many bands can be said to have started their career as "alternative" simply because they are little known and therefore non-mainstream, but as they become more successful and consequently incorporated into the mainstream, they are no longer "alternative" even though they may have changed their music little.

"We proved that alternative music is a viable commodity."
Krist Novoselic, Nirvana

Mainstream bands such as Radiohead, U2 and INXS have all at some point in their careers been described as "alternative". Confused? You should be! Just don't take this "alternative" category too rigidly!

Stateside, the first two alternative bands of lasting significance were REM and Hüsker Dü, both of whom emerged in the mid-1980s. REM started off as a guitar pop band, inspiring many bands in their wake, and went on to become one of the biggest and most successful bands on the planet; Hüsker Dü's speed pop was similarly influential although they never broke into the mainstream.

Thom Yorke from England's Radiohead. Receiving critical acclaim for albums such as The Bends *(1995) and* OK Computer *(1997), Radiohead's musical style continues to evolve with each record they release.*

A Broad, Wide *Scene*

In the 1990s, the most influential alternative band was Nirvana, who emerged from the so-called Seattle-based grunge scene, with *Nevermind* (1991), breaking down the barrier between hard rock and alternative.

Influenced by the Pixies' use of dynamics (that is, quiet passages followed by loud passages as heard on 'Smells Like Teen Spirit') as on 'Surfer Rosa' (1988), Nirvana were described as "the Guns 'n' Roses it's OK to like" — melodic hard rock without the macho and misogynistic trappings that traditionally accompany many hard rock bands.

The alternative scene is so broad that it encompasses experimental bands such as the Butthole Surfers from Austin, Texas, and Sonic Youth, who emerged from the New York Noise scene. At the other end of the spectrum, it includes bands with traditional rock influences such as Jane's Addiction and the Smashing Pumpkins, led by alternative guitar hero Billy Corgan, who "widdles" with the best of them on 1993's *Siamese Dream*. Nine Inch Nails took traditionally conservative heavy metal into new areas with drum machines in industrial metal and Danzig took metal into new musical territories with *Danzig III: How The Gods Kill* (1992).

Lollapalooza Festival

Key Artists:

REM
Hüsker Dü
Nirvana
The Smiths

Perry Farrell, the Jane's Addiction singer, packaged the alternative scene into the Lollapalooza tour in the 1990s, a travelling musical circus showcasing many of the alternative bands but also celebrating alternative counter-culture 1990s-style with tattooing and piercing stands. Controversy was caused in 1996 when the festival was headlined by Metallica, again illustrating the broadness of the "alternative" category. Metallica certainly started out as a broadly alternative band, albeit of the speed metal variety, but many alternative purists felt they were really unreconstructed heavy metal dinosaurs.

The Smashing Pumpkins' Siamese Dream (1993) was rock with extra texture.

smashing pumpkins ★ siamese dream

Indie in the *UK*

The indie rock scene in the UK has many parallels with the alternative scene in the US. Inspired by the DIY ethic of the punk rockers, many independent small labels sprung up offering a refreshing alternative to the big, lumbering corporate labels who were perceived as boring and run by men in suits. Ironically, many of these labels became absorbed by the major record labels.

Although indie rock is more pop-based than the alternative scene in the US, it similarly encompasses several other styles such as the shoegazers, My Bloody Valentine being the leaders of this movement, Madchester, as celebrated by the Happy Mondays, Brit pop, as exemplified by Blur and Oasis, and goth rock, represented by the Sisters of Mercy.

The longest-lasting and most prolific indie rock band is probably the Fall, led by Mark E. Smith. Despite an ever-changing line-up, the Fall's unique sound – courtesy of Smith's half-sung, half-spoken vocals, backed by spiky and sometimes almost cacophonic guitar and keyboards (as on 1980's *Grotesque (After The Gramme)*) – has changed little over the years.

Key Albums:

Dragnets The Fall
Land Speed Record Hüsker Dü
Murmur REM
Nevermind Nirvana
The Smiths The Smiths

The Smiths self-titled debut album in 1984 heralded the most influential British guitar rock of the 1980s and, like REM across the pond, the Smiths were influenced by 1960s guitar pop like the Byrds but with singer Morrissey's uniquely English slant on life.

Morrissey was the spokesman for a disillusioned generation with his bleak sound and thought-provoking lyrics.

Shoegazing

Originally coined as a criticism of the bands' static stage performances – band members were said to stand stock still staring at their shoes – the so-called shoegazers played slow- or medium-paced rock, generally with heavily distorted or heavily reverbed guitars topped by dreamy, melodic and ethereal vocals.

Influenced by the use of distorted guitars by the Jesus & Mary Chain and the otherworldliness of the Cocteau Twins, the shoegazers were primarily a British movement, the most prominent exponent being My Bloody Valentine.

My Bloody Valentine took a long and tortuous path from their debut recording *This Is Your Bloody Valentine*, released in 1985, to their masterpiece album *Loveless* in 1991. Starting as a goth band, their distinctive sound began to emerge with the addition of singer Bilinda Butcher and the development of bandleader Kevin Shields' guitar sound.

"We try to make the music the personality and keep ourselves quite anonymous." Andy Bell, Ride

Retreating to the recording studio for two years to further refine their sound, spending around £200,000 ($310,000) in studio time and nearly bankrupting their label, Creation, the band's painstaking attention to sound detail is confirmed by the "engineered and assisted by" credit that runs to 18 different names (including two band members). Centring around Shields' awesome guitar sounds and the sensual interplay between Shields and Butcher's airy vocals, *Loveless* defines the shoegazing sound.

My Bloody Valentine pioneered the ethereal sound that came to define shoegazing.

Bandwagon

Such was My Bloody Valentine's hold on the shoegazer style that some bands inspired by *Loveless* were accused of jumping on the shoegazer bandwagon – Curve in particular suffered from such bad press, although *Doppelganger* (1992) sees them finding their own take on the *Loveless* sonic landscape. The Verve emerged from darkest Wigan with a psychedelic take on the shoegazer sound, as heard on *A Storm In Heaven* (1993).

Insular

A rather inward-looking and insular movement, some of the shoegazer bands such as Ride, Chapterhouse, Curve, Slowdive and Lush struggled to develop their sound. Others managed to evolve and reach a wider audience. The shoegazer influence can be heard on Blur's *Leisure* (1991), but by the time of *Parklife* (1994) they had established themselves as forerunners of Britpop.

The Verve broke into the mainstream with their massive hit single 'Bitter Sweet Symphony' from *Urban Hymns* (1997). Similarly, the Boo Radleys' *Everything's Alright Forever* (1992) reveals a debt to the shoegazer sound, but by *Wake Up!* (1995) they were more of a straightforward pop band.

Key Artists:

My Bloody Valentine
Curve
The Verve
Ride
Chapterhouse

The shoegazer bands' notoriously static live performances didn't endear them as live acts and few were able to move in new directions. Even Kevin Shields found it hard to follow up *Loveless* and My Bloody Valentine still hadn't recorded a full-length follow-up album when Shields joined Primal Scream as a guitarist on a semi-permanent basis in the late 1990s. The shoegazers influence can be heard in trip hop.

Toni Halliday, whose languid vocals cut through Curve's multi-layered, dreamy sound. Halliday went on to contribute guest vocals to Leftfield's 'Original' on their 1995 album Leftism.

US Underground & Garage *Rock*

Taking their name from the meagre rehearsal facilities of its early practitioners, garage rock began in the US during the mid-1960s. The loud, fuzz-toned guitars often failed to disguise links to UK pop mentors like the Beatles, the Rolling Stones and the Who. Later acid rock bands such as the Electric Prunes incorporated progressive and psychedelic influences.

Mostly, however, the first wave of garage rock bands were destined for short-lived cult appeal, then obscurity. Garage rock became rawer and more raucous, evolving into something more politicized during the early 1970s. Among the first indications that something was afoot, future Patti Smith guitarist Lenny Kaye assembled *Nuggets, Vol 1: The Hits*, a legendary double compilation that cherrypicked the likes of the Chocolate Watch Band, the Electric Prunes, Blue Cheer, Seeds and Todd Rundgren's Nazz, even coining the term "punk rock" for the first time in his sleeve notes.

Prose and Punk Rock

By 1975, Kaye was providing musical backing for Patti Smith's poetry readings. Smith's watershed album *Horses* (1975) had successfully married her adventurous prose to a proto-garage rock sound, making it one of the most influential albums in the growth of punk rock. Elsewhere, an early single sleeve of John F. Kennedy being shot had rendered the Misfits so notorious that labels were genuinely afraid to release their product. Eventually, such albums as 1982's *Walk Among Us* – or, perhaps more accurately, the patronage of thrash metal giants Metallica, who covered 'Last Caress' during the 1980s – belatedly secured the place of the New Jersey punks in the annals of underground rock.

America's alternative rock scene was thriving. West coast punk act Black Flag had played their part, though by 1986 guitarist Greg Ginn had disbanded the group, his SST label introducing the world to the Meat Puppets, Sonic Youth, Hüsker Dü, Soundgarden, Screaming Trees, the Minutemen and Firehose, becoming one of the most important independent imprints of its day. SST also distinguished itself by issuing *I Against I*, by Washington D.C.-based fusionists the Bad Brains, and the Black Sabbath-flavoured sludge rock of St Vitus.

Underground queen Patti Smith, who has described her unique sound as "three chord rock merged with the power of the word". Smith's 1975 debut Horses *was the first underground rock album to enter the Billboard Top 50.*

Twisted *Eclecticism*

The Butthole Surfers and Big Black crystalized the twisted eclecticism of the US underground, which mutated hard and punk rock with alternating strains of psychedelia, art rock, folk and even country. Both were formed in 1982 and lead by gifted, uncompromising mavericks in the shape of Gibby Haynes and Steve Albini, making music that was powerful, cynical, crazed and often wryly amusing.

The unhinged Haynes, in particular, based his career upon shockingly bad behaviour, though he remained forgiveable while creating records as brilliantly frazzled as 1987's *Locust Abortion Technician*. Splitting up at their peak, Big Black lasted for just five short years, Albini becoming a producer (or to use the term he prefers "recording engineer") of distinction through his work with Nirvana, the Pixies and even his heroes Cheap Trick.

Unlike their rivals REM, Minneapolis bands Hüsker Dü and the Replacements never quite became household names. However, the songwriting skills of guitarist Bob Mould and drummer Grant Hart remain among the most celebrated of the US underground. Like Sonic Youth, Hüsker Dü moved onto a major label as the 1980s drew to a close, although the band split up in January of 1988 when the long-running rivalry between Mould and Hart became unworkable. The Replacements, meanwhile, formed in 1979, playing some of the noisiest and most chaotic gigs of the following decade, although sometimes they were unable to complete shows due to drunkenness – or worse. A reluctance to make accessible videos also speeded up the Replacements' demise, though singer/songwriter Paul Westerberg has a cult solo career and former bassist Tommy Stinson toured with Guns 'n' Roses.

Key Artists:

Patti Smith Group
Dinosaur Jr.
Hüsker Dü
Sonic Youth
Jon Spencer Blues Explosion

Sonic Youth emerged from New York's "no-wave" scene with a ferocious sound, blending infectious melodies and intense instrumentation, which the band refined over time.

Continuing *Successes*

At least Sonic Youth were sussed enough to have ensured that their contract gave them total creative control when they signed with the Geffen Records offshoot DGC, offering genuine hope that independent artistry could work hand-in-hand with corporate distribution and marketing. However, since then, the twin driving forces of guitarist Thurston Moore and bassist Kim Gordon have regained indie credibility through the formation of their own label SYR Records.

In common with many garage rock acts, Pussy Galore were also plagued by substance problems. The bass guitar-less Washington DC quartet, who took their name from the female James Bond character, created a scuzzy, nihilistic wall of sound that was jointly inspired by the New York Dolls and the Velvet Underground. When the band split in 1990, frontman Jon Spencer adopted the tongue-in-cheek name of the Blues Explosion (aka JSBX) for his new project, while guitarist Neil Haggerty formed the similarly confrontational Royal Trux with vocalist Jennifer Herrema. The latter were once described as sounding like: "two hopeless junkies in a cheap studio making up a horrid squall of off-key guitars, out-of-time drums, and tuneless moaning in lieu of vocals as they go along", so it's no surprise that of the two acts, JSBX have fared better.

The Jon Spencer Blues Explosion's energetic blend of punk, funk, rockabilly and soul was equally hard to ignore, and the support of Steve Albini further validated the band's credentials. Now onto their eighth album, the acclaimed *Plastic Fang* (2002), the Explosion's future success is assured.

Key Tracks:

'Last Caress' Patti Smith Group
'Freak Scene' Dinosaur Jr.
'Teenage Riot' Sonic Youth

Albini has also worked with Californian art rockers Neurosis, another band that have helped to erode the boundaries of underground rock with their highly charged industrial metal and progressive-influenced arrangements. The success of both Tool and A Perfect Circle have certainly helped to break down barriers in that respect, though nothing, it seems, is sacred any more.

Jon Spencer, the charismatic frontman of the Jon Spencer Blues Explosion (or JSBX). The band play a manic mixture of musical styles which combines punk rock with blues-flavoured grooves.

A Garage Rock *Revival*

In recent years garage rock has undergone a revival, a new wave of often besuited upstarts from around the planet re-invigorating the style. Between them, Sweden's the Hives, New York five-piece the Strokes and the Detroit-based duo White Stripes have somehow injected urgency and fashionability into a form of music that was in danger of becoming redundant.

Rolling Stone magazine had no hesitation in putting Jack and Meg White of the White Stripes on their prestigious front cover, touting the minimalist pair as the "next big thing".

Among the acts snapping at the heels of this elite bunch are the Vines, the Australians whose debut album *Highly Evolved* debuted in August 2002 at number 11 on the *Billboard* 200, plus fellow Detroit combo the Von Bondies, New Zealand's the Datsuns and D4, the BellRays from Britain and Finland's the Flaming Sideburns.

Key Albums:

Bug Dinosaur Jr.
Confusion Is Sex Sonic Youth
New Day Rising Hüsker Dü
Now I Got Worry Jon Spencer Blues Explosion
Walk Among Us Patti Smith Group

(Right) Australian garage rock band the Vines burst onto the music scene with their critically acclaimed debut Highly Evolved *(2002).*
(Above) The White Stripes' 2001 album White Blood Cells *showcased the band's raw, garage rock sound.*

Progressive *Metal*

Canadian trio Rush had little idea of the magnitude of their actions when they released *Caress Of Steel* in September 1975. Just seven months after the group's second album, *Fly By Night*, it saw them board a creative wave that for many fans would peak with their next studio release, 1976's conceptual album *2112*.

Though still recognizeable as a Led Zeppelin/Cream-inspired bar act, the increasingly progressive Caress... introduced 'The Necromancer' and 'The Fountain Of Lamneth' – twelve and a half minutes and twenty minutes long, respectively – epic numbers which were infused with an adventurous new spirit and embellished by drummer Neal Peart's sci-fi lyrics.

"Every day's a test of friendship for this band..."
Mike Portnoy, Dream Theater

Then as now, critics dismissed the trio's endeavours as overblown and pretentious, but the fans did not care. Rush would release better focused albums than *Caress Of Steel* over the course of a still unfolding thirty-year career, though it undoubtedly served as a launch pad for their own endeavors, as well as a sub-genre now known as progressive metal.

Heirs to Rush's Throne

In the 1980s, with Rush busy exploring synthesizers, bands like Watchtower and Fate's Warning took up the baton, mostly missing the point with their combination of unnecessarily shrill vocals and super-technical instrumentation. However, Queensrÿche and King's X eventually emerged as fitting heirs to the throne, with Savatage lurking not too far behind.

Rush are Canada's biggest rock act and have retained a large fan base throughout their lengthy career, despite frequent panning by critics – as well as sometimes by the fans themselves.

Progressing *Steadily*

In 1988, Queensrÿche unveiled *Operation: Mindcrime*. Offering power in the Iron Maiden mould and soaring melodies, the Seattle quintet found themselves billed as the thinking man's hard rock band.

The album tipped its hat at Rush's own *2112* for its concept of futuristic censorship, and also to Michael Kamen for its lavish orchestral arrangements, yet Queensrÿche's masterwork is rightly regarded as a power metal watershed moment in its own right. *Operation: Mindcrime* stayed on the American charts for a year, selling over a million copies, though even those figures were eclipsed in the 1990 *Empire* album, with its haunting hit 'Silent Lucidity'.

The departure of guitarist Chris DeGarmo accelerated Queensrÿche's gradual process of unravelling. Things reached a nadir with the dreary *Q2K* in 1999, by which time the band had a serious rival. Originally known as Majesty, Dream Theatre's earliest recording line-up had shown potential on 1989's debut *When Dream And Day Unite*. Replacing frontman Charlie Dominici with beefy Canadian James LaBrie helped the quintet to gain invaluable MTV exposure for their excellent 1992 follow-up, *Images And Words*, after which they never looked back. The group's insistence upon performing lengthy drum, keyboard, guitar and bass solos infuriated reviewers, only cementing the enthusiasm of their following. In creative terms, Dream Theater peaked in 1999 with *Metropolis Pt 2: Scenes From A Memory*, an ambitious conceptual piece that the band had modeled upon *Dark Side Of The Moon* and *The Wall* by Pink Floyd, Genesis' *The Lamb Lies Down On Broadway* and even *OK Computer* by Radiohead.

Key Artists:

Rush
Queensrÿche
Dream Theatre
Opeth
King's X

Most of the best progressive metal now emanates from Scandinavia, such groundbreaking acts as Opeth, Meshuggah and Therion proving that a little serious thought is all it takes to carve new and unique ideas from what's gone before.

Lengthy drum solos, in the style of Led Zeppelin's John Bonham, have found a home in the progressive metal genre.

Black *Metal*

By the end of the 1980s, thrash metal was on its last legs. Metallica and Slayer were on the path towards acceptance by the mainstream and it seemed as though heavy metal was in danger of losing not only the extremity upon which it had been founded, but also its shock value. How ill-founded those assumptions turned out to be.

In America, death metal had already raised the stakes, but an even more violent new breed of metal musician was lurking in Norway. Jointly inspired by the Satanic writings of Aleister Crowley and the groundbreaking evil noise of UK trio Venom, whose 1982 watershed release *Black Metal* effectively gave the new style its name, groups like Mayhem, Burzum and Emperor were soon to achieve worldwide notoriety.

Satanic Crimes

The bleak, icy extremity of black metal was quickly rendered infamous through a succession of twisted, criminal acts. The features of its protagonists were disguised by "corpse paint", a ghostly white type of facial make-up, their identities further cloaked by such grim pseudonyms as Count Grishnackh, Euronymous and Dead. Such anonymity allowed them to pursue a variety of alleged causes, including satanism, paganism and nationalism, not forgetting self-promotion.

"He died from one stab to the head, through the skull. I actually had to knock the knife out."
Count Grishnackh of Burzum after he had murdered Mayhem's Euronymous

Although rivalry between the early front-runners was fierce, a ten-man "inner circle" eventually established itself. Together they swore to rid Norway of Christianity and would torch wooden Christian churches by night and afterwards openly boast of their satanic influence. Ultimately, many of their number would eventually die – some at the hands of fellow conspirators– while others ended up imprisoned for murder, arson or grave desecration.

Venom's penchant for using extreme pyrotechnic effects during their stage act significantly reduced their choice of venues.

Murder and *Mayhem*

Chillingly, none of those apprehended went on to express remorse for their deeds. Indeed, Mayhem frontman Euronymous – stabbed to death in his underwear in 1993 by former friend Count Grishnackh of Burzum – once stated: "I don't want to see people respecting me, I want them to hate and fear." Grishnackh (real name Varg Vikernes) is likely to be freed in October of 2006, though he has added to the Burzum catalogue since his incarceration.

Of all the black metal bands, Emperor became the most popular and influential. Having dropped the corpse paint and refined their sound with *Anthems To The Welkin At Dusk* in 1997, the quartet had seemed on the verge of big things before announcing a decision to retire from touring. This was followed by a full-blown split in 2001.

Black metal has gradually divided into numerous offshots, newcomers like Dimmu Borgir choosing to add keyboards and proceed down more orchestrally embellished routes. But while many of the music's original goals have thankfully been laid to rest, its popularity continues to thrive.

Key Artists:

Emperor
Burzum
Venom
Mayhem

In late 2002, Norwegian duo Satyricon and Capitol Records offered the genre's first major label release, *Volcano*, and in the UK the Sony corporation have also entered the market via the signing of Cradle Of Filth. With their *Damnation And A Day* album, the self-styled vampiric rockers from Suffolk are optimistic of reaching sales of a cool half-million copies.

Burzum's Count Grishnackh, who ended up behind bars after killing fellow black metal star Euronymous, from the band Mayhem.

Grunge

With lyrics written minutes before they were recorded and the most ramshackle production imagineable, Nirvana's 1989 debut album *Bleach* didn't sound like the work of a group capable of toppling MTV's fixation with hairspray rock; nor did its initial sales of around 15,000 copies. But that's exactly what the trio from Aberdeen, Washington, went on to achieve.

Armed with just the simplicity of guitarist/vocalist Kurt Cobain's songs and a refreshingly fundamentalist view of what making music should really be about, Nirvana went on to revolutionize rock music as it was known in the 1990s and beyond.

Such was the impact of the band's addictive breakthrough single 'Smells Like Teen Spirit', it mattered little that the track's riff was borrowed from 'More Than A Feeling' by melodic rock radio staples Boston. With hindsight, Nirvana were doing little that the Pixies hadn't already attempted over a cult four-album career, though the group's talismanic 1991 album *Nevermind* was greeted by media overkill. Indeed, the grunge phenomenon eventually found itself suffering from many of the ailments that it had seemed like curing.

"A lot of kids were looking for something that felt more real and had more passion..."
Butch Vig, Nevermind producer

Seattle Stars

Third-rate imitators were soon crawling out of the woodwork, though the credentials of fellow Seattle originals like Soundgarden, Pearl Jam, Alice In Chains and Mudhoney were never in doubt. The same couldn't be said for Stone Temple Pilots, who despite achieving major stardom with their three-million-selling *Core* debut in 1992, were cast as plagiarists. Strange then that along with Pearl Jam, STP were among the few grunge acts with any real staying power. The fickle nature of fortune also ensured that one of the longest lasting and most talented of the Seattle bands, the Screaming Trees, also fell by the wayside (though vocalist Mark Lanegan is now a member of Queens Of The Stone Age).

Dave Grohl, Krist Novoselic and Kurt Cobain (left to right) of Nirvana, the band which both created and epitomized the grunge movement. Their album Nevermind *became an anthem for the so-called "Generation X".*

A New Stripped-Down *Style*

The pressure of stardom was too much for the waif-like, increasingly self-destructive Cobain. The singer attempted suicide many times, and had several heroin overdoses; in 1993 after another overdose, he failed to complete a rehabilitation programme and went missing.

Many conspiracy theories suggest otherwise, but it's certain that Kurt shot himself on 5 April 1994, leaving behind a wife, Courtney Love of Hole, and daughter Frances Bean. Love's marriage and subsequent tragedy obscured her own musical achievement with Hole, whose breakthrough 1993 album *Live Through This* was widely acclaimed.

Pearl Jam's popularity is only marginally diminished. Meanwhile, drugs terminated the life of singer Layne Staley and the career of his band Alice In Chains. Staley died of a heroin overdose eight years to the day after Cobain's suicide.

Key Artists:

Nirvana
Pearl Jam
Soundgarden
Alice in Chains
Hole

Elsewhere, the Soundgarden frontman Chris Cornell is now a member of Audioslave, who are completed by the three instrumentalists from Rage Against The Machine. A self-titled album has received rave reviews.

The glory days of what we traditionally recognize as grunge rock are long gone, but Nirvana drummer Dave Grohl has found success with the Foo Fighters and Creed, Live, Silverchair, Bush, Everclear and 3 Doors Down have all borrowed liberally from grunge's stripped-down formula, reaping their own multi-platinum rewards.

Pearl Jam, dismissed as "corporate" by Kurt Cobain, have remained true to their ideals by playing less-established venues – in a bid to enrage the all-pervasive Ticketmaster – and by voicing their opinions, however controversial (notably against the war in Iraq in 2003).

Funk Metal

Funk stars of the 1970s like The Ohio Players, Sly & The Family Stone and Funkadelic didn't realize for a decade that hard rock ears had been paying attention. That same decade, Aerosmith's combination of white-boy electric blues and propulsive arena hard rock had been deemed as unique, with just Grand Funk Railroad working along the similar lines.

It would be more than ten years before a revamped version of Aerosmith's 'Walk This Way', recorded with Run-DMC, took the mixture of styles to its logical conclusion, and when the collaboration charted all over the globe it opened the floodgates for an avalanche of other like-minded acts. In 1986, the Beastie Boys, whose rock-fuelled *Licensed To Ill* was the first hip hop album to top the American chart.

"Living in Portland was a great mixture of the east and west coasts. At the same time as we got AC/DC, we also got Sly & The Family Stone. We got Cameo, we got Parliament, Humble Pie, Free and Bad Company." Dan Reed

Aerosmith frontman Steven Tyler himself had described the Red Hot Chili Peppers as "fuckin' great", and the Chilis' breakthrough arrived with their 1991 album, the Rick Rubin-produced *Blood Sugar Sex Magik*. By this time broader-based material like 'Under The Bridge', 'Give It Away' and 'Breaking The Girl' had rewarded them with a popularity that only drug addiction had seemed likely to destroy.

The irrepressible Red Hot Chili Peppers.

Thrills and *Spills*

Faith No More paired a simmering internal tension with a pooled record collection that included punk, heavy metal and Tibetan Buddhism. In 1989, it all came to the boil for an album called *The Real Thing*, but the stardom that such hits as 'Epic' and 'Midlife Crisis' brought the San Francisco five-piece affected them in so many different ways that they simply could not last.

In 1988, the Prince-meets-Van Halen groove of the Dan Reed Network's self-titled debut had thrilled and puzzled in equal measures. However, frontman Reed's humanitarian streak meant he was not cut out for the music business, and the DRN went their separate ways in 1993. Formed the following year, New York's Mick Jagger-approved Living Colour burned brightly at first but fragmented after four albums. However, the group has since reformed.

Ska Meets Funk Metal

Sugar Ray and the ska-flavoured *No Doubt* have brought the funk metal sound into the new millennium, though when *Californication* (1999) and *By The Way* (2002) came around, the Chilis' had long since moved onto more mellow, stadium-friendly strains of rock. Newcomers like the Bloodhound Gang have since taken Anthony Kiedis and company's harmless innuendo to its vulgar limits. "You and me baby ain't nuthin' but mammals/So let's do it like they do on the Discovery Channel", sing the vacant Philadelphia crew on 2000's *Hooray For Boobies*, setting both funk-rock and the male species back several generations in one fell swoop. Fortunately, old-timers Fishbone remain determined to uphold traditional values, even if it means proceeding down the independent label route.

Key Artists:

Red Hot Chilli Peppers
Faith No More
The Beastie Boys
Dan Reed Network

Faith No More struggled with their conflicting opinions of the rock mainstream, of which they unwittingly became a part.

Riot *Grrrl*

A potent though short-lived force in the early 1990s, lyrically, riot grrrl had a strong feminist agenda, whilst musically it was strongly influenced by punk rock. The spiritual roots of riot grrrl can be traced back to the all-female British punk band the Slits from the 1970s.

With its origins in America, and an agenda of "cutting the tripwires of alienation that separate girls from boys", riot grrrl was pioneered by Bikini Kill in the US, and by their spiritual cousins Huggy Bear in the UK. The movement sought to by-pass the traditional male-dominated structures of the music business by generally recording for small, independent labels and using fanzines to reach their followers while refusing to play the media game of giving interviews to the traditional mainstream music press.

In keeping with their political agenda, Bikini Kill even recorded for the Olympia, Washington-based Kill Rock Stars label. *The CD Version Of The First Two Records* (1992) draws together the band's first two albums – angry, aggressive and confrontational, but also intelligent. Bikini Kill teamed up with Huggy Bear for *Yeah! Yeah! Yeah!* (1992), each band taking one side of the twelve-inch release.

"Because we don't wanna assimilate to someone else's (Boy) standards of what is or isn't."
From Kathleen Hanna's Riot Grrrl Manifesto.

Bikini Kill's *Pussy Whipped* (1994) is more experimental, varied and accessible, but the band's preference for enthusiastic performances over polished production values doesn't help broaden their listening appeal. Ex-Runaways singer and solo artist Joan Jett helped address this by producing Bikini Kill's 'New Radio' single, included on *The Singles* (1998).

The UK's Brighton-based Huggy Bear comprised two male and three female members and scored hits with songs such as 'Her Jazz'.

Female-Friendly *Gigs*

At live shows, audiences were asked to allow women to the front. At a Huggy Bear gig in England in 1993, a male member of the audience objected to the "girls only at the front" policy, the resulting melée meaning the gig ended in chaos. Bikini Kill would invite female members of the audience to take the microphone and discuss matters of sexual misconduct and sexual abuse.

Negative Publicity

The British and American media were keen to run stories on riot grrrl, but a lack of co-operation from the bands meant media publicity was outside the bands' influence. Huggy Bear attracted controversy when they disrupted UK youth culture programme *The Word* because they objected to an item on "bimbos". In the States, Bikini Kill's singer Kathleen Hanna gained similar non-musical publicity when she was punched in the face by Hole's Courtney Love – not much sisterhood there, then!

Key Artists:
Bikini Kill
Huggy Bear
Sleater-Kinney
Babes In Toyland
Tribe 8

Ironically, despite having a valid feminist agenda, particularly regarding sexism in the music industry, refusing to give interviews to the music press limited the movement's impact, and musically neither Bikini Kill nor Huggy Bear were able to move forward or capture a wider audience.

Some of the spirit and influence of riot grrrl can be heard in British band Bis and in American bands L7, Babes In Toyland and Hole. The movement largely faded away with Kathleen Hanna going to graduate school in 1998, although Sleater-Kinney formed from the remnants of two first generation riot grrrl bands and kept the flag flying with *Call The Doctor* (1996).

As pioneers of the riot grrrl movement, Bikini Kill offered a similar brand of aggressive musical frustration and promises of female liberty to 1990s women as the Slits had done to female punks in the 1970s.

Nu Metal

As the genre's name so boldly implies, timing and image were both of critical importance to the realm of nu metal. In pure musical terms there was little to unite the scene's leading exponents, save for the radical detuning of their instruments and a desire to distance themselves from such old-school hard rock favourites as Iron Maiden and Metallica.

From the rap-flavoured pop rock of Limp Bizkit to the hate-driven, theatrical metal of Slipknot, the nu metal crowd was indeed a disparate gathering. Marilyn Manson and Nine Inch Nails, for example, were both established names before the critics began lumping them in with an array of musical misfits.

Although Faith No More will forever be irked by the suggestion, the San Franciscan quintet's provocative, chaotically eccentric brand of funk metal helped to define the roots of nu metal during the mid-1980s. Later that decade, the grunge of Nirvana also helped to tear down lyrical, philosophical and visual barriers, paving the way for a far darker, nihilistic and stripped-down approach.

"There is good and evil within all of us, and I enjoy searching to bring that out through my music. I like it that there are questions brought out by my music."
Marilyn Manson

Among the first act to crystallize the nu metal sound were Korn, a five-piece from Bakersfield in California. Railing against the suffocation of smalltown USA, Korn were lead by vocalist and former undertaker Jonathan Davis. The group's compellingly miserable self-titled debut album surfaced in 1994, overseen by Ross Robinson, the producer whose name quickly became a watermark of approval from within the nu metal circle. Davis' violent lyrics addressed such previously taboo subjects as childhood bullying and even sexual abuse, connecting with many confused souls in the process. *Korn* was a slowburner, though it eventually sold two million copies, and two years later the band confirmed their star quality with *Life Is Peachy*. Three more studio albums and seven years later, Korn have set standards of consistency and longevity that other nu metal acts can only dream of. However, their chief rivals are Slipknot and Limp Bizkit.

Korn brought about the 1990s renaissance of metal music, with their raw, hip hop-tinged sound and honest songs that spoke to misunderstood teenagers everywhere.

Other *Agendas*

Hailing from Des Moines, Iowa, the nine members of Slipknot also used the repressions of their own collective youth as highly effective subject matter for songs like 'Wait And Bleed', 'Spit It Out' and 'People = Shit'.

Fusing jagged, grinding riffs with barbaric percussion, plus samples and keyboards, Slipknot became overnight heroes after signing to Roadrunner Records in 1999 for their platinum-selling second album, Slipknot (their first album, 1997's *Mate. Feed. Kill. Repeat*, was self-financed). The group's refusal to be photographed without their trademark scary masks and boiler suits polarized opinions on levels of musicianship and validity, though to most it only heightened their mystique.

Proof of Slipknot's mushrooming popularity arrived in 2001 when their third album, Iowa, entered the *Billboard* chart at number three. However, with the group busying themselves in a variety of side-projects like the Murderdolls, Stone Sour and DJ Starscream – and even stating: "We've [got] one more album in us, then we'll call it a day" – question marks must be raised against their long-term future.

The very public face of nu metal, Limp Bizkit's Fred Durst is as famous for his red baseball cap and cheeky grin as for a series of childish feuds and disposable one-liners. The ubiquitous Durst astutely plotted the route to his current, enviable position of influence. It was Durst who appointed turntable wizard DJ Lethal to play on Limp Bizkits's first album, 1997's *Three Dollar Bill, Y'All$*, and who discovered future US chart-toppers Staind. He also recognized the importance of internet file-trading, controversially aligning the group to a tour sponsored by the music industry's avowed bête noire, Napster.

Key Artists:

Limp Bizkit
Slipknot
Korn
System Of A Down
Marilyn Manson

2000's American chart-topping third album, *Chocolate Starfish And The Hotdog Flavored Water* proved Limp Bizkit's high point. Guitarist Wes Borland left in 2001 and rejoined in 2004, but vital momentum was lost and their moment passed.

The constantly masked band Slipknot consists of nine members, including three percussionists, two guitarists, a bassist, a DJ, a sampler and a lead singer. This line-up shows a marked departure from the traditional rock band and gives some idea of how rock music is evolving.

Unpredictable *Antics*

If one single factor unites nu metal, it's the genre's sheer unpredictability. From the chameleon-like, shock rock-inspired antics of Marilyn Manson to the electrifying unconformity of Armenian-American four-piece System Of A Down and the commercially infused Linkin Park, bands once again seem happy to take chances.

The power of the electric guitar – sometimes offered in seven-string format – remains central to the appeal of acts like Papa Roach, Staind, Amen and Taproot, but integration of electronica, hip hop, gothic and dance music is steadily growing.

Key Albums:

Iowa Slipknot
Korn Korn
Life Is Peachy Korn
Three Dollar Bill, Y'All$ Limp Bizkit

Just a decade ago, it would have been hard to accept the notion of a hard rock group brave enough to absorb the Cure's influence, in the case of Sacramento's Deftones, or Duran Duran and Depeche Mode in that of Linkin Park. However, the mounting Grammy nominations and sales figures suggest that, for the moment at least, the listening public cannot get enough of such avid cross-pollination.

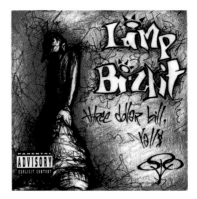

(Right) Limp Bizkit guitarist Wes Borland, whose departure from the band in 2000 left a gaping hole. He later rejoined, but the band's heyday was over. (Above) Limp Bizkit's promising sound, as heard on thier debut album Three Dollar Bill Y'All$ (1997) helped set them apart from their peers.

New Rock *Revolution*

As rock rang up its first half-century from Elvis Presley's 'Heartbreak Hotel', in 2006 it looked all manner of challenges in the face. Digital devices such as the iPod were changing the way music was consumed. Downloaded MP3 computer files were now chart-eligible money-making items rather than Napster-available freebies, while hit singles became mobile-phone ringtones and vice versa.

Not everyone had thrown convention to the winds, however, and the Darkness, Britain's top band of 2004, were all in favour of traditional virtues – from long hair to the glossy production values once favoured by Queen, not to mention some Spinal Tap-inspired videos. Their debut album *Permission To Land* (2003) topped the charts worldwide, but linking with Queen producer Roy Thomas Baker and ousting moustachio'd bassist Frankie Poullain suggested they were taking themselves way too seriously. The success of late 2005's *One Way Ticket To Hell And Back* suggested the joke had yet to wear fatally thin, however.

On a more streetwise level, the Libertines were a band seemingly intent on taking their cues from the Clash: indeed, that band's Mick Jones was employed to produce them, and in Pete Doherty and Carl Barat they had a frontman duo to rival the Strummer-Jones combination. Unfortunately it all went downhill after the promising 2002 debut *Up The Bracket* – and though the eponymous follow-up went in at the top two years later, Doherty was now persona non grata. The songs detailed the split that paralleled the Clash's own messy break-up.

"We're a recognizable band for the simple fact that we've got long hair."
The Darkness' Dan Hawkins

Doherty's adventures with hard drugs and an on-off relationship with supermodel Kate Moss kept the tabloids busy in 2005, making his music, as Babyshambles, an irrelevance to many, while Barat looked to emerge from the Libertines' shadow with his Dirty Pretty Things.

With a sound often likened to that of the Jam, the Kinks and the Clash, the Libertines received critical acclaim for their quintessentially English take on punk rock. Pete Doherty is seated on the left.

Britain *Booms*

Razorlight stemmed from the same London roots as the Libertines, but Johnny Borrell's frontman posturing harked back to the likes of Mick Jagger (or possibly Jarvis Cocker) rather than punk for inspiration.

Chart rivals the Kaiser Chiefs started 2005 as indie hopefuls but by October had a double platinum album (*Employment*) and three Brixton Academy sell-outs via Glastonbury and a U2 support slot. Two of their tracks, 'I Predict A Riot' and 'Oh My God', were in the *Q* magazine readers' Top 5 tracks of 2005. Cartoon rockers Gorillaz started life as Blur's Damon Albarn's side project before eclipsing the band he started with.

Scotland's Franz Ferdinand scooped the Mercury Music Prize en route to becoming the key successors to the likes of Pulp and the Smiths. Matt Bellamy from Muse nailed their appeal, stating that they "combined dance music and rock music in a really cool way without samples or sequencers". Franz labelmates Arctic Monkeys made a play for the Babyshambles market when second single 'I Bet You Look Good On The Dancefloor' took the Sheffield guitar-scrubbers to a UK number one in late 2005, while the similarly streetwise Hard-Fi, hailing from under the Heathrow flight path, made their debut album *Stars Of CCTV* for the princely sum of £300.

Key Artists:

The Libertines
The Kaiser Chiefs
Franz Ferdinand
Green Day
The Killers

Coldplay had come forward to fill the gap left by Radiohead's intermittent activity. Led by Chris Martin, whose marriage to screen queen Gwyneth Paltrow added glamour to their drab image, the four ex-London University students were derided as U2-lite, but sired three best-selling albums in five years, aided by some undeniably catchy singles.

Martin and company's political savvy also found them prime movers in the G8 movement of 2005. Meanwhile Keane in turn had taken advantage of Coldplay's quiet year to turn in 2004's *Hopes And Fears*, an album so sincere it ached.

Influenced by 1980s post-punk, garage rock and new wave, Franz Ferdinand's spectacular 2004 self-titled debut album entered at number three in the UK album chart.

Rocking it *Stateside*

The American noughties scene was dominated by the Foo Fighters and Green Day, the latter having transcended their punk roots to become a major money-making machine. The demise of the likes of Blink 182 left Billie Joe Armstrong's band undisputed leaders in their field, their four million-selling 2004 album *American Idiot* displaying a sure grasp of what it took to win over the airwaves while delivering a strong anti-Bush message.

Dave Grohl's Foo Fighters initially benefited from his association with Nirvana – but his decision to emerge from behind the drum kit to take the role of lead singer and guitarist ensured the music bore little resemblance. Using the medium of video to snare the MTV generation via sharp, witty clips directed by the best in the business ensued the Foos' five albums issued between 1995 and 2005 enjoyed ever-increasing commercial reward. They also became a favourite with the festival generation.

The Killers blew out of Las Vegas with the breakthrough *Hot Fuss*, the fifth best-selling UK album of 2005; a follow-up with Alan Moulder (Nine Inch Nails) and Flood (U2) at the controls could break Brandon Flowers' band even bigger.

Key Albums:

American Idiot Green Day
Employment Kaiser Chiefs
Franz Ferdinand Franz Ferdinand
Hot Fuss The Killers
Up The Bracket The Libertines

Meanwhile the White Stripes, Jack and Meg White, continued to cement their place as the loudest and most influential two-piece in rock. Another US-based left-field bid for glory came from Antony and the Johnsons, the Mercury Music Prize 2005 winner from New York led by Antony Hegarty. First album guest stars Lou Reed, Rufus Wainwright and Boy George give clues as to their off-the-wall appeal.

Thanks to hits like 'This Is A Call' and 'Everlong', and with five studio albums under their belt, Dave Grohl's Foo Fighters have earned a strong worldwide following.

Biographies

Foreword: **Sir George Martin**

Sir George Martin has produced more than 700 recordings in a 50-year career that has encompassed a wide range of musical genres – jazz, rock, classical, comedy and film soundtracks, including an unprecedented 30 number one Beatles and post-Beatles hits. Martin is arguably the most influential and prolific record producer in history. He has worked with artists like Stan Getz and Judy Garland, establishing himself as a jazz, classical and light music producer, and produced a string of hit comedy records with Peter Ustinov and the Goons, before in 1960, as head of Parlophone, the Temperance Seven gave him his first number one hit. But it was the 1960s which saw him make his greatest impression, with the emergence of the Beatles. In 1963, Martin spent a record-breaking 37 weeks at the number one spot, as the producer of the Beatles and other artists. Martin produced almost every Beatles single and album during their career. In the 1970s and 1980s, he produced albums by the Mahavishnu Orchestra, America, Jeff Beck, Neil Sedaka, Jimmy Webb, Cheap Trick and Kenny Rogers. He was knighted in 1996, and received a Lifetime Achievement Award at the Grammys the same year. A year later, Martin produced his 30th number one hit in the UK, Elton John's 'Candle In The Wind 1997', a charity single recorded after Diana, Princess of Wales' death, that became the bestselling single of all time and, in Martin's words, "...probably my last single. It's not a bad one to go out on."

General Editor: **Michael Heatley**

Michael Heatley was the editor of *The History Of Rock*, a ten volume series on popular music (1981–84). Since then, he has written over 50 music, sport and television books, contributed to *Music Week*, *Gold Mine (US)*, *Record Collector*, *Radio Times* and many other magazines. He is the founder of Northdown Publishing, producers of many quality music books.

Consultant Editors

Ian Anderson is the founder and editor of the renowned folk music magazine, *fROOTS*, radio presenter, occasional record producer, semi-retired musician and completely retired festival and tour organizer.

Paul Du Noyer has written for the *NME*, edited *Q* magazine, launched *Mojo* and is now associate editor of *Word*. With hundreds of interviews to his credit he has been face to face with Madonna, Bruce Springsteen and David Bowie. He also collaborated with Paul McCartney on three world tour magazines. His books include *We All Shine On*, about the songs of John Lennon, and *Liverpool: Wondrous Place*, a history of his home town's music scene.

Geoff Brown is a writer on popular music at *Mojo* magazine. He spent several years with *Melody Maker* and *Black Music* magazine, and is currently production editor for *Mojo* magazine. His most recent book was *Otis Redding: Try a Little Tenderness*.

Richard Buskin used to be senior editor and bureau chief of *Performance*, as well as a researcher and on-screen music expert for the BBC (also see following page).

Paul Kingsbury is a freelance writer and former director of special projects at the Country Music Hall of Fame and Museum in Nashville, Tennessee, and was the editor for the Hall of Fame's press and its *Journal of Country Music*. Books he has written and edited include *The Grand Ole Opry History of Country Music* and *Country: The Music and the Musicians*.

Chrissie Murray is a freelance journalist and former jazz consultant to London's Capital Radio. She was co-founder/launch editor of the groundbreaking magazine *The Wire* and was relaunch editor of *Jazzwise* magazine. She is currently an associate editor of *Jazz At Ronnie Scott's* and freelances for *JazzUK*.

Michael Paoletta is the dance/electronic music editor and album reviews editor for *Billboard* magazine. Prior to this he was a freelance journalist whose by-line has appeared in numerous publications, including *Vibe*, *Spin*, the *Advocate*, *Paper*, *Detour*, and *Time Out*.

Philip Van Vleck is currently the pop music critic for the *Durham Herald-Sun* newspaper. He also covers world music, blues, jazz and world jazz for *Billboard* magazine, and is a regular contributor to College Music Journal's *New Music Monthly* magazine, *Dirty Linen* magazine and *www.BMGmusic.com*.

Authors

Bob Allen is a country music journalist, historian and critic. He is a former editor and regular contributor to the Nashville-based *Country Music Magazine*. His writing has appeared in *Esquire*, *Rolling Stone*, the *Washington Post*, the *Atlanta Journal*, and the *Baltimore Sun*. He is the author *The Life And Times Of A Honky Tonk Legend*, the biography of singer George Jones, and has contributed to various historical and reference books on country music in recent years.

Lloyd Bradley toured the USA as a member of ParliamentFunkadelic. For the last 20 years he has written about music for *Mojo*, *Q*, the *Guardian*, *NME* and *Blender*, amongst others. He is the author of *Bass Culture: When Reggae Was King*, *Reggae: The Story Of Jamaican Music* and was associate producer of the BBC2 series of the same name.

Richard Brophy wrote for the Dublin fanzine *Club Dub* before becoming a music correspondent for Irish music magazine *Hot Press*. He has written for UK dance magazines *Jockey Slut* and *DJ* magazine as well as contributing articles to newspapers like the *Irish Times* and the *Evening Herald*. He is also the creator of the pioneering dance music website www.etronik.com.

Richard Buskin is a *New York Times* best-selling author and a full-time freelance journalist specializing in popular music, film, television and cultural affairs. Having written for numerous music and film magazines around the world, he has also authored more than a dozen pop culture books. Recent publications include *Inside Tracks: A First-Hand History of Popular Music from the World's Greatest Record Producers and Engineers*.

Leila Cobo is *Billboard* magazine's Latin/Caribbean bureau chief and is considered one of the leading experts in Latin music in the country. She is regularly interviewed and consulted by outlets such as CNN, VH1, the BBC, Reuters, the *Los Angeles Times*, the *Washington Post* and *USA Today*.

Cliff Douse has written hundreds of articles and columns for many of the UK's foremost music and computer magazines including *Guitarist*, *Computer Music*, *Future Music*, *Rhythm* and *Mac Format*. He is also the author and co-author of several music books. He is currently the editor of *Guitarist Icons* magazine and is working on a number of new books and music software projects.

Colin Irwin was assistant editor of *Melody Maker* and editor of *Number One* magazine before turning to freelance writing. He has presented several BBC series on folk music, both on radio and television. He is also a regular contributor to *Mojo* and *fROOTS* magazines, has written for *The Times*, the *Guardian* and the *Independent* and also wrote *The Name Of The Game*, a biography of ABBA.

Dave Ling is a music journalist who has written for *Sounds*, *Kerrang!*, *Metal Hammer*, *RAW* and *Frontiers* magazines, plus various websites. In November 1998 he was a co-founder of *Classic Rock* magazine, the fastest growing music title in the UK. He also edits *Subterranea*, a monthly extreme music supplement to *Metal Hammer* magazine.

Carl Loben has written about dance music for the music weekly *Melody Maker* as well as for more specialized dance publications. He is currently the features editor of the widely respected *DJ* magazine.

Bill Milkowski is a New York-based music writer, whose work has appeared in several magazines, including *Down Beat*, *Jazz Times*, *Jazziz*, *Guitar Player*, *Guitar World*, *Bass Player* and *Modern Drummer*. He is also the author of *JACO: The Extraordinary and Tragic Life of Jaco Pastorius* and *Swing It! An Annotated History of Jive*.

Garry Mulholland is a music writer who has contributed features and interviews on pop, rock, dance and black music to the *NME*, *Select*, the *Guardian*, the *Sunday Times*, the *Independent* and *Time Out*. His first book *This is Uncool: The 500 Greatest Singles Since Punk and Disco* was published in 2002.

Douglas J Noble has written books on Jimi Hendrix and Peter Green as well as a guitar tuition book – *The Right Way To Play Guitar* – and has contributed to several books on the electric guitar. He is the music director of *UniVibes* magazine, and is an examiner for Rock School/ Trinity College of Music. He has contributed to several music magazines and has interviewed many of the world's top guitarists.

Ed Potton is a regular contributor of articles on music, film and literature to *The Times*. He has also written for *Elle*, the *Independent on Sunday*, *Muzik* and the BBC, and is co-author of *Into the Woods: the Definitive Story of the Blair Witch Project*. He has been an associate producer for Channel 4 television and a broadcast journalist for BBC radio.

Picture Credits

Arbiter Group plc:
335; Millennium Products: 491

Foundry Arts:
36, 49, 57, 72, 81, 117, 147, 161, 166, 175, 189, 201, 209, 231, 235, 245, 263, 277, 299, 307, 334, 340, 365, 367, 377, 380, 387, 411, 419, 421, 428, 432, 437, 444, 450, 458, 473, 486, 512

Kobal Collection Ltd:
Film Four/Lafayette Films: 261

London Features International:
34, 111, 131, 257; D. De Roos: 249; C. Gunther: 127; T. Sheehan: 286

Mary Evans Picture Library: 61

With grateful thanks to **Referns** and the following list of photographers:
Richie Aaron: 409; Glenn A Baker Archives: 89, 103, 149, 169, 179, 187, 215, 239, 351, 369, 371, 385, 431; Michael Ochs Archives: 4 (all), 13, 21, 27, 29, 31, 33, 37, 39, 41, 43, 45, 51, 53, 63, 65, 69, 73, 75, 79, 83, 85, 87, 91, 95, 113, 123, 133, 137, 173, 181, 279, 349, 357, 359, 391, 393, 395, 397; R. Baras: 499; Paul Bergen: 6, 227, 273, 283, 317, 321, 347; Keith Bernstein: 413; Chuck Boyd: 379, 389; George Chin: 461; Fin Costello: 191, 243, 251, 383, 399, 443, 459, 489, 493; Nigel Crane: 343, 513; Grant Davis: 237, 295, 297; Ian Dickson: 427, 433; Kieran Doherty: 309;

Debbie Doss: 155; Erica Echenberg: 505; David Warner Ellis: 405; Brigitte Engl: 463, 509; JM Enternational: 285, 329; Tabatha Fireman: 517; Patrick Ford: 275, 311, 479; Gems: 59, 97, 373; Suzi Gibbons: 247, 477; Steve Gillett: 129; Harry Goodwin: 47; Tim Hall: 265; Olivia Hemingway: 289; Ron Howard: 145; Richie Howell: 101; Clive Hunte: 467; Mick Hutson: 7, 271, 345, 439, 449, 451, 453, 485, 495, 503, 511; Salifu Idriss: 341; Benedict Johnson: 331; Max Scheler/K&K Studios: 71; Robert Knight: 361; Martin Langer: 207; BBC Photo Library: 363, 375, 447; Michel Linssen: 315, 325, 355, 469, 497; Haley Madden: 471, 487; Gered Mankowitz: 17, 233, 455; Sue Moore: 465; Keith Morris: 153, 157, 241, 417; Leon Morris: 151; Stuart Mostyn: 293, 323; Jan Olofsson: 139; Martin Philbey: 519; Andrew Pulter: 143; Christina Radish: 333; RB: 109, 119, 163; David Redfern: 67, 93, 99, 115, 121, 135, 403, 407; Redferns: 159, 183, 337; Lorne Resnick: 401; Rick Richards: 55; Steve Richards: 445; Simon Ritter: 319; Ebet Roberts: 193, 253, 381, 429, 435, 441, 457, 481, 483, 501, 507; John Rodgers: 125; Kerstin Rodgers: 475; S&G: 229; S&G Press Agency: 105; Donna Santisi: 423; Nicky J. Sims: 269, 291, 301; Colin Streater: 287; Jon Super: 327, 339; Virginia Turbett: 255; Lex Van Rossen: 515; Toby Wates: 415; Des Willie: 313; Bob Willoughby: 19; Val Wilmer: 107; Jon Wilton: 15; Charlyn Zlotnik: 141

With grateful thanks to **S.I.N.** and the following list of photographers:
David Corio: 5, 167, 171, 197, 203; Joe Dilworth: 221; Steve Double: 303; Greg Freeman: 281; Martin Goodacre: 211; Jane Houghton: 223; Anna Meuer: 205, 225; Alessio Pizzicannella: 213; Leo Regan: 259; Roy Tee: 177; Andy Willsher: 305

Sylvia Pitcher Photo Library:
B. Smith: 35

Topham Picturepoint:
23, 25, 77, 165, 185, 199, 217, 219, 353, 425; PA: 267; Richard Lucas/The Image Works: 195

Further Reading

POP

Brend, Mark, *American Troubadors: Groundbreaking Singer-Songwriters of the 60s*, Backbeat Books, San Francisco, 2001

Buskin, Richard, *Inside Tracks: A First-Hand History of Popular Music from the World's Greatest Record Producers and Engineers*, Avon, 1999

Carr, Roy, and Farren, Mick, *Elvis: The Complete Illustrated Record*, Eel Pie, London, 1982

Cooper, Kim, *Bubblegum Music is the Naked Truth*, Feral House, 2001

Escott, Colin, with Hawkins, Martin, *Good Rockin' Tonight: Sun Records and the Birth of Rock 'n' Roll*, St. Martin's Press, New York, 1992

Fong-Torres, Ben, *The Hits Just Keep On Coming: The History of Top 40 Radio*, Backbeat Books, San Francisco, 2001

Fox, Ted, *In the Groove*, St. Martins Press, New York, 1986

Kozinn, Allan, *The Beatles*, Phaidon, London, 1995

Larkin, Colin, *Encyclopedia of Popular Music*, Virgin Publishing, London, 2002

Larkin, Colin, *The Guinness Who's Who of Sixties Music*, Guinness Publishing, London, 1992

Lewisohn, Mark, *The Complete Beatles Chronicle*, Harmony Books, New York, 1992

Logan, Nick, and Woffinden, Bob (eds.), *The Illustrated New Musical Express Encyclopedia of Rock*, Hamlyn, London, 1976

Marcic, Dorothy, *Respect: Women and Popular Music*, Texere, New York, 2002

Marcus, Greil, *Mystery Train: Images of America in Rock'n'Roll Music*, E P Dutton, 1975

Morath, Max, and Feinstein, Michael, *The Npr Curious Listener's Guide to Popular Standards*, Perigee, New York, 2002

Mulholland, Garry, *This Is Uncool: The 500 Greatest Singles Since Punk and Disco*, Cassell, London, 2002

Olsen, Eric et al, *The Encyclopedia of Record Producers*, Billboard, New York, 1999

Pascall, Jeremy, *The Golden Years of Rock & Roll*, Phoebus Publishing, New York, 1974

Ramsey, Guthrie P., *Race Music: Black Cultures from Bebop to Hip-Hop*, University of California Press, Berkeley, 2003

Smith, Joe, *Off the Record: An Oral History of Popular Music*, Warner Books, 1988

Swern, Phil, and Greenfield, Shaun, *30 Years of Number Ones*, BBC Books, London, 1990

Thompson, David, *Pop*, Collectors Guide Publishing, 2000

Unterberger, Richie, *The Rough Guide to Music USA*, Rough Guides, London, 1999

Whitburn, Joel, *Billboard Top 1000 Singles 1955–2000*, Hal Leonard Publishing, Milwaukee, 2001

White, Charles, *The Life and Times of Little Richard*, Harmony Books, 1984

Wolfe, Tom, *The Kandy-Kolored Tangerine-Flake Streamline Baby*, Simon & Schuster, New York, 1965

ROCK

Asbjornsen, Dag Erik, *Scented Gardens of the Mind: A Comprehensive Guide to the Golden Era of Progressive Rock: 1968–1980*, Borderline Productions, New York, 2001

Azerrad, Michael, *Our Band Could Be Your Life: Scenes from the American India Underground 1981–1991*, Little Brown & Company, New York, 2001

Billboard Guide to American Rock and Roll, Billboard Books, New York, 1997

Blush, Steven, *American Hardcore: A Tribal History*, Feral House, 2001

Bogdanov, Vladimir (ed.), et al, *All Music Guide to Rock*, Backbeat, London, 2002

Christe, Ian, *The Sound of the Beast: The Complete Headbanging History of Heavy Metal*, William Morrow, New York, 2003

Cohn, Nik, *Awopbopaloobopalopbamboom: The Golden Age of Rock*, Grove Press, New York, 2003

Cole, Richard, and Trubo, Richard, *Stairway to Heaven: Led Zeppelin Uncensored*, HarperEntertainment, New York, 2000

Ellinham, Mark, *The Rough Guide to Rock*, Rough Guides, London, 1996

Gassen, Timothy, *The Knights Of Fuzz*, Borderline Productions, Columbia, 1996

George-Warren, Holly, et al, *The Rolling Stone Encyclopedia of Rock & Roll*, Fireside, New York, 2001

Graff, Gary, and Durchholz, Daniel, *MusicHound Rock: The Essential Album Guide*, Gale, 1998

Harrison, Hank, *Kurt Cobain, Beyond Nirvana: The Legacy of Kurt Cobain*, The Archives Press, 1994

Ingham, Chris, *The Book Of Metal*, Carlton Books, London, 2002

Jeffries, Neil (ed.), *The "Kerrang!" Direktory of Heavy Metal: The Indispensible Guide to Rock Warriors and Headbangin' Heroes*, Virgin Books, London, 1993

Juno, Andrea, *Angry Women In Rock*, Juno Books, 2003

Larkin, Colin, *The Virgin Encyclopedia of Heavy Rock*, Virgin Books, London, 1999

Larkin, Colin, *The Virgin Illustrated Encyclopedia of Rock*, Virgin Books, London, 1999

McIver, Joel, *Nu-Metal: The Next Generation Of Rock And Punk*, Omnibus Press, London, 2002

McNeil, Legs and McGain, Gillian (eds.), *Please Kill Me: The Uncensored Oral History of Punk*, Penguin USA, New York, 1997

Moynihan, Michael and Søderlind, Didrik, *Lords Of Chaos: The Bloody Rise Of The Satanic Underground*, Feral House, 2003

Porter, Dick, *Rapcore: The Nu-Metal Rap Fusion*, Plexus Publishing, New Jersey, 2002

Reynolds, Simon, *The Sex Revolts: Gender, Rebellion and Rock'n'roll*, Harvard University Press, Harvard, 1995

Spicer, Al, *The Rough Guide to Rock (100 Essential CDs)*, Rough Guides, London, 1999

Strong, Martin C., *The Great Metal Discography*, Mojo Books, London, 2002

Strong, Martin C., *The Great Rock Discography*, Canongate Publications, Edinburgh, 2002

Index

Index